Legal and Ethical Issues in Human Language Technologies and Multilingual De-Identification of Sensitive Language Resources (LEGAL-MDLR 2022)

Held at LREC 2022

Marseille, France
20 June 2022

Editors:

Mickael Rigault
Victoria Arranz
Ingo Siegert

ISBN: 978-1-7138-6126-3

Printed from e-media with permission by:

Curran Associates, Inc.
57 Morehouse Lane
Red Hook, NY 12571

CURRAN ASSOCIATES INC. proceedings.com

Some format issues inherent in the e-media version may also appear in this print version.

Association for Computational Linguistics
209 N. Eighth Street
Stroudsburg, Pennsylvania 18360

Phone: 1-570-476-8006
Fax: 1-570-476-0860

acl@aclweb.org

Additional copies of this publication are available from:

Curran Associates, Inc.
57 Morehouse Lane
Red Hook, NY 12571 USA
Phone: 845-758-0400
Fax: 845-758-2633
Email: curran@proceedings.com
Web: www.proceedings.com

LREC 2022 Joint Workshop
Language Resources and Evaluation Conference
20-25 June 2022

Legal and Ethical Issues In Human Language Technologies and Multilingual De-Identification of Sensitive Language Resources (LEGAL - MDLR)

PROCEEDINGS

Editors: Mickaël Rigault, Victoria Arranz, Ingo Siegert

Proceedings of the LREC 2022 Joint Workshop on Legal and Ethical Issues in Human Language Technologies and Multilingual De-Identification of Sensitive Language Resources (LEGAL - MDLR 2022)

Edited by:
Mickaël Rigault, Victoria Arranz, Ingo Siegert

For more information:
European Language Resources Association (ELRA)
9 rue des Cordelières
75013, Paris
France
http://www.elra.info
Email: lrec@elda.org

Preface

The legal framework affecting access to and re-use of language data in the European Union has evolved very significantly since the last LREC conference (7-12 May 2018). The main objective of the workshop is to discuss the major issues around legal and related technological directions of Human Language Technologies.

The workshop is meant to study different interactions between legal and technical aspects of data collection, processing, and distribution. Such interactions may concern text crawling, speech and voice recordings and the impact of the text and speech data mining exception introduced by the European legislation in 2018. These interactions may also concern the compatibility of the legal requirement for (text, audio, video) data collection and their processing as imposed by the GDPR, together with the technical feasibility of the different anonymisation and pseudonymisation techniques. This workshop looks into the various approaches to effective and reliable text de-identification, focusing on some particularly sensitive domains such as the medical and legal domains, but not only.

This workshop also aims to discuss larger issues such as ethics and morality, as well as trust and their interactions as a whole on data collection and distribution and how they may be inserted into binding legal instruments (code of ethics, best practices). The purpose of this workshop will attempt to build bridges between technology and legal experts and discuss current legal and ethical issues in the Human Language Technology sector. This will be addressed by bringing together researchers and scholars working on Intellectual Property, Public Sector Information, Personal Data and possibly ethics, both from the legal and technical perspectives.

This volume documents the Proceedings of the LREC Joint Workshop on Legal and Ethical Issues In Human Language Technologies and Multilingual De-Identification of Sensitive Language Resources, held on Friday, June 24, 2022, as part of the LREC 2022 Conference (International Conference on Language Resources and Evaluation).

We would like to thank our keynote speakers for their enlightening speeches, as well as the authors who contributed to this workshop with their papers and discussions. We are also very grateful to the members of the Program Committee for the time and effort devoted to the reviewing of the papers.

LEGAL Organizing Committee

Ingo Siegert – Otto von Guericke University Magdeburg (GERMANY)
Mickaël Rigault – ELDA/ELRA (FRANCE)
Khalid Choukri – ELDA/ELRA (FRANCE)
Pawel Kamocki – IDS Mannheim (GERMANY)
Andreas Witt – IDS Mannheim (GERMANY)
Krister Linden – University of Helsinki (FINLAND)
Claudia Cevenini – University of Bologna (ITALY)

MDLR Organizing Committee

Victoria Arranz – ELDA/ELRA (FRANCE)
Montse Cuadros – Vicomtech Foundation (SPAIN)
Aitor García Pablos – Vicomtech Foundation (SPAIN)
Cyril Grouin – Université Paris-Saclay, CNRS, LISN (FRANCE)
Manuel Herranz – Pangeanic (SPAIN)

Program Committee:

Khalid Choukri, ELDA/ELRA (FRANCE)
Hercules Dalianis, Stockholm University (SWEDEN)
Amando Estela, Pangeanic (SPAIN)
Thierry Etchegoyhen, Vicomtech Foundation (SPAIN)
Albert Gatt, Malta University (MALTA)
Lucie Gianola, Université Paris-Saclay, CNRS, LISN (FRANCE)
Ona de Gibert, BSC (SPAIN)
Marwa Hadj Salah, ELDA/ELRA (FRANCE)
Udo Hahn, University of Jena (GERMANY)
Thomas Kleinbauer, COMPRISE Project (GERMANY)
Maite Melero, BSC (SPAIN)
Patrick Paroubek, Université Paris-Saclay, CNRS, LISN (FRANCE)
Naiara Perez, Vicomtech Foundation (SPAIN)
Stelios Piperidis, Athena Research and Innovation Center (GREECE)
Prokopis Prokopidis, Athena Research and Innovation Center (GREECE)
Mike Rosner, Malta University (MALTA)
Roberts Rozis, TILDE (LATVIA)
Özlem Uzuner, George Mason University (U.S.A.)
Emmanuel Vincent, Inria Nancy-Grand Est (FRANCE)
Rinalds Vīksna , TILDE (LATVIA)
Pierre Zweigenbaum, Université Paris-Saclay, CNRS, LISN (FRANCE)

Table of Contents

Conference Program

Friday, June 24, 2022

09:00–09:15 *Welcome and Introduction*
Ingo Siegert, Victoria Arranz

09:15–10:10 Keynote Speech - Major Developments in the Legal Framework Concerning Language Resources
Pawel Kamocki, IDS Mannheim

10:10–10:30 Session A: COVID Issues and Policy Amendments

10:10–10:30 *Sentiment Analysis and Topic Modeling for Public Perceptions of Air Travel: COVID Issues and Policy Amendments*
Avery Field, Aparna Varde and Pankaj Lal

11:00–12:00 Session B: GDPR and Legal Aspects

11:00–11:20 *Data Protection, Privacy and US Regulation*
Denise DiPersio

11:20–11:40 *Pseudonymisation of Speech Data as an Alternative Approach to GDPR Compliance*
Pawel Kamocki and Ingo Siegert

11:40–12:00 *Categorizing Legal Features in a Metadata-Oriented Task: Defining the Conditions of Use*
Mickaël Rigault, Victoria Arranz, Valérie Mapelli, Penny Labropoulou and Stelios Piperidis

Friday, June 24, 2022 (continued)

12:00–13:00 Session C1: Data Protection: Anonymisation, De-Identification and Legal Aspects

12:00–12:20 *About Migration Flows and Sentiment Analysis on Twitter data: Building the Bridge between Technical and Legal Approaches to Data Protection*
Thilo Gottschalk and Francesca Pichierri

12:20–12:40 *Transparency and Explainability of a Machine Learning Model in the Context of Human Resource Management*
Sebastien Delecraz, Loukman Eltarr and Olivier Oullier

12:40–13:00 *Public Interactions with Voice Assistant – Discussion of Different One-Shot Solutions to Preserve Speaker Privacy*
Ingo Siegert, Yamini Sinha, Gino Winkelmann, Oliver Jokisch and Andreas Wendemuth

14:00–15:00 Keynote Speech - Anonymisation and the GDPR
Brij Mohan Lal Srivastava, Co-Founder of Nijta Startup Studio, Lille

15:00–16:00 Session C2: Data Protection: Anonymisation in Practice

15:00–15:20 *Cross-Clinic De-Identification of Swedish Electronic Health Records: Nuances and Caveats*
Olle Bridal, Thomas Vakili and Marina Santini

15:20–15:40 *Generating Realistic Synthetic Curricula Vitae for Machine Learning Applications under Differential Privacy*
Andrea Bruera, Francesco Aldà and Francesco Di Cerbo

15:40–16:00 *MAPA Project: Ready-to-Go Open-Source Datasets and Deep Learning Technology to Remove Identifying Information from Text Documents*
Victoria Arranz, Khalid Choukri, Montse Cuadros, Aitor García Pablos, Lucie Gianola, Cyril Grouin, Manuel Herranz, Patrick Paroubek and Pierre Zweigenbaum

Friday, June 24, 2022 (continued)

16:30–17:30 Session D: Privacy and Ethical Challenges in Data

16:30–16:50 *PriPA: A Tool for Privacy-Preserving Analytics of Linguistic Data*
Jeremie Clos, Emma McClaughlin, Pepita Barnard, Elena Nichele, Dawn Knight, Derek McAuley and Svenja Adolphs

16:50–17:10 *Legal and Ethical Challenges in Recording Air Traffic Control Speech*
Mickaël Rigault, Claudia Cevenini, Khalid Choukri, Martin Kocour, Karel Veselý, Igor Szoke, Petr Motlicek, Juan Pablo Zuluaga-Gomez, Alexander Blatt, Dietrich Klakow, Allan Tart, Pavel Kolčárek and Jan Černocký

17:10–17:30 *It is not Dance, is Data: Gearing Ethical Circulation of Intangible Cultural Heritage Practices in the Digital Space*
Jorge Yánez and Amel Fraisse

17:30–18:00 *Closing Ceremony*

Dr. iur. Paweł Kamocki, IDS Mannheim

Major developments in the legal framework concerning language resources

Introductory Talk for the Workshop on Legal and Ethical Issues in Human Language Technologies, LREC 2022, *Marseille, 24 June 2022*

The legal framework affecting access to and re-use of language data in the European Union has evolved very significantly since the last LREC conference (7-12 May 2018).

The General Data Protection Regulation (GDPR) entered into application on 25 May 2018, and although its content was already well-known and discussed at length during the last LREC, best practices and guidelines are still emerging. Today, we know much more especially about such aspects of the GDPR as Privacy by Design, the controller/processor dichotomy, or the data subject's right of access. In particular, specific guidelines on Virtual Voice Assistants were issued by the European Data Protection Board in 2021.

Among the directives adopted since 2018, two are of particular relevance for the language community: the Open Data Directive (of 20 June 2019) and the Directive on Copyright in the Digital Single Market (of 17 April 2019); both had to be implemented by mid-2021. The Open Data Directive has replaced the Public Sector Information Directive. Its scope is now significantly larger: while its predecessor facilitated access to and re-use of data held by public administrations as well as museums, libraries and archives, the new rules cover also data held by public undertakings and research data resulting from public funding. This opens a wealth of new data for use in language resources and language technology projects.

The Directive on Copyright in the Digital Single Market contains, among many other interesting provisions, a long-awaited copyright exception for text and data mining purposes. The mechanism is in fact two-fold, with one exception (Article 3) for research organisations and cultural heritage institutions, and another one (Article 4) for the general public. *Prima facie*, these rules allow for very wide re-use of copyright-protected material for language technology purposes, but they are in fact full of caveats and gray areas.

Finally, in 2020 the European Commission launched the European Strategy for Data. A series of proposals for Regulations (labelled, in the Anglo-Saxon way, "Acts") were adopted based on this consultation, including the Data Governance Act and the Artificial Intelligence Act. In particular, the Data Governance Act, which is now at the final stages of the legislative process and is expected to enter into application in mid-2023, contains interesting provisions on data altruism, a solution enabling individuals to 'donate' their data to registered organisations (legal entities established to meet objectives of general interest, operating on a non-profit basis and independently from any for-profit entities). The same Act also strengthens the rules concerning providers of data-sharing services.

The talk will discuss all the above-mentioned changes in the legal framework, and try to predict their impact on the language community.

The Legal and Ethical issues Workshop @LREC2022, pages 2–8
Marseille, 20 June 2022

Sentiment Analysis and Topic Modeling for Public Perceptions of Air Travel: COVID Issues and Policy Amendments

Avery Field[1], Aparna S. Varde[2], Pankaj Lal[3]
1. Computational Linguistics, 2. Computer Science, 3. Earth and Environmental Studies
Montclair State University, Montclair NJ 07043, USA
{fielda1, vardea, lalp}@montclair.edu

Abstract

Among many industries, air travel is impacted by the COVID pandemic. Airlines and airports rely on public sector information to enforce guidelines for ensuring health and safety of travelers. Such guidelines can be policy amendments or laws during the pandemic. In response to the inception of COVID preventive policies, travelers have exercised freedom of expression via the avenue of online reviews. This avenue facilitates voicing public concern while anonymizing / concealing user identity as needed. It is important to assess opinions on policy amendments to ensure transparency and openness, while also preserving confidentiality and ethics. Hence, this study leverages data science to analyze, with identity protection, the online reviews of airlines and airports since 2017, considering impacts of COVID issues and relevant policy amendments since 2020. Supervised learning with VADER sentiment analysis is deployed to predict changes in opinion from 2017 to date. Unsupervised learning with LDA topic modeling is employed to discover air travelers' major areas of concern before and after the pandemic. This study reveals that COVID policies have worsened public perceptions of air travel and aroused notable new concerns, affecting economics, environment and health.

Keywords: Anonymization. Coronavirus, Freedom of Expression, Global Policy, Online Reviews, Transparency

1. Introduction

The COVID pandemic continues to be a great disruptor to many industries, including air travel. In a global health crisis, people expect public sector organizations to provide information that can be used to create policies and laws to ensure the protection and safety of people across all industries and institutions. During the COVID pandemic, public health organizations, e.g. Centers for Disease Control and Prevention (CDC, 2022), and World Health Organization (WHO, 2022) enforced policies such as mask wearing, COVID testing and social distancing, to help prevent the spread of the virus (TSA, 2022). Doing so consequently changed the process of air travel. In an unprecedented situation such as a pandemic, it is important to rely on the public sector for guidance. It is equally important for people affected by these changes to freely express their own opinions on implementation of new policies to ensure transparency, maintaining anonymity as needed.

As travelers are poised to keep up with the latest COVID preventative guidelines, they must comply with the protective measures deemed appropriate by their location of departure, destination and air carrier. Consequently, while flying during the pandemic and its immediate aftermath, travelers have voiced their experiences online via reviews, anonymizing or concealing their own identity if needed. Our study therefore aims to explore the impact of COVID related policy amendments on the public perceptions of air travel, while protecting user identity and preserving ethical issues. We investigate how travelers' perceptions have changed since March 2020 and comprehend the concerns that have increased and emerged ever since preventative measures have been executed via public sector information. In this process, we deploy publicly accessible sources to collect data (e.g. TripAdvisor), however, the user identities are not revealed in our work to protect their privacy.

2. Related Work

The significance of mass opinion is highlighted in numerous studies that cater to public policy, some of which pertain to work in our own research teams. This is surveyed in a recent paper addressing its importance in various environmental issues (Du et al., 2019). It is emphasized in smart governance through mining ordinances and their public reactions (Puri et al., 2022, Puri et al., 2018). It is discussed in work on sentiment analysis for partially labeled data (Gandhe et al., 2018). Additionally, it mentioned in some studies on policy related areas such as hydro-informatics (Pathak et al., 2020). It is a subject of research in work on air quality assessment (Du et al., 2016). Moreover, it is evident from work in infrastructure improvements relevant to social sciences (Wieczerak et al., 2022). While implementing policy amendments and laws during a health crisis, public opinion is a primary constraint (Treloar and Fraser, 2007). Needle and syringe programs have prevailed in the public sector in Australia to battle the opioid epidemic. Failure to consider public opinion in releasing information about these programs has led to instances of hasty political response, thereby evoking negative public reaction, and often causing chaos.

The COVID pandemic has resulted in rapidly evolving and sometimes, contradictory public policies (Sheluchin et al., 2020). The public health sector has put forth policies throughout the pandemic and then had a change of heart. For example, public health agencies in both the U.S. and Canada have revised guidance on the utility of masks. In 2020, a research study gauging public response to the mask usage reversal laws in Canada revealed that throughout the tumultuous changes in policy, It is noticed that Canadians have remained compliant with the guidelines of their country.

According to a recently published case study, Italian air travelers flying during the COVID pandemic have been increasingly more concerned about the compensations, cancellations than the coronavirus itself (Piccinelli et al., 2021). As per this analysis, travelers' feelings have been mixed and unpredictable. Many air travelers have become apprehensive with the irregularity of flights and have swarmed to online platforms to express their concerns.

3. Data

In order to gather traveler insights, data is generated from online reviews of airlines and airports from June 2017 until March 2022. The airlines being reviewed in our data are Delta Airlines, American Airlines and Southwest Airlines, which are the top three most flown airlines in the United States (Salas, 2022). Since this study only focuses on English-language data, airport reviews come from the United States, Canada and the United Kingdom. These reviews are obtained from TripAdvisor.com and AirlineEquality.com using a web-scraping tool built from the Selenium web driver library in python (Selenium, 2022). These websites are chosen because they both serve as focused platforms which allow travelers to connect and share travel related experiences through reviews and comments.

The total number of reviews obtained in this study is 17,145. There are 164 reviews from 2017; 577 from 2018; 5965 from 2019; 5437 from 2020; 4321 from 2021; and 681 from 2022. Figure 1 presents some snapshots from reviews on TripAdvisor.

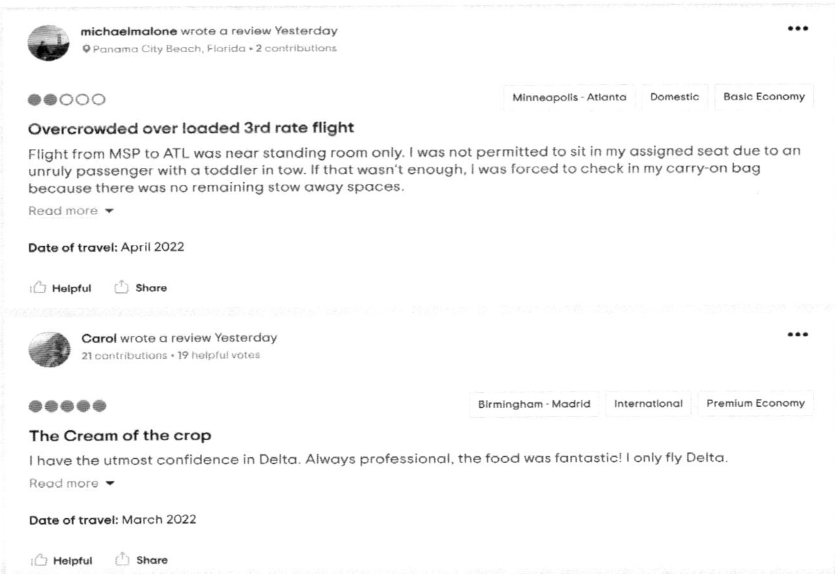

Figure 1: Sample reviews from TripAdvisor.com

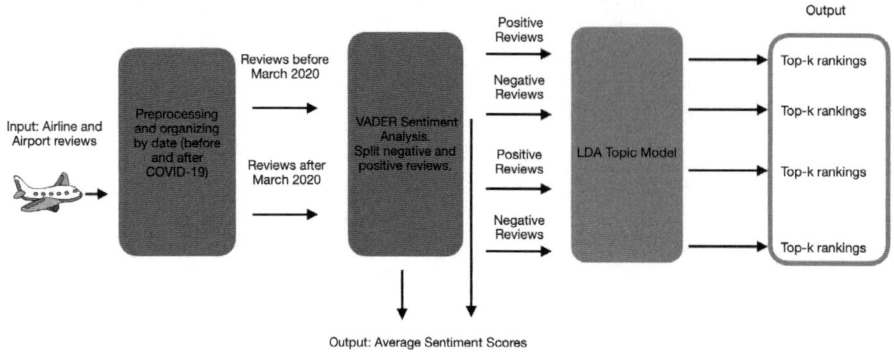

Figure 2: Proposed approach for the study

4. Methods

After data collection, the first step in our study is to organize the data into temporal categories. Using the "pandas" library in Python, reviews are categorized as: "before COVID" / "after COVID" and placed into respective csv files. For the purposes of this study, March 15, 2020 denotes the beginning of the pandemic period since it is the start date of the CDC implementing its policies.

The natural language toolkit (nltk) library of Python helps to preprocess text in our review data. In the preprocessing stage, non-character text such as punctuation, emojis and stop words are removed. This is because stop words do not contribute any significant meaning to the text as a whole in this context. While emojis and punctuations may at times convey sentiment, that is often expressed through the terms in the text itself, especially in online reviews on platforms such as TripAdvisor that tend to be somewhat more formal (as opposed to informal posts on Twitter and Facebook).

As a next step, suitable n-grams in the text are processed, i.e. clusters of n number of words that have a singular meaning when grouped together, such as "customer service" and "social distancing". Thereafter, an analysis of the preprocessed data occurs. This entails two methods widely used in data science and linguistics studies, i.e. sentiment analysis, and topic modeling.

The supervised learning method of sentiment analysis is useful in this work because it helps to gauge the opinions of the travelers, thus enabling the prediction of future reactions on similar policies, and hence guiding decision-making by leveraging transparency and openness. In order to perform sentiment analysis, VADER: Valence Aware Dictionary and Sentiment Reasoner (Hutto and Gilbert, 2014) is used which is included in Python's nltk library. This provides a numerical sentiment score to each review, -1 being the most negative a review can be and +1 being the most positive a review can be. The average sentiment score is calculated for reviews before and after COVID in order to ensure that the change in public opinion of air travel is observable.

Furthermore, in order to extract and highlight the major areas of concern expressed by various air travelers, the unsupervised learning method of topic modeling is useful. We harness LDA: Latent Dirichlet Allocation (Blei et al., 2003) for this purpose. LDA topic modeling uses statistical methods to group related words in a document together to create "topics" discussed in the document. We consider four different categories of reviews, separated based on sentiment score. These are: positive reviews before COVID, negative reviews before COVID, positive reviews after COVID and negative reviews after COVID.

A coherence score is calculated to determine how many topics should be generated for each review category to provide the most coherent and readable information. This topic modeling thereby helps to rank topics of interest based on the most significant to least significant ones that arouse concern among air travelers. It is yet another means to comprehend their reactions, to support future decision-making while shaping public sector policies, incorporating user involvement via transparency.

Based on this discussion, the algorithm proposed in this study for sentiment analysis and topic modeling is outlined next as a pseudocode in Algorithm 1. This is implemented into our program and is used to conduct experiments, with a summary of the results presented in the following section.

Algorithm 1: Sentiment Analysis, Topic Modeling for Reviews

```
READ Review_Data
FOREACH review
IF review date is after "3-15-2020"
THEN Add review to After_Covid
ELSE Add review to Before_Covid

FOREACH review in After_Covid
COMPUTE Avg_Sent_Score
IF Avg_Sent_Score > 0.7
THEN Add review to Pos_After_Covid
ELSE Add review to Neg_After_Covid
FOREACH review in Before_Covid
COMPUTE Avg_Sent_Score
IF Avg_Sent_Score > 0.7
THEN Add review to Pos_Before_Covid
ELSE Add review to Neg_Before_Covid
OUTPUT Avg_Sent_Scores

SET categories: Pos_After_Covid, Neg_After_Covid, Pos_Before_
Covid, Neg_Before_Covid
FOREACH category
COMPUTE topic model using LDA
SET value of k
OUTPUT top-k rankings
```

5. Results

The sentiment analysis reveals that ever since COVID policies have been in place through organizations such as the CDC and the WHO, public perceptions of air travel have become increasingly more negative. The results also indicate that this negative shift in public opinion is greater in airline reviews than airport reviews. Figures 3 and 4 present a summary of the sentiment analysis outcomes.

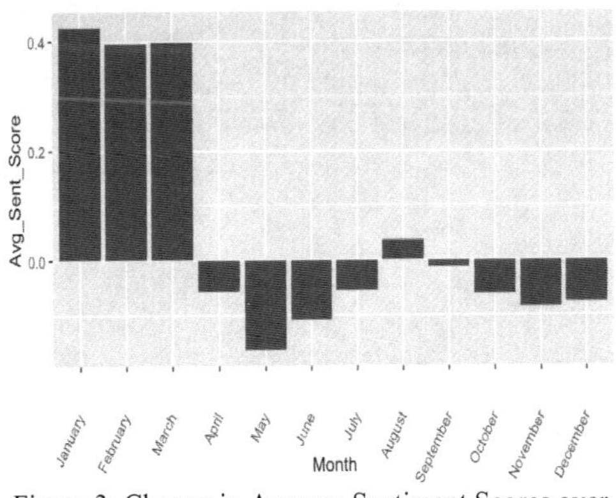

Figure 3: Change in Average Sentiment Scores over all the 12 months in 2020

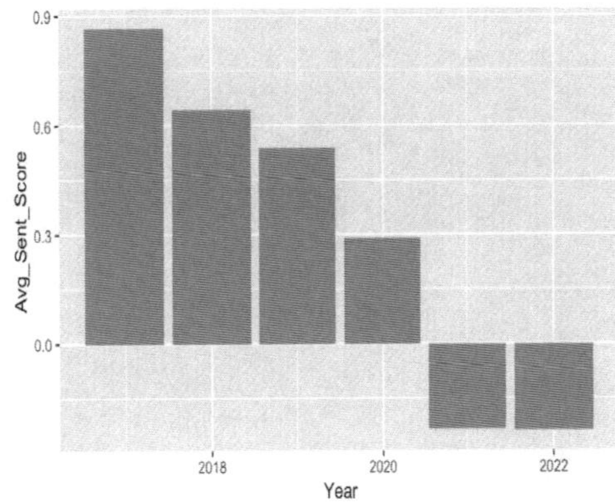

Figure 4: Change in Average Sentiment Scores all across the years 2017-2022

According to the topic models generated, air travelers' greatest areas of concern before the pandemic are: waiting time, customer service quality, and unexpected changes (e.g. flight rescheduling / seat alterations). After the pandemic, all these concerns persist. New concerns emerging are: mask mandates enforced unprofessionally by airline and airport staff, COVID guidelines poorly followed in airports, and COVID related measures being lackluster on airplanes. Accordingly, considering the value of $k=30$, Figures 5 to 8 synopsize the topic modeling results. Other such results are obtained for different k values.

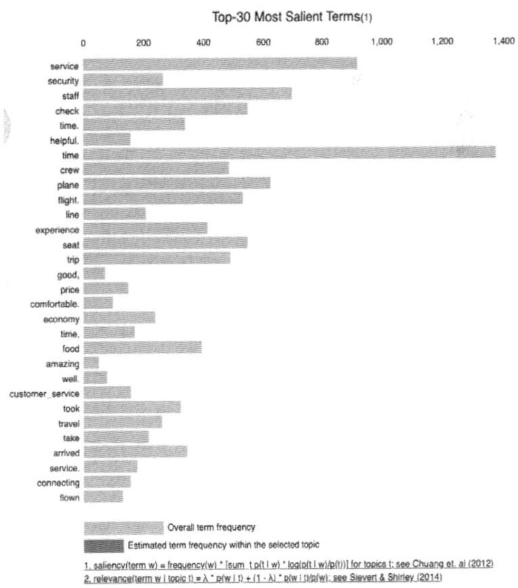

Figure 5: Top-k rankings of topic modeling for positive reviews before March 2020

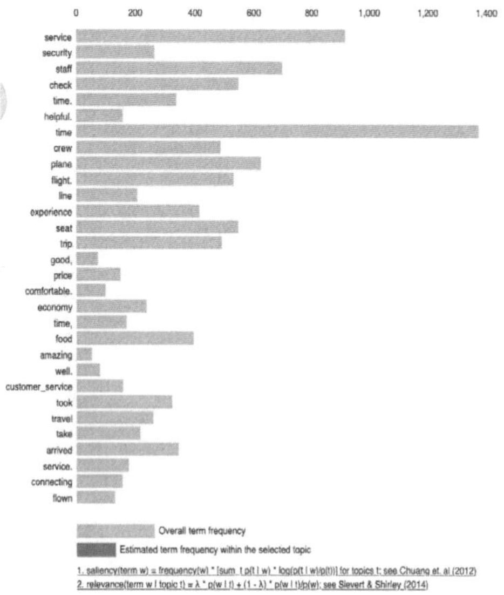

Figure 6: Top-k rankings of topic modeling for positive reviews after March 2020

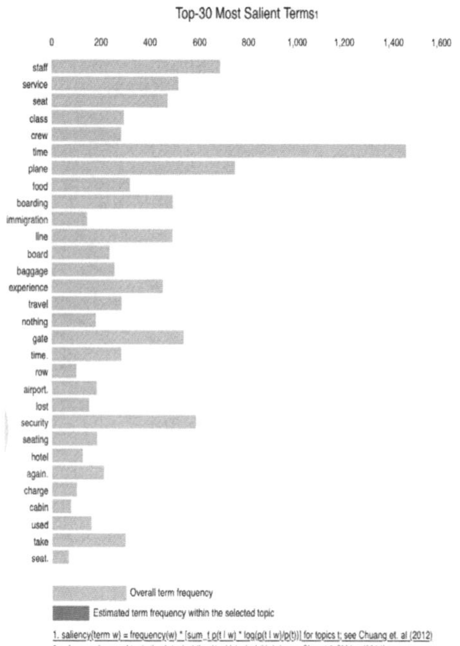

Figure 7: Top-k rankings of topic modeling for negative reviews before March 2020

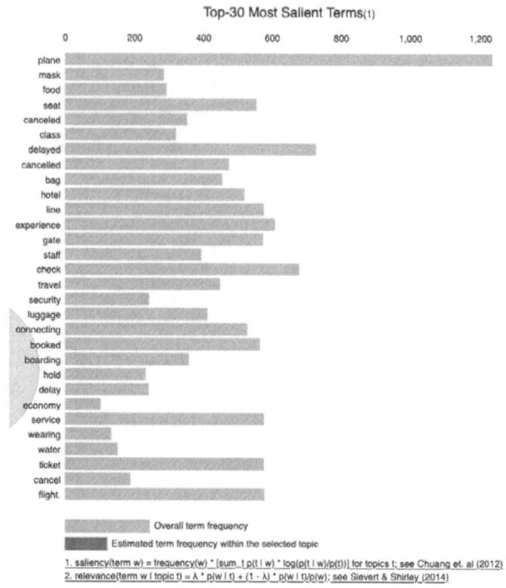

Figure 8: Top-k rankings of topic modeling for negative reviews after March 2020

We present Word Cloud visualizations about these reviews in Figures 9 to 12. Overall, our results indicate that the implementation of new COVID preventive policies from public sector organizations are adding to the potential concerns of air travelers.

Figure 9: Word cloud for positive reviews before March 2020

Figure 10: Word cloud for positive reviews after March 2020

Figure 11: Word cloud for negative reviews before March 2020

Figure 12: Word cloud for negative reviews after March 2020

6. Conclusions and Ongoing Work

This study uses data science approaches of sentiment analysis and topic modeling to examine impacts of public sector information (by CDC and WHO) as per policy amendments on a private industry (air travel) due to a global pandemic. The emergence of COVID policies in March 2020 significantly influenced air travelers' opinions about flying, as discovered by sentiment scores and ranking of issues in topic modeling. This study provides initial support that several public laws and policy amendments negatively affect travelers' opinions of airports and airlines, thus being adversely associated with air travel. Air travelers already had concerns related to flying pre-pandemic. Additionally, air travelers have new concerns related to public guidelines crafted to maintain the health and safety of air travelers throughout the pandemic.

The results of this study can be useful in future decision-making by private industries such as airlines, and public sector organizations, e.g. airports, health-related bodies and other policymakers. While health and safety is of the utmost importance, it is useful to garner public satisfaction vis-à-vis economic and environmental impacts. Moreover, it is insufficient to just draft health policies, their effective practice is paramount to ensure that health objectives are met, e.g. in this case the manner in which airline and airport staff apply COVID preventive measures. Such aspects appear in the outcomes of our study, and can be useful for future planning and enhancement.

Our ongoing work includes making the results of this study more visible, examining areas of concern more closely to provide suggestions for improvement, and researching long-term impacts of this work from various health, safety, environmental and economic perspectives. The theme of this study fits Smart Governance, much encouraged in the world today. This focuses on transparency, openness, and freedom of expression in shaping public policy.

Note: The main resources for this work are available at (Field and Varde, 2022). Additional information can be provided upon request.

7. Acknowledgements

Aparna Varde acknowledges the NSF grants 2018575 (MRI: Acquisition of a High-Performance GPU Cluster for Research & Education); and 2117308 (MRI: Acquisition of a Multimodal Collaborative Robot System (MCROS) to Support Cross-Disciplinary Human-Centered Research & Education). She is a visiting researcher at Max Planck Institute for Informatics, Germany.

8. References

Blei, D. M., Ng, A. Y., and Jordan, M. I. (2003), Latent Dirichlet Allocation. *Journal of Machine Learning Research*, 3(Jan), 993-1022.

CDC. (2022), Find local COVID-19 Guidance, *Centers for Disease Control and Prevention*, Retrieved April 2022, from https://www.cdc.gov/

Du, X., Kowalski, M., Varde, A. S., de Melo, G., and Taylor, R. W. (2019), Public opinion matters: Mining social media text for environmental management. *ACM SIGWEB*, (Autumn Issue), 5:1-5:15.

Du, X., Emebo, O., Varde, A., Tandon, N., Chowdhury, S. N., and Weikum, G. (2016), Air quality assessment from social media and structured data: Pollutants and health impacts in urban planning. *IEEE ICDE - International Conference on Data Engineering, workshops*, pp. 54-59.

Field, A,, and Varde, A. (2022), https://github.com/avery-field/MSCL_Project

Gandhe, K., Varde, A.S., and Du, X. (2018), Sentiment Analysis of Twitter Data with Hybrid

Learning for Recommender Applications, *IEEE Annual Ubiquitous Computing, Electronics & Mobile Communication Conference (UEMCON),* pp. 57-63.

Hutto, C., and Gilbert, E. (2014), Vader: A parsimonious rule-based model for sentiment analysis of social media text. *AAAI conference on web and social media*, Vol. 8, No. 1, pp. 216-225.

Piccinelli, S., Moro, S., and Rita, P. (2021), Air-travelers' concerns emerging from online comments during the COVID-19 Outbreak. *Tourism Management*, 85, 104313. https://doi.org/10.1016/j.tourman.2021.104313

Pathak, D., Varde, A. S., De Melo, G., and Alo, C. (2020), Hydroinformatics and the web: Analytics and dissemination of hydrology data for climate change and sustainability. *ACM SIGWEB,* (Autumn Issue), 3:1-3:17.

Puri, M., Varde, A.S. and de Melo, G. (2022), Commonsense based text mining on urban policy. *Language Resources & Evaluation (LREV),* https://doi.org/10.1007/s10579-022-09584-6

Puri, M., Varde, A. S., and Dong, B. (2018), Pragmatics and semantics to connect specific local laws with public reactions. *IEEE International Conference on Big Data*, pp. 5433-5435.

Salas, E. B. (2022, March 11). U.S. Airline Industry Market Share 2019. Statista. Retrieved April 20, 2022, from https://www.statista.com/statistics/250577/domestic-market-share-of-leading-us-airlines/

WebDriver. Selenium. (2022). Retrieved May 14, 2022, from https://www.selenium.dev/documentation/webdriver/

Sheluchin, A., Johnston, R. M., and Van Der Linden, C. (2020), Public responses to policy reversals: The case of mask usage in Canada during COVID-19. *Canadian Public Policy*, 46(S2). https://doi.org/10.3138/cpp.2020-089

Treloar, C., and Fraser, S. (2007), Public opinion on needle and syringe programmes: Avoiding assumptions for policy and Practice. *Drug and Alcohol Review*, 26(4), 355–361. https://doi.org/10.1080/09595230701373867

TSA. (2022), Coronavirus (COVID-19) information. Coronavirus (COVID-19) information | *Transportation Security Administration*. Retrieved April 2022, from https://www.tsa.gov/coronavirus

WHO. (2022), COVID-19 Pandemic All Information, *World Health Organization*, Retrieved April 2022, from https://www.who.int/

Wieczerak, T., Lal, P., Witherell, B., and Oluoch, S. (2022), Public preferences for green infrastructure improvements in Northern New Jersey: A discrete choice experiment approach, *Springer Nature Social Sciences* 2 (2), 1-20.

The Legal and Ethical issues Workshop @LREC2022, pages 9–16
Marseille, 20 June 2022

Data Protection, Privacy and US Regulation

Denise DiPersio
Linguistic Data Consortium, University of Pennsylvania
3600 Market Street, Suite 810, Philadelphia, PA 19104 USA
dipersio@ldc.upenn.edu

Abstract

This paper examines the state of data protection and privacy in the United States. There is no comprehensive federal data protection or data privacy law despite bipartisan and popular support. There are several data protection bills pending in the 2022 session of the US Congress, five of which are examined in Section 2 below. Although it is not likely that any will be enacted, the growing number reflects the concerns of citizens and lawmakers about the power of big data. Recent actions against data abuses, including data breaches, litigation and settlements, are reviewed in Section 3 of this paper. These reflect the real harm caused when personal data is misused. Section 4 contains a brief US copyright law update on the fair use exemption, highlighting a recent court decision and indications of a re-thinking of the fair use analysis. In Section 5, some observations are made on the role of privacy in data protection regulation. It is argued that privacy should be considered from the start of the data collection and technology development process. Enhanced awareness of ethical issues, including privacy, through university-level data science programs will also lay the groundwork for best practices throughout the data and development cycles.

Keywords: data protection, privacy, regulation

1. Introduction[1]

This is an interesting time for the field of language resources and related technologies. From the first days of natural language processing research represented by early machine translation, document understanding and speech recognition systems, we are today surrounded by human language technologies that are part of our daily lives. How we got here is a story about lots of good people doing good work in academia and industry and not least, sharing data broadly among the community. Data sharing has been fraught with legal issues, principally copyright rights and related licensing considerations, and depending on the data type, ethics and privacy concerns. Some of those issues persist in commercial language technologies, affecting how the systems work and how an individual's data is protected. The work grew faster than the law, so we find ourselves trying to match law and ethics with today's research and business realities. Tensions abound.

This paper examines the state of data protection and privacy in the United States, where the catching-up process has a long way to go. There is still no comprehensive federal data protection or data privacy law that addresses key issues. In the meantime, several US states have passed laws of their own (and more are in the works), and some federal agencies, principally the US Federal Trade Commission, investigate data-related consumer harms. The lack of an overarching philosophy or schema is a real problem.

There are several data protection bills pending in the 2022 session of the US Congress, five of which are examined in Section 2 below. Although it is not likely that any will be enacted, the growing number reflects the concerns of citizens and lawmakers about the power of big data.

Recent actions against data abuses, including data breaches, litigation and settlements, are reviewed in Section 3 of this paper. These reflect the real harm caused when personal data is misused.

Section 4 contains a brief US copyright law update on the fair use exemption, highlighting a recent court decision and indications of a re-thinking of the fair use analysis.

In Section 5, some observations are made on the role of privacy in data protection regulation. It is argued that privacy should be considered from the start of the data collection and technology development process. Enhanced awareness of ethical issues, including privacy, through university-level data science programs will also lay the groundwork for best practices throughout the data and development cycles.

2. Data Protection

2.1 Lack of US Progress

As reported at LREC2018, there is no comprehensive data protection law in the United States, and those that exist apply mostly to government use of personal information or to special circumstances (e.g., health information, personal credit information, student education records, children's online activity). (DiPersio, 2018). Private organizations face little regulation with respect to the collection, storage and use of data collected from or about individuals in the course of their business. This cuts across all industries, but is especially problematic with respect to the large technology companies that dominate the US, and to some extent, the global, economy.

Enacting a comprehensive US data protection scheme is an issue that has some level of bipartisan political support in Congress as well as broad popular appeal, but little progress has been made to date. The situation is becoming urgent, however, as individuals become increasingly aware of the ways in which their personal information is being used (and exploited) in the digital space. Companies claim to self-regulate, but those efforts often fall short. Several states have their own data protection statutes, but standards and provisions vary. Victims of data breaches and other unfair or deceptive data practices can resort to the courts

[1]This paper does not provide legal advice and nothing in this paper should be construed to constitute legal advice.

and to some government agencies under various theories and laws, with the attendant possibility of inconsistent outcomes.

In an age of virtual, cross-border data flows, this data protection gap also affects US relations with other countries, a growing number of which, led by the European Union and the GDPR, have enacted comprehensive data privacy laws. Indeed, some believe that the effect of the *Schrems II* decision, in which the European Court of Justice found that US data surveillance laws did not pass muster under the GDPR, could be ameliorated to some extent by US laws mandating standards for companies' collection and storage of personal information, thus in turn, limiting the reach of the US government's access to such information.

2.2 Pending Data Protection/Privacy Legislation

Several bills around the privacy and protection of an individual's personal data are pending in the 2021-2022 session of the US Congress. These include proposals that were introduced in the previous Congressional session (2019-2020), were not acted upon and were re-introduced in the current session. Most commentators believe that it is unlikely that any will be considered or enacted in this session, absent a showing of strong will from Congress and the Executive Branch.

Five of these bills are described below. Of these, three were introduced by members of the Democratic party (President Biden's party) (D), and two were introduced by members of the Republican party (R). Only one has co-sponsors from both parties. Four were pending in the 2019-2020 session and were re-introduced in 2021; no action (hearings, debates, etc.) has been taken on any of these bills in 2022 as of this writing.

These schemes represent varying approaches. Some are more comprehensive than others, some would preempt state data protection/privacy laws, some create new government agencies, and some rely on existing government infrastructure for investigation and enforcement. The more comprehensive proposals have some exemption for research-related activities. In all cases, existing federal data privacy/protection laws would remain in effect.

2.2.1 Information Transparency & Personal Data Control Act (D)

The **Information Transparency & Personal Data Control Act** (H.R. 1816) was introduced into the US House of Representatives in March 2021. This proposed law focuses on strengthening the powers of the US Federal Trade Commission (FTC), the agency with the authority to investigate unfair trade practices and to date the leading US regulator to take action on complaints alleging data abuses. It would provide the FTC with the authority to regulate the collection, processing, use, and storage of "sensitive personal information," an inclusive category that covers categories like financial account numbers, usernames and passwords, genetic data, citizenship, gender identity, web browsing history and more. Organizations that collect, store, process, sell, share or otherwise use sensitive personal information from more than 250,000 people annually would be required to undergo a privacy audit every two years. The act's restrictions do not apply to activities in the "public interest" including research, as long as processing does not create "significant harm" to users. [2] This bill would also preempt state privacy laws. H.R. 1816 is considered to be more business-friendly than other proposals.

2.2.2 Data Protection Act (D)

In June 2021, the **Data Protection Act of 2021** (S. 2134) was introduced in the US Senate (S. 2134). (A similar bill was introduced in 2020, but no action was taken before the 2019-2020 Congressional session ended.) It provides for the creation of a federal Data Protection Agency that would be charged with developing and enforcing data protection rules. It includes sections around agency authority to review mergers involving large technology companies, or any merger that involves the transfer of the personal data from more than 50,000 individuals; the establishment of an Office of Civil Rights; and the ability to impose fines and punitive penalties for unlawful, unfair, deceptive, abusive or discriminatory data practices.

The bill focuses on "data aggregators" and "high risk data practices," both of which may require some further clarification regarding research-related uses. A data aggregator is defined as any person collecting, using or sharing personal data that is not "de minimis," exempting individuals who collect, user or share such data for non-commercial purposes.[3] "High risk data practices" include "a systematic processing of publicly accessible data on a large scale." [4]

Although the term "personal identifying information" is used throughout the US research community, including by US government agencies, it has no conclusive definintion. The Data Protection Act takes a broad approach, defining "personal data" as electronic data that "identifies, relates to, describes, is capable of being associated with, or could reasonably be linked, directly or indirectly, with a particular individual, household or device." [5]

There are no provisions addressing research-related exemptions, except perhaps implicitly by the above reference to those who collect and share data for non-commercial purposes. State laws offering greater protections than those under this act would not be preempted (e.g., California's data privacy law).

2.2.3 Filter Bubble Transparency Act (R, D co-sponsors)

The Filter Bubble Transparency Act, previously incorporated in the 2019 version of the SAFE DATA Act (see below), was re-introduced in June 2021 as separate legislation in the Senate (S. 2024). This act would require internet platforms to provide users with "the option to engage with a platform without being manipulated by

[2] H.R. 1816, Section 3(b)(1)(G).

[3] S. 2134, Section 2 (6).

[4] Ibid., Section 2 (11).

[5] Ibid., Section 2 (16). Compare to GDPR Article 4 (1) where "personal data" can refer to name, identification number, location, online presence, or physical, genetic, economic, cultural or social identity.

algorithms driven by user-specific data."[6] Specifically, users would have the option of a "filter bubble-free view" of information, the presentation or order of which is not determined by an "opaque" algorithm.

A platform conducting not-for-profit research is exempt from the bill.[7] The FTC would enforce violations of the act under its jurisdiction to investigate unfair or deceptive acts or practices.[8]

Google has publicly expressed concern about the act, telling its business users that it "could disrupt many of the digital tools you use" and "[m]ake it harder for customers to find you."[9]

2.2.4 Setting an American Framework to Ensure Data Access, Transparency and Accountability Act (SAFE DATA Act) (R)

Another bill from the 2019-2020 Congressional session reintroduced in July 2021 is the SAFE DATA Act (S. 2499). This Senate bill aims to give users control over how their data is accessed, used and maintained, to require businesses to follow transparent data practices, and to strengthen the FTC's rulemaking ability and enforcement authority. The legislation would preempt state privacy laws.

Of interest here is the definition of research. Processing data for a research purpose means that the "advancement of scientific knowledge" is the primary purpose of the activity, but it can also be for the commercial benefit of the entity processing the data.[10] Exempt from the bill are data collection, processing, and related activities conducted for research (peer-reviewed, public, historical, statistical) that follow applicable privacy and ethical laws including Institutional Review Board review under the federal regulations for human subjects research.[11]

2.2.5 Online Privacy Act (D)

Like most of the current propsals, the **Online Privacy Act** was pending in the 2019-2020 Congressional session but failed to advance. In November 2021, the bill (H.R. 6027) was reintroduced in the US House of Representatives. It gives users the right to access, correct or delete their data, limits the amount of data companies can collect, allows users to decide how long companies can maintain their data, and requires that companies obtain consent from users. A new Data Privacy Agency would be responsible for enforcement and investigation. Qualified research entities conducting work for non-commercial purposes would be exempt from the act's ban on re-identifying de-identified data.[12]

2.3 The Pitfalls of Lagging Behind

The divergent approaches to US data protection legislation illustrated in the selected bills above suggest that finding common ground will be a challenging task. In addition to an extremely partisan congressional atmosphere, other high priority issues such as infrastructure, the Ukraine war, climate change and more vie for lawmakers' attention. The likelihood that a data protection law will be enacted before the current session ends in January 2023 is doubtful. Nevertheless, at a Global Privacy Summit in April 2022, Congressional aides indicated that talks have been ongoing behind the scenes and as a result, some compromises are possible. The main points of contention are federal preemption (the continued viability of state privacy laws) and whether individuals/groups can sue companies for money damages under a federal law. A compromise that allows some state law provisions to remain and that permits a limited right of private action is apparently gaining traction.[13] But the timing of any solution is still unclear.

The recent settlement proposal in the Clearview AI litigation, a case brought by the ACLU and others based in part on Illinois' biometric data statute (which requires user consent to the use of biometric data, including faces), reveals the shortcomings when state laws must fill the data protection gap. (See Section 3.2 below). The settlement will have some broad applicability to the extent that Clearview will not be able to sell its faces database to most US companies, but only photographs taken in, or uploaded from, Illinois will be removed from the database. The lack of a federal law regulating personal biometric information means in this case a less than satisfactory result

A larger issue, however, is that the United States is out of step with the global community in its piecemeal approach, shunning a data protection law that cuts across specific use cases. This is not new; traditional American thinking regards regulation as an impediment to innovation and US competitive standing. The GDPR, on the other hand, reflects broad goals regarding fundamental rights and economic and social issues.[14] Indeed the GDPR is viewed as setting the international standard for data protection and privacy. Other countries are moving forward with their own data protection and privacy regimes, many of which are based on, or are similar to, the GDPR model.[15]

---

[6]S. 2024, Preamble.

[7]Ibid., Section 2(4)(B)(III)(ii).

[8]Ibid., Section 4(a).

[9]Boyle, Christopher. *Google Fear of Looming "Filter Bubble Transparency Act" Legislation Which Would Force Fairness, Disclosure and Accountability.* Available at : https://www.publishedreporter.com/2021/11/24/google-scared-of-looming-filter-bubble-transparency-act-which-would-force-fairness-disclosure-and-accountability/.

[10]S. 2499, Section 2(16).

[11]Ibid., Section 108(a)(10).

[12]H.R. 6027, Section 205(c).

[13]Lima, Cristiano. The debate over a privacy bill is inching forward on Capitol Hill. Available at: https://www.washingtonpost.com/politics/2022/04/13/debate-over-privacy-bill-is-inching-forward-capitol-hill/.

[14]Roberts, Huw and Luciano Floridi. The EU and the US: two different approaches to AI governance. Available at: https://venturebeat.com/2022/03/21/why-2022-is-only-the-beginning-for-ai-regulation/.

[15]Those include the United Kingdom, Switzerland, Turkey, Australia, China, India, Indonesia, Japan, New Zealand, Philippines, Singapore, Thailand, South Africa, Saudi Arabia and

The 2020 decision of the European Court of Justice in *Schrems II* that US privacy safeguards were not "adequate" within the meaning of the GDPR is one example of how the philosophy gap between the United States and other countries affects international commerce.[16] The European court was concerned specifically about US intelligence laws that allow broad access to individual data.[17] In March 2022, the US and EU reached a tentative agreement on the dispute, with the US agreeing to make some administrative adjustments to intelligence law procedure that the parties believe will support a US claim that US safeguards are "necessary and proportionate in the pursuit of defined national security objectives." [18] However, because US law will not be changed, many believe that this latest agreement will be challenged in court as well. Again, the US line, here its stated need for surveillance, is at odds with the EU's focus on personal data protection.[19]

3. Data Breaches, Litigation, Settlements

Data breaches caused by events like cyberattacks, human errors, malicious activity and negligence are a daily threat for anyone whose personal information is stored in some organization's database. The full extent of the damage caused by US data breaches is often hard to assess since there are few regulations requiring that breaches be reported and the scope of any damage revealed. Too often, users discover that their personal information was compromised long after the event. The US Privacy Rights Clearinghouse is a non-profit organization with the goal to protect privacy for all. As part of that work, it has tracked reported US data breaches since 2005. It currently reports that over 11 billion records were compromised in more than 9000 reported US data breaches since 2005.[20] The actual numbers are likely much higher.

In the meantime, victims of data breaches or data misuse have been calling companies to account. Below are some recent examples.

3.1 Data Abuse Victims React

Selected challenges to US data breaches and related violations in 2021-2022 include the following.

Online merchandise platform **CafePress** settled FTC claims that it failed to secure users' sensitive personal data and failed to disclose a major data breach that allowed hackers to access millions of email addresses, passwords, social security numbers, credit card information and more. The company's former owner will pay $500,000 to data breach victims and along with the current owner, will implement security measures to address the circumstances leading to the data breach. Financial services company **Plaid, Inc.** will pay $58 million to settle a legal action in which Plaid was accused of accessing personal banking information without consent from users of financial applications such as Robinhood and Venmo. **Zoom** agreed to an $85 million settlement in a California federal lawsuit alleging that it engaged in unauthorized sharing of user data, misrepresented its encryption services and allowed hackers to disrupt meetings. **OpenX Technologies**, an advertising platform, must pay $2 million to settle claims by the FTC that it collected data from children in violation of the agency's Children's Online Privacy Protection Act Rule. **TikTok** settled consolidated litigation alleging that it shared users' personal data without consent, improperly handled users' biometric data and engaged in ad targeting for $92 million; the case involved roughly 89 million users. **Meta/Facebook** agreed to settle two privacy class-action lawsuits: it will pay $650 million to resolve allegations that it tagged biometric information in violation of Illinois law (2020) and $90 million to settle claims made in 2012 that it tracked users' activity after they logged off the platform (2022).

3.2 Clearview AI Litigation

In 2020, US facial recognition company Clearview AI claimed that it had developed a database of three million human images scraped from the web and annotated for biometric characteristics which it made available to law enforcement organizations and other paying customers. That generated a series of lawsuits from affected groups alleging breach of privacy and related theories. The cases were consolidated in a Chicago, Illinois federal court; they include claims under Virginia, California and New York law and under Illinois' Biometric Information Privacy Act (BIPA). BIPA constrains how companies can collect, use and store biometric information and requires that such information cannot be collected or used without users' written consent. It also permits individuals to bring actions under the statute on their own behalf.

Brazil. Gibson Dunn. International Cybersecurity and Data Privacy Outlook and Review – 2022. Available at: https://www.gibsondunn.com/international-cybersecurity-and-data-privacy-outlook-and-review-2022/.

[16]The so-called "privacy shield" relates to cross-border data transfers of personal information.

[17]Schaetzel, Lucas, J. U.S. and E.U. Reach New Trans-Atlantic Data Flow Agreement To Replace Privacy Shield. Available at: https://www.beneschlaw.com/resources/us-and-eu-reach-new-trans-atlantic-data-flow-agreement-to-replace-privacy-shield.html.

[18]FACT SHEET: United States and European Commission Announce Transatlantic Data Privacy Framework. Available at: https://www.whitehouse.gov/briefing-room/statements-releases/2022/03/25/fact-sheet-united-states-and-european-commission-announce-trans-atlantic-data-privacy-framework/.

[19]Ikeda, Scott. EU and US Move Closer to Privacy Shield Replacement With Agreement on Data Transfer Deal. Available at: https://www.cpomagazine.com/data-privacy/eu-and-us-move-closer-to-privacy-shield-replacement-with-agreement-on-data-transfer-deal/.

[20]Privacy Rights Clearinghouse. Available at: https://privacyrights.org/.

YouTube, Twitter and others demanded that Clearview stop collecting images from their sites in early 2020, claiming that the company's acts violated the sites' terms of use.

In the meantime, the company continued to conduct business. It announced that it was collecting 100 billion photos for its database, processing around 1.5 billion images monthly.

The presiding judge in the Illinois case ruled against Clearview's motion to dismiss the complaint in February 2022. In May 2022, a proposed settlement to the litigation was announced under which Clearview agreed to change its business model. Specifically, it will only sell its algorithm to customers, not its faces database. Additionally, it will not work with Illinois police or government organizations for five years and will remove from its database all photos taken in, or uploaded from, Illinois.[21]

This result shows the value of a statute like BIPA. Clearview's business practices are also under review in various foreign venues.[22]

3.3 Data Brokers, Cloud Services, Cyberattacks

A recent lawsuit involving two US **data brokers** illustrates the downstream risks associated with the collection of individuals' personal data. The litigation involves Outlogic (formerly known as X-Mode) and NybSys. X-Mode sells location data it collects from various apps, and it licensed that data to NybSys. X-Mode claims that NybSys unlawfully resold the information to another data broker, that in turn resold it to others. The suit is based on contract and trade secret claims. The case was referred to private mediation in March 2022.

Cloud services have become vital to everyday life, comparable in some ways to essential business such as power companies. Yet, those services are controlled by a few actors – Alphabet, Amazon, Microsoft – that are essentially unregulated. Missing are obligations around reporting data breaches. A model for oversight could be a recently-enacted US law requiring "key businesses" to report **cyberattacks/hacks** within 72 hours to the government's Cybersecurity and Infrastructure Security Agency, part of the US Department of Homeland Security. Covered businesses include banks and utilities. Any ransomware payments must be reported within 24 hours of the payment. Details on coverage, reporting, deadlines and so on are to be worked out in forthcoming regulations. Industry groups have criticized the measure as likely to result in large amounts of non-meaningful information that will hinder government analysis; they urge time for companies to assess the extent of any breach and to assemble information targeting actual harm.

4. US Copyright Update

The trend in US courts has been to recognize that copyrighted materials used for machine learning purposes are eligible for the US copyright law's fair use exception. Principally based on the transformative nature of the machine learning use case, such rulings have included unmodified full-text searchable databases within the exception, as discussed in previous LREC workshops (DiPersio, 2018).

An interesting 2021 case involving photographs of the musical artist Prince raised the relationship between derivative works under US copyright law (in which the original rightsholder shares copyright with the derivative works author) and fair use. Finding that "[i]t does not follow . . . that any secondary work that adds a new aesthetic or new expression to its source material is necessarily transformative," a US federal court held that changes made by Andy Warhol to the Prince photographs without the original author's permission were "substanially similar" to the orignal works and therefore more derivative than transformative.[23] Although this ruling may be deemed applicable to artistic works only, it bears watching to the extent courts could be influenced to take a harder look at transformation generally.

This ties in with the view of some that the emphasis on transformativeness in the fair use analysis overlooks the traditional thinking that fair use is supposed to benefit the less powerful non-rights holder against the monopoly of the copyright holder. Instead, as one scholar claims, "[t]oday's tech business turns this structure on its head," allowing "big users" to monetize lots of "little content" that includes allowing machines to learn from the way authors express ideas.[24] Moreover, with respect to the fair use factor around whether a substitute market (e.g., for machine learning) exists for the original rightsholder, a question that courts have in the past answered in the negative, one can imagine that text owners today would take advantage of the existing market for training data, for example. The data science and machine learning communities have benefited from the fair use copyright exception, but the growing power of technology, its insatiable need for data and the demonstrated ways in which individuals are harmed by big

[21]Harwell, Drew. Clearview AI to stop selling facial recognition tool to private firms. Available at: https://www.washingtonpost.com/technology/2022/05/09/clearview-illinois-court-settlement/.

[22]France 24. Clearview AI agrees to limit sales of facial recognition data after ACLU lawsuit. Available at: https://www.france24.com/en/americas/20220510-clearview-ai-settles-suit-agrees-to-limit-sale-of-facial-recognition-database (referencing proceedings in Canada, Italy, France, Austria and the United Kingdom).

[23]The Andy Warhol Foundation for the Visual Arts, Inc. V. Lynn Goldsmith, Lynn Goldsmith, Ltd., 11 F.4th 26, 38, 42 (2d Cir. 2021). The US Supreme Court has agreed to hear an appeal of this decision in its fall 2022 term.

[24]Sobel, B. L. W. (2017). Artificial Intelligence's Fair Use Crisis. The Columbia Journal of Law & The Arts, 41(1), pp. 45–97, 87, 89. Available at : https://doi.org/10.7916/jla.v41i1.2036.

data may cause policymakers and courts to rethink their approach.

5. Privacy and Regulation

A final word about privacy. Even as the number of US bills to address technology-related data protection and personal privacy issues increase in number, some question using established legal principles to address the ways the digital world impacts personal information. Protecting persons from intrusion is rooted in the idea of a private space sacrosanct to the individual. Thus, the notions of "zones of privacy" and a person's "expectation of privacy" – developed in the late 19th century in connection with the inventions of the telephone and photography and applied to new, related technologies (e.g., wiretapping) through the 20th century and beyond (Chertoff, 2018) – were coined to describe such boundaries. A companion principle is that information provided "voluntarily" to third parties is not protected. The distinction between public and private information, however, is blurred in the digital space.

Privacy should therefore be considered less rigidly, as something that applies variously depending on the information and the context. (Hartzog, 2018). The suggestion has been made that *autonomy* or *human values* are better expressions of the notions underlying privacy because they take into account the mass of personal information collected, processed, repurposed and resold today. (Ibid.; Chertoff, 2018). Moreover, to be effective, such personal human values should be considered at the beginning of the development process, not after the technology or application is finished and operational, because assumptions that implicate privacy are incorporated at the start: "[w]e shape our tools and thereafter our tools shape us."[25] This can be as innocuous as including features for convenience or responding to corporate pressure to generate data so that it can be monetized downstream. Some of this behavior is occasionally explained as resulting in unintended consequences. Nevertheless, design choices are not necessarily value neutral; they can favor certain societal interests over others. (Ibid.).

The move to create or enhance data science programs in US colleges and universities offers an opportunity to make ethics, privacy and related issues part of the curriculum, and many institutions offer such courses and training. (Baumer, et al. 2022; Davis, 2020). It is also encouraging to note that some large companies, including Google, Apple and Facebook, have implemented internal processes for evaluating privacy and ethical issues in their data collection and research activities.[26] Behind the scenes, however, is the specter of artificial intelligence and its boundless capabilities. Companies are spending substantial sums on "AI" research.[27] Academic research, sometimes with industry partners, reflects this trend as well. Thus, the tension between the technology industry's continued need for more researchers (software engineers, linguists) to advance the corporate mission and the goal of developing technology that serves all interests of society.

6. Conclusion

This paper has attempted to unite several themes around the regulation of data protection and privacy in the United States: the state of federal legislative initiatives, legal proceedings relating to data abuses, and thinking about how traditional notions about privacy relate or not to the realities of digital life. As discussed above, the current failure of a principled approach to regulating data protection and privacy in the United States means that those most vulnerable – everyone whose data is collected, analyzed, shared and sold – have little clarity on achieving effective relief. Pending legislation addresses some aspects of the problem, but until federal laws are enacted, data abuse victims must resort to the courts and to administrative remedies under a variety of legal frameworks. Those developing the means to exploit, or those exploiting user data, are the beneficiaries for now, although recent legal decisions and settlements suggest that the situation may be changing. Nevertheless, the United States lags behind its international partners in dealing with the digital world. The *Andy Warhol Foundation* copyright case illustrates another prospect for change, namely a re-thinking of how the transformation test could be applied in future cases involving machine learning applications. Similarly, a new notion of privacy that abandons the traditional US legal concept could lead to more effective regulation with respect to personal information in the digital space. And providing students and the professional community with ethics training and better tools for navigating the research and development process has the prospect of mitigating the occurrence of unintended consequences.

7. Bibliographical References

Altman, Micha, et al. (2018). Practical approaches to big data privacy over time. International Data Privacy Law, 8 (1), pp. 29-51.

Associated Press. *Facebook, YouTube demand facial recognition company stop scraping faces from sites.* Available at: https://www.nbcnews.com/tech/security/facebook-youtube-demand-facial-recognition-company-stop-scraping-faces-sites-n1131786.

Baumer, Benjamin S. et al. (2022). Integrating data science ethics into an undergraduate major; A case study. Available at https://arxiv.org/pdf/2001.07649.pdf.

Boyle, Christopher. *Google Fear of Looming "Filter Bubble Transparency Act" Legislation Which Would Force Fairness, Disclosure and Accountability.*

[25] Hartzog, Woodrow. (2018). *Privacy's Blueprint,* 8 n.11. Cambridge, Massachusetts: Harvard University Press (quoting Marshall McLuhan).

[26] Altman, Micha, et al. (2018). Practical approaches to big data privacy over time. International Data Privacy Law, 8 (1), pp. 29-51, 38.

[27] Rosenbush, Steven. *Big Tech Is Spending Billions on AI Research. Investors Should Keep An Eye Out.* Available at: https://www.wsj.com/articles/big-tech-is-spending-billions-on-ai-research-investors-should-keep-an-eye-out-11646740800.

Available at : https://www.publishedreporter.com/2021/11/24/google-scared-of-looming-filter-bubble-transparency-act-which-would-force-fairness-disclosure-and-accountability/.

Channick, Robert. *Nearly 1.6 million Illinois Facebook users could get their $400 checks soff after appeals court upholds $650 million settlement.* Available at: https://www.chicagotribune.com/business/ct-biz-facebook-privacy-settlement-illinois-appeal-decision-20220317-e4s3jqzm7bfvxliwh2uibbfo7y-story.html.

Chertoff, M. (2018). *Exploding Data, Reclaiming Our Cybersecurity In The Digital Age*. New York, New York: Atlantic Monthly Press.

Davis, Karen C. (2020). Ethics in Data Science Education. *In American Society for Engineering Education Virtual Conference.* Available at: https://peer.asee.org/ethics-in-data-science-education.pdf.

Dean, Graham and Ronald Raether. *U.S. Senators Reintroduce Privacy Legislation*. Available at: https://www.jdsupra.com/legalnews/u-s-senators-reintroduce-privacy-4527842/#_ftn6.

DiPersio, D. (2018). *A US Perspective on Selected Legal and Ethical Issues Affecting the Development of Language Resources and Related Technology.* In Nicoletta Calzolari (Conference Chair), et al., editors, *Proceedings of the Eleventh International Conference on Language Resources and Evaluation (LREC'18), W21, Legal Issues and Ethics*, Miyazaki, Japan, May. European Language Resource Association (ELRA).

EU General Data Protection Regulation (GDPR): Regulation (EU) 2016/679 of the European Parliament and of the Council of 27 April 2016 on the protection of natural persons with regard to the processing of personal data and on the free movement of such data, and repealing Directive 95/46/EC (General Data Protection Regulation), OJ 2016 L 119/1.

FACT SHEET: United States and European Commission Announce Transatlantic Data Privacy Framework. Available at: https://www.whitehouse.gov/briefing-room/statements-releases/2022/03/25/fact-sheet-united-states-and-european-commission-announce-trans-atlantic-data-privacy-framework/.

Federal Trade Commission. *Advertising Platform OpenX Will Pay $2 Million for Collecting Personal Information from Children in Violation of Children's Privacy Law.* Available at: https://www.ftc.gov/news-events/news/press-releases/2021/12/advertising-platform-openx-will-pay-2-million-collecting-personal-information-children-violation.

Federal Trade Commission. *FTC Takes Action Against CafePress for Data Breach Cover Up.* Available at: https://www.ftc.gov/news-events/news/press-releases/2022/03/ftc-takes-action-against-cafepress-data-breach-cover.

France 24. *Clearview AI agrees to limit sales of facial recognition data after ACLU lawsuit.* Available at: https://www.france24.com/en/americas/20220510-clearview-ai-settles-suit-agrees-to-limit-sale-of-facial-recognition-database.

Gibson Dunn. *International Cybersecurity and Data Privacy Outlook and Review – 2022.* Available at: https://www.gibsondunn.com/international-cybersecurity-and-data-privacy-outlook-and-review-2022/.

Gold, Ashley. *Exclusive: New bipartisan bill takes aim at algorithms.* Available at: https://www.axios.com/algorithm-bill-house-bipartisan-5293581e-430f-4ea1-8477-bd9adb63519c.html.

Haasch, Palmer. *TikTok may owe you money from its $92 million data privacy settlement.* Available at: https://www.businessinsider.com/tiktok-data-privacy-settlement-how-to-submit-claim-2021-11.

Hammer, Alex. *Facial Recognition firm Clearview AI says it will soon have 100 BILLION photos in its database to ensure 'almost everyone in the world will be identifiable' and wants to expand beyond law enforcement.* Available at: https://www.dailymail.co.uk/news/article-10523739/Clearview-AI-seeking-100-billion-photos-facial-recognition-database.html.

Hartzog, Woodrow. (2018). *Privacy's Blueprint.* Cambridge, Massachusetts: Harvard University Press.

Harwell, Drew. *Clearview AI to stop selling facial recognition tool to private firms.* Available at: https://www.washingtonpost.com/technology/2022/05/09/clearview-illinois-court-settlement/.

Holland, Makenzie. *Federal data privacy law efforts fizzle.* Available at: https://www.techtarget.com/searchcio/news/252512860/Federal-data-privacy-law-efforts-fizzle?vgnextfmt=print.

Ikeda, Scott. *EU and US Move Closer to Privacy Shield Replacement With Agreement on Data Transfer Deal. Available* at: https://www.cpomagazine.com/data-privacy/eu-and-us-move-closer-to-privacy-shield-replacement-with-agreement-on-data-transfer-deal/.

Jaehnig, Johnathan. *YouTube Claims to Be "Explicitly Clear" on Facial Recognition, But Is It Really?* Available at: https://www.makeuseof.com/youtube-claims-to-be-explicitly-clear-on-facial-recognition-but-is-it-really/.

Keegan J. and Alfred Ng. *Lawsuit Highlights How Little Control Brokers Have Over Location Data.* Available at: https://themarkup.org/privacy/2022/03/21/lawsuit-highlights-how-little-control-brokers-have-over-location-data.

Keegan J. and Alfred Ng. *There's a Multibillion-Dollar Market for Your Phone's Location Data.* Available at: https://themarkup.org/privacy/2021/09/30/theres-a-multibillion-dollar-market-for-your-phones-location-data.

Kerry, Cameron F. *One year after Schrems II, the world is still waiting for U.S. privacy legislation.* Available at: https://www.brookings.edu/blog/techtank/2021/08/16/one-year-after-schrems-ii-the-world-is-still-waiting-for-u-s-privacy-legislation/.

Lexis/Nexis. *AI in Academia: How the Need for Future Data Scientists & the Availability of Big Data is Transforming Universities.* Available at: https://www.lexisnexis.com/community/insights/professional/b/trends/posts/ai-in-academia.

Lima, Cristiano. *Europe is lapping the U.S. on tech regulation – again.* Available at: https://www.washingtonpost.com/politics/2022/03/28/europe-is-lapping-us-tech-regulation-again/.

Lima, Cristiano. *The debate over a privacy bill is inching forward on Capitol Hill.* Available at: https://www.washingtonpost.com/politics/2022/04/13/debate-over-privacy-bill-is-inching-forward-capitol-hill/.

Meltzer, Joshua P. *The Court of Justice of the European Union in Schrems II: The impact of GDPR on data flows and national security.* Available at: https://www.brookings.edu/research/the-court-of-justice-of-the-european-union-in-schrems-ii-the-impact-of-gdpr-on-data-flows-and-national-security/.

Michaels, Daniel and Sam Schechner. *U.S., EU Reach Preliminary Deal on Data Privacy.* Available at: https://www.wsj.com/articles/u-s-eu-reach-preliminary-deal-on-data-privacy-11648200085.

Privacy Rights Clearinghouse. Available at: https://privacyrights.org/

Roberts, Huw and Luciano Floridi. *The EU and the US: two different approaches to AI governance.* Available at: https://venturebeat.com/2022/03/21/why-2022-is-only-the-beginning-for-ai-regulation/.

Rosenbush, Steven. *Big Tech Is Spending Billions on AI Research. Investors Should Keep An Eye Out.* Available at: https://www.wsj.com/articles/big-tech-is-spending-billions-on-ai-research-investors-should-keep-an-eye-out-11646740800.

Roth, Emma. *Plaid, the service used by Venmo, Acorns, Robinhood, and more, may owe you some money.* Available at: https://www.theverge.com/2022/1/23/22898009/plaid-financial-venmo-acorns-robinhood-class-action-lawsuit.

Sobel, B. L. W. (2017). Artificial Intelligence's Fair Use Crisis. The Columbia Journal of Law & The Arts, 41(1), pp. 45-97. Available at; https://doi.org/10.7916/jla.v41i1.2036.

Spangler, Todd. *Meta to Pay $90 Million to Settle Decade-Old Facebook Data Privacy Lawsuit.* Available at: https://variety.com/2022/digital/news/facebook-90-million-privacy-lawsuit-settlement-1235182172/.

Stempel, Jonathan. *Zoom reaches $85 mln over user privacy, 'Zoombombing'.* Available at: https://www.reuters.com/technology/zoom-reaches-85-mln-settlement-lawsuit-over-user-privacy-zoombombing-2021-08-01/.

The Federal Trade Commission Act. 15 USC 41-58, as amended.

The YouTube Team. *Updates to YouTube's Terms of Service.* Available at: https://blog.youtube/news-and-events/updates-to-youtubes-terms-of-service/.

Turkewitz, Neil. *Fairness to Whom? Reimagining a New Paradigm for Considering Fair Use.* Available at: https://medium.com/@nturkewitz_56674/fairness-to-whom-reimagining-a-new-paradigm-for-considering-fair-use-c871797ceb60.

Uberti, David. *Fearing More Cyberattacks, Congress Requires Key Businesses to Report Digital Breaches.* Available at: https://www.wsj.com/articles/fears-of-cybersecurity-attacks-may-increase-disclosure-requirements-for-businesses-11647444384?mod=hp_lista_pos3.

Ziegler, Bart. *Should Amazon, Microsoft, Google and Other Cloud Companies Face More Government Oversight?* Available at: https://www.wsj.com/articles/should-amazon-google-microsoft-cloud-companies-face-more-government-oversight-11646430816.

8. Legal Case References

In re Clearview AI, Inc., Consumer Privacy Litigation, Case No. 21-cv-0135, Memorandum Opinion and Order (N.D. Ill. Feb. 14, 2022).

Outlogic, LLC v. NybSys, Inc., Case No. 21-cv-09592-VKD (N.D. Cal. 2021), First Amended Complaint.

The Andy Warhol Foundation for the Visual Arts, Inc. v. Lynn Goldsmith, Lynn Goldsmith, Ltd., 11 F.4th 26 (2d Cir. 2021).

The Legal and Ethical issues Workshop @LREC2022, pages 17–21
Marseille, 20 June 2022

Pseudonymisation of Speech Data as an Alternative Approach to GDPR Compliance

Paweł Kamocki[1] **and Ingo Siegert**[2]
[1]Leibniz Institut für Deutsche Sprache, Mannheim, Germany
[2]Mobile Dialog Systems, Otto von Guericke University Magdeburg, Germany
kamocki@ids-mannheim.de, siegert@ovgu.de

Abstract

The debate on the use of personal data in language resources usually focuses — and rightfully so — on anonymisation. However, this very same debate usually ends quickly with the conclusion that proper anonymisation would necessarily cause loss of linguistically valuable information. This paper discusses an alternative approach — pseudonymisation. While pseudonymisation does not solve all the problems (inasmuch as pseudonymised data are still to be regarded as personal data and therefore their processing should still comply with the GDPR principles), it does provide a significant relief, especially — but not only — for those who process personal data for research purposes. This paper describes pseudonymisation as a measure to safeguard rights and interests of data subjects under the GDPR (with a special focus on the right to be informed). It also provides a concrete example of pseudonymisation carried out within a research project at the Institute of Information Technology and Communications of the Otto von Guericke University Magdeburg.

Keywords: Pseudonymisation, GDPR, Personal Data, Speech Data

1. Introduction

In European law, personal data are defined in a very broad manner as 'any information related to an identified or identifiable natural person'. This definition, currently in §4 of the GDPR, is in fact much older than the GDPR itself, and can be traced back to the 1981 Council of Europe's Convention 108, or even to the 1977 German Federal Data Protection Act (itself inspired by the 1970 Data Protection Act of the State of Hessen). This very general and broad approach is the cornerstone of European privacy law.

Under this approach, even information that is not nominative (i.e. does not contain the person's name and surname) or directly identifying (e.g. a social security number) should be regarded as personal data, as long as it can be related to a person. Therefore, a huge part of language data, especially in speech and multi-modal resources, fall within the scope of data protection laws. As such, the processing of such data should abide by the GDPR principles of lawfulness, fairness, transparency, purpose limitation, data minimisation, accuracy, storage limitation, integrity, confidentiality, and accountability. A good overview on reflections on legal and technical issues regarding speech data and GDPR is given in (Nautsch et al., 2019).

These principles no longer apply to data that have been anonymised, i.e. processed in such a manner that the person they originally referred to can no longer be identified 'by any means likely reasonably to be used'. However, anonymisation should be permanent and irreversible (WP29 (Article 29 Data Protection Working Party), 2014), which almost always entails a loss of potentially valuable linguistic information (Siegert et al., 2020). Moreover, taking into account the growing availability of online data that can be used to re-identify the person, the technical standard for anonymisation (set high by the 2014 WP29 opinion on anonymisation techniques) is constantly getting higher. Therefore, apart from being a technological and organisational challenge (with many tasks that still have to be performed manually), anonymisation is necessarily a costly procedure.

Pseudonymisation, which should be clearly distinguished from anonymisation, may be an alternative solution. Rather than permanently breaking the relation between the person and the data, pseudonymisation consists of the processing of the data in such a manner that it can no longer be attributed to a specific person without the use of additional information (e.g. a pseudonym or an ID number). This additional information (which can be referred to as 'the key') shall be kept separately from the data, and be subject to technical and organisational measures to prevent re-identification of data subjects (cf. definition of pseudonymisation in §4 of the GDPR).

Under the GDPR, pseudonymisation is one of the possible safeguards for the rights and freedoms of data subjects (Section 2), which, if applied correctly, reduces the legal burden at various stages of data processing (also, for example, regarding the data subjects' right to information; Section 3). It is therefore an interesting option to consider in research projects, for example in the field of speech data (Section 4).

2. Pseudonymisation in the GDPR

Unlike the 1995 Personal Data Directive (in force until 2018), the GDPR explicitly introduces pseudonymisation as a safeguard that can 'reduce the risks to the data subjects concerned and help controllers and processors to meet their data-protection obligations' (Recital 28 of the GDPR). This has several practical consequences, especially regarding the so-called 'purpose extension' (WP29 (Article 29 Data Protection Working Party), 2013), and the processing of personal data for research purposes. Purpose extension is the principle according to which data lawfully collected for one purpose can be subsequently re-used (without e.g. the need to obtain new consent from data subjects) for a 'compatible purpose'. By means of exception, scientific research shall always be regarded as a compatible purpose (as per Article 5.1 (b) of the GDPR). However, if the purpose is different from scientific research, then it is for the data controller to assess the compatibility of the new purpose with the initial purpose. Article 6.4 of the GDPR lists five elements that can be taken into account in this assessment (the list is not exhaustive); the existence of safeguards such as pseudonymisation is one of them. Therefore, pseudonymisation facilitates the use of lawfully collected data for a new purpose, as it enlarges the scope of 'compatible' purposes.

When the processing is carried out for research purposes, Article 89 of the GDPR allows the Member States to adopt a number of exceptions and derogations from the general data protection framework. These derogations concern e.g. the purpose limitation principle (scientific research is always regarded as a 'compatible purpose'), the storage limitation (for research purposes, data can be stored for longer than 'necessary'), as well as some rights of data subjects (information, erasure, right to object). An important caveat, however, is that in order to be able to qualify for all these derogations, the processing should be not only carried out exclusively for scientific research purposes (including commercial research), but also it should be subject to 'appropriate safeguards'. Article 89 of the GDPR expressly lists pseudonymisation as an example (the only example) of such a safeguard. Arguably, pseudonymisation is in most cases the cheapest safeguard, and the easiest to implement.

Before we discuss a concrete example of pseudonymisation, it should be pointed out that pseudonymisation, in order to meet the requirements of the GDPR, should involve appropriate technical and organisational security measures to prevent unauthorised access to the 'key' and identification of data subjects. Such organisational security measures, as per Articles 32 and following of the GDPR, can include a Data Breach Policy — an internal procedure to follow in case of an event which may constitute a data breach, and the criteria to determine the related risks for data subjects. It should be reminded here that a breach, if it is likely to result in a risk for the rights and freedoms of natural persons, should be notified to the supervisory authority, and if the risk is high — also communicated to data subjects.

3. Data Subject's Right to Information under the GDPR

As discussed in the previous section, pseudonymised data are still to be regarded as personal data, and therefore their processing should in principle still observe the General Data Protection Regulation. This means that, among other obligations, data subjects can still exercise their rights, unless a statutory exception applies.

Information is the most fundamental right of data subjects. According to Article 12 of the GDPR, the controller shall take appropriate measures to inform data subjects about the processing in 'a concise, transparent, intelligible and easily accessible form, using clear and plain language, in particular for any information addressed specifically to a child'. The information should be provided in writing, including in electronic form. Oral transmission of information is not excluded, but it is much harder to document, which is especially important since according to the accountability principle, the controller should be able to demonstrate compliance with the GDPR. Moreover, the sheer amount of information that, according to Articles 13 and 14, should be communicated to the data subject (see below), transmission in writing is also more practicable.

Importantly, data subjects shall be provided with information regardless of whether their consent is asked for in the process and regardless of whether the data were obtained directly from them or from other sources (including publicly available sources such as public LinkedIn profiles). In the first case (data obtained directly from the subject), the information should be provided at the time when the data is obtained; in the second (data obtained from other sources) - within a reasonable period of time, but no later than a month after the data have been obtained, or - if the data are disclosed to another recipient (e.g. shared with another research team) - at the latest at the moment of this disclosure.

Regarding the elements that data subjects should be provided with, the GDPR contains two lists: Article 13 applies when the data are collected directly from the data subject; Article 14 - in other cases. For the most part, both lists overlap; they both include such elements as (among others) the identity and contact details of the data controller, the purposes and the legal basis for the processing (including, where this basis applies, the legitimate interest pursued by the controller), the period for which the data will be stored in unanonymised form (or at least how the period will be determined), the persons (or categories of persons) the data will be disclosed to (recipients) and, if applicable, intended transfers of the data outside the European Economic Area. Both Article 13 and 14 also require information about the rights of the data subject, including the right to withdraw consent (if the processing is based on consent) or to lodge a complaint with a supervisory authority. The most important difference in the content of information between the two articles is that where the data are not obtained directly from the data subject (Article 14), he or she has to be informed about the categories of data collected and about the source it was obtained from (including information on whether the source is publicly available).

It shall be noted that in practice, most of these elements

Table 1: Overview of selected information provided to data subjects.

<table>
<tr><th></th><th>Data collected directly from subject (13 GDPR)</th><th>Data obtained from another source (14 GDPR)</th></tr>
<tr><td>When to inform</td><td>At the time of collection</td><td>Max. 1 month after obtaining data</td></tr>
<tr><td>Exception 1</td><td colspan="2">Subject already has the information</td></tr>
<tr><td>Exception 2</td><td></td><td>provision is impossible or requires disproportionate effort</td></tr>
<tr><td>Controller's identity and contact</td><td colspan="2">+</td></tr>
<tr><td>Data protection officer's contact</td><td colspan="2">+</td></tr>
<tr><td>Purpose(s) of the processing</td><td colspan="2">+</td></tr>
<tr><td>Categories of processed data</td><td>-</td><td>+</td></tr>
<tr><td>Legal basis of the processing (or legitimate interest)</td><td colspan="2">+</td></tr>
<tr><td>Recipients</td><td colspan="2">+</td></tr>
<tr><td>Transfers outside European Economic Area, if intended</td><td colspan="2">+</td></tr>
<tr><td>Data retention period (or criteria to determine it)</td><td colspan="2">+</td></tr>
<tr><td>Right to lodge a complaint</td><td colspan="2">+</td></tr>
<tr><td>Right to withdraw consent</td><td colspan="2">+</td></tr>
<tr><td>Whether the provision of data is required (by law or by contract), and consequences of refusal</td><td>+</td><td>-</td></tr>
<tr><td>Source data was obtained from</td><td>-</td><td>+</td></tr>
<tr><td>Existence of automated decision-making (see 22 GDPR)</td><td colspan="2">+</td></tr>
</table>

can be covered in a boilerplate text (with some modifications to fit specific scenarios), it is therefore highly recommendable to work on a re-usable model for an information form (sometimes referred to as 'consent form', rather mistakenly, since the information has to be provided even when there is no need to obtain consent, i.e. when processing is based on other grounds, such as legitimate interests).

The main interest in distinguishing between the situation when the data are obtained from the data subject and when they are obtained from other sources is in the exceptions. In the first scenario, Article 13.4 allows for only one exception: the information does not have to be provided when the data subject already has it. However, when the data are not obtained directly from the data subject, there is considerably more leeway; the obligation to provide information can be derogated from (Article 14.5) also when it proves impossible or would involve a disproportionate effort or in so far as the provision of information is likely to render impossible or seriously impair the achievement of the objectives of that processing. This is particularly relevant when the processing (of the data) is carried out for research purposes, and the application. In assessing whether the obligation can be derogated based on disproportionate efforts, account should be taken of three elements (WP29 (Article 29 Data Protection Working Party), 2018): the number of data subjects (the higher the number, the bigger the effort), the age of the data (the older the data, the bigger the effort) and any appropriate safeguards adopted. In this approach, the use of safeguards such as pseudonymisation may be a factor that 'tilts the scales' on the side of the derogation. The differences between Article 13 and Article 14 are summarized in Table 1.

However, even if the derogation from the obligation to provide information applies, transparency of the processing should still be observed. In such case, the controller should take appropriate measures to protect the data subject's rights and freedom, e.g. by making the information about the processing publicly available. In the context of research projects, when the data are collected directly from the subjects, and where measures such as pseudonymisation are applied, publishing a note with all required elements on the institution's (or the project's) website would often be enough to comply with the obligation.

4. Pseudonymisation of Speech Data: A Case Study

Naturalistic data recordings are an important resource for speech-based analyses. Therefore, data should be of high quality, including long and elaborate interactions, non-verbal events, and having a reliable and versatile emotion annotation. Ideally, the data set should contain contextual information about the speakers, such as age, sex, or personality traits, see (Böck et al., 2019).
The reported case study concerns a dataset recorded under a transfer project within the DFG-funded SFB/TRR-62 "A Companion Technology for cognitive technical systems"[1] at the Institute of Information Technology and Communications of the Otto von Guericke University Magdeburg in collaboration with a German call centre agency. The aim was to automatically support the agent in the handling of affective customer signals. It was aimed to give feedback to the agents regarding their dialogue with the customer and to give suggestions for customer-oriented dialogues. As call centre agents are mostly dealing with the factual level of the conversations and are rather insensitive to signals on the relational level (Watzlawick et al., 1967). The project ran from 2015 until 2016.
To support this hypothesis and develop a suitable recognition system, suitable data of sufficient amounts have to be available. To exclude side effects, which prevent a satisfactory classification performance on the expected less expressive emotional expressions, data having the same context and the same acoustic conditions are necessary (Douglas-Cowie et al., 2005; Zeng et al., 2009). Therefore, a larger data collection to train the recognition models and to obtain a sufficient number of different caller and agent behaviour was conducted at the beginning of the project. This recording has on the one hand to protect the personal data of both the agent and the caller and on the other hand allowing to record and analyse the recorded voice data.
The audio stream of both agent and caller was recorded. To later inspect the recordings for peculiarities, the agent was video-recorded as well. The callers were informed about the fact that the call was being recorded by preceding information that "the conversation is recorded due to quality reasons and the customers can refuse to accept this recording at any time". The agents took part voluntarily and their name has never been disclosed to the academic partner. As it is known that the emotional reaction is heavily dependent on personality ((Larsen and Ketelaar, 1991)), the agent's evaluation regarding the Big Five personality traits ((Costa and McCrae, 1995)) and the stress-coping questionnaire ((Jahnke et al., 2002)) are stored as well. As for the agents, also age, gender, and personality information were recorded, an agent code (Agent1 ... Agent4) was used to pseudonymise this information.
To conduct the recording, a separate recording carrel

[1] http://www.sfb-trr-62.de/

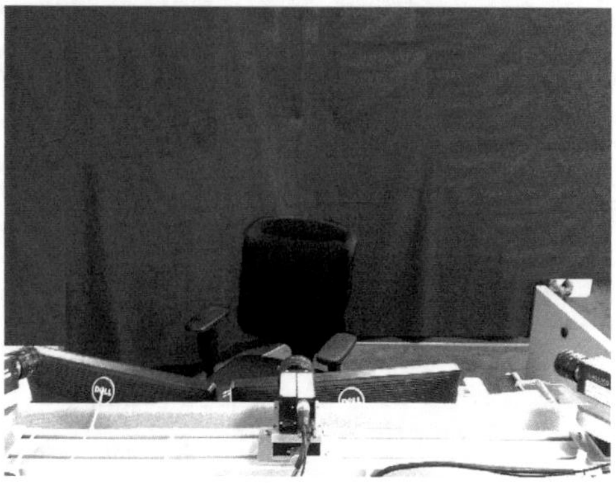

Figure 1: Picture of the separate recording carrel

was established. Thereby surrounding noise could be minimized, for the video recordings the privacy of people not involved could be preserved and a uniformly illuminated scene was enabled. All of these recordings took place in-house at the call centre agency. Furthermore, a special button was installed to interrupt the recording if a customer withdraws the initially given consent for recording.
The dataset ((Siegert and Ohnemus, 2015)) comprised real telephone-based conversations of in total 1 447 dialogues with 46 610 turns, which comprises approx. 93 hours of speech data. The topics of the calls range from simple informative calls and notifications of changes of customer data to complaint calls. In order to enable a comprehensive analysis of the material, four agents were selected, and their conversations were recorded on a daily basis.
As the phone calls were authentic customer dialogues, they had to be "pre-anonymised" first. Therefore, specially trained employees carefully listened to all recordings. All passages where personal information was disclosed were replaced by corresponding silence passages. The employees used Audacity for this task. Although most of the procedure could be sped up by using specialized keyboard shortcuts, this task had a processing time from 6 times the original recording time. To pseudonymise the remaining data, each recorded dialogue is stored under a consecutive number. A separate file holds the detailed information of the specific recording time for each dialogue. This file connects the consecutive number of each dialogue (the filename, e.g. 0001.wav) with its recording time (e.g. 31. February 2016, Dialogue 55). This file is stored on a separate external hard disk, in a locked cabinet, where only the lead scientists have access.

5. Conclusion

Pseudonymisation should not be mistaken for anonymisation; pseudonymised data are still to be considered personal data, but if the pseudonymisation is done correctly (also with regard to organisational and technical security measures to prevent de-identification), it may allow for the data to be lawfully processed for scientific research purposes, without losing all the relevant information. It may also be less costly than anonymisation. The pseudonymised data allows for research on prosodic-acoustic analyses by distributing extracted characteristics for acoustic modelling and by allowing in-house listener evaluations. Pseudonymisation of audio data is still an open issue, especially, as techniques to anonymize the speaker (obfuscating the speaker ID) while preserving relevant speech and emotional content is still under development (Sinha and Siegert, 2022; Tomashenko et al., 2021). Therefore, it should always be considered as an alternative way to GDPR compliance for scientific research projects, especially those involving processing of speech data, which are particularly hard to anonymise.

6. Bibliographical References

Böck, R., Egorow, O., Höbel-Müller, J., Requardt, A. F., Siegert, I., and Wendemuth, A., (2019). *Anticipating the User: Acoustic Disposition Recognition in Intelligent Interactions*, pages 203–233. Springer International Publishing, Cham.

Costa, P. T. and McCrae, R. R. (1995). Domains and Facets: Hierarchical Personality Assessment Using the Revised NEO Personality Inventory. *J Pers Assess*, 64:21–50.

Douglas-Cowie, E., Devillers, L., Martin, J.-C., Cowie, R., Savvidou, S., Abrilian, S., and Cox, C. (2005). Multimodal databases of everyday emotion: facing up to complexity. In *Proc. of the INTERSPEECH-2005*, pages 813–816, Lisbon, Portugal.

Jahnke, W., Erdmann, G., and Kallus, K. (2002). *Stressverarbeitungsfragebogen mit SVF 120 und SVF 78*. Hogrefe, Göttingen, Germany, 3 edition.

Larsen, R. J. and Ketelaar, T. (1991). Personality and susceptibility to positive and negative emotional states. *J Pers Soc Psychol*, 61:132–140, 07.

Nautsch, A., Jasserand, C., Kindt, E., Todisco, M., Trancoso, I., and Evans, N. (2019). The GDPR & Speech Data: Reflections of Legal and Technology Communities, First Steps Towards a Common Understanding. In *Proc. Interspeech 2019*, pages 3695–3699.

Siegert, I. and Ohnemus, K. (2015). A new dataset of telephone-based human-human call-center interaction with emotional evaluation. In *Proc. of the 1st International Symposion on Companion Technology (ISCT 2015)*, pages 143–148, Ulm, Germany, September.

Siegert, I., V.Silber-Varod, Carmi, N., and Kamocki, P. (2020). Personal data protection and academia: Gdpr issues and multi-modal data-collections "in the wild". *The Online Journal of Applied Knowledge Management: OJAKM*, 8:16 – 31.

Sinha, Y. and Siegert, I. (2022). Performance and quality evaluation of a mcadams speaker anonymization for spontaneous german speech. In *Fortschritte der Akustik - DAGA 2022*, pages 1185–1188, Stuttgart, Germany.

Tomashenko, N., Wang, X., Vincent, E., Patino, J., Srivastava, B. M. L., Noé, P.-G., Nautsch, A., Evans, N., Yamagishi, J., O'Brien, B., et al. (2021). The voiceprivacy 2020 challenge: Results and findings. *arXiv preprint arXiv:2109.00648*.

Watzlawick, P., Beavin, J. H., and Jackson, D. D. (1967). *Pragmatics of Human Communication: A Study of Interactional Patterns, Pathologies, and Paradoxes*. Norton, Bern, Switzerland.

WP29 (Article 29 Data Protection Working Party). (2013). Opinion 03/2013 on purpose limitation.

WP29 (Article 29 Data Protection Working Party). (2014). Opinion 05/2014 on anonymisation techniques.

WP29 (Article 29 Data Protection Working Party). (2018). Opinion guidelines on transparency under regulation 2016/679, revised.

Zeng, Z., Pantic, M., Roisman, G., and Huang, T. (2009). A Survey of Affect Recognition Methods: Audio, Visual, and Spontaneous Expressions. *IEEE Trans. Pattern Anal. Mach. Intell.*, 31:39–58.

The Legal and Ethical issues Workshop @LREC2022, pages 22–26
Marseille, 20 June 2022

Categorizing Legal Features in a Metadata-Oriented Task: Defining the Conditions of Use

Mickaël Rigault[1], Victoria Arranz[1], Valérie Mapelli[1], Penny Labropoulou[2], Stelios Piperidis[2]
[1]ELDA/ELRA,
[1]9 rue des Cordelières, 75013 Paris, France, [2]Institute for Language and Speech Processing
[2]Artemidos 6 & Epidavrou, GR-151 25 Maroussi, Athens Greece
mickael@elda.org, arranz@elda.org, mapelli@elda.org, penny@athenarc.gr, spip@athenarc.gr

Abstract

In recent times, more attention has been brought by the Human Language Technology (HLT) community to the legal framework required to render Language Resources (LR) and tools available for later use. Licensing is now an issue that is foreseen in most research projects and that is essential to provide legal certainty for repositories when distributing resources. Some repositories such as Zenodo or Quantum Stat do not offer the possibility to search for resources by licenses which can turn the searching for relevant resources into a very complex task. Other repositories such as Hugging Face propose a search feature by license which may make it difficult to figure out what use can be made of such resources.
During the European Language Grid (ELG) project, we moved a step forward to link metadata with the terms and conditions of use. In this paper, we document the process we undertook to categorize legal features of licenses listed in the SPDX license list[1] and widely used in the HLT community as well as those licenses used within the ELG platform.

Keywords: Copyright, Open-Source Licenses, Licensing, Metadata

1. Introduction

Nowadays, the number of licenses that exist to define the framework of use of tools and Language Resources (LRs) in the field of Human Language Technologies (HLT) is tremendously high. There are several widely known license suites available for research teams to make their content available (Creative Commons[2], MIT[3], ELRA[4], META-NET[5], CLARIN[6], BSD[7]…). Therefore, it is increasingly difficult for researchers and potential users to have clear information on the terms and conditions of use of a particular resource. Therefore, repositories transcribe legal concepts into metadata information to allow for the display of legal information to users and thus allow both a) to know what can be done with a resource at first glance and b) the implementation of search functions within catalogues of resources for popular conditions of reuse. A thorough study was initiated within the Meta-Share project (Piperidis, 2012; Piperidis et al., 2014) to highlight licenses and related concepts that apply to HLT tools and LRs (Choukri et al. 2012,). ELDA also built a License Wizard[8] that enables users to select licenses depending on the legal metadata used as search criteria.

Following upon Meta-Share, the European Language Grid (ELG)[9], a project funded by the European Union, has developed a platform to enable access and use of HLT tools and LRs.

To support the ELG platform (Rehm 2020), the project team developed a metadata schema (Labropoulou et al. 2020) for the description of Language Resources and Technologies (LRTs). For the free text search and faceted view, the ELG platform uses a subset of the metadata elements deemed important for discovery by the users. Findability[10] is a crucial feature in the lifecycle of an LRT.

In this paper we relate the research that we performed to power this search engine with legal metadata features.

For this purpose, we identified general legal concepts and transcribed those into metadata values, we cross-checked a list of licenses through the lens of these general concepts and categorized these licenses according to their conditions of use and the corresponding metadata values.

2. License Framework

The main purpose of this task was to define legal categories and add them to the ELG metadata scheme[11]. This work was done through a thorough investigation of the licenses available on the SPDX license list[12] and those used for LRTs already included in the ELG platform, which provides a list of commonly used licenses in the open-source community. All the different aspects analyzed and addressed are described in the coming sections.

[1] https://spdx.org/licenses/
[2] https://creativecommons.org/about/cclicenses/
[3] https://opensource.org/licenses/MIT
[4] http://www.elra.info/en/services-around-lrs/distribution/licensing/
[5] http://www.meta-net.eu/
[6] https://www.clarin.eu/content/licenses-and-clarin-categories
[7] https://opensource.org/licenses/BSD-3-Clause
[8] http://wizard.elda.org/
[9] https://www.european-language-grid.eu/
[10] Please refer to (Wilkinson et al., 2016) for the FAIR Principles.
[11] https://european-language-grid.readthedocs.io/en/stable/all/A2_Metadata/Metadata.html
[12] https://spdx.org/licenses/

3. Licensed Rights

In the general theory of copyright, the set of rights granted by the law aims to foster innovation and protect creators with respect to their original works. Moreover, the law allows copyright owners to deal freely with the rights they own. Generally, this can be done through "proprietary licenses" where copyright owners or allowed licensees keep control over who has the right to use the set of rights to the underlying original works.

However, in recent years, under the influence of the open-source movement, specific licenses were designed so that creators could allow redistribution and reuse of their works' contents with fewer restrictions

In the following sub-sections we will detail the set of rights that may be granted by those licenses. It should be noted that we tried our best to generalize legal concepts found in licenses that may not be expressed with the same terms in all licenses and/or may have differences in the semantic nuances and presentation in the texts (Rodriguez-Doncel and Labropoulou 2015).

3.1 Right to Reuse

Copyright protection prevents third parties from reusing the intellectual property to create copies of the original work and create derivative works or products based on the original.

During our investigation we found out that some of the licenses that allow open access to their content, widely called "open-source" licenses, provide or imply that the licensor grants licensees the right to reuse the content of the protected works for their own use. This right to reuse will also help us imply some further reuse possibilities down the line when we will deal with the items linked to restrictions and conditions attached to reuse in Section 5.

3.2 Right to Copy

The core of copyright is to allow the creator of the original work to have copies made of its work and to allow for their exploitation. We can see this type of exploitation in several industries such as edition, cinema and many others.

In research, the right to copy is useful towards the training of a language tool or the modification of a software. Therefore, the majority of "open-source" licenses grant licensees the right to copy content from the original work and to reuse this content for subsequent use. One exception of note is the *Community Data License Agreement – Permissive, version 1.0*[13]. This license provides resource users the right to use and publish data but grants no other rights.

3.3 Right to Redistribute

The distribution rights of a copyrighted work are the exclusive rights granted to the copyright owners. Copyright owners or allowed licensors can either distribute their work through proprietary licenses where they may restrict the distribution rights or through "open-source" licenses which can allow third parties to redistribute the work.

This right to redistribute is essential in open science to promote the works that have been produced and allow others to evaluate the quality of research.

Therefore, most "open-source" licenses provide third parties obtaining content placed under those licenses the right to redistribute the original work. In opposition, as an example of proprietary license, the LDC User Agreement for non-members[14] does not allow redistribution of the work protected by the license.

3.4 Right to Distribute Derivatives

We can define a derivative work as a work that includes major elements of copyrighted work that would otherwise be infringing the law if not authorized by the creator of the original work.

This right is essential, especially in research, where we usually need to rework on preexisting works. These preexisting works may be existing copyrighted works on language resources or software that are available prior to any new licensing to third parties. Researchers may need to combine and reuse data available and be allowed to create new works to be distributed to the public.

Usually in "open-source" licenses, this will be provided as a right to rework upon the original work which grants the licensee the right to use a part or the entirety of a work in a derivative work.

However, in the case of the Creative Commons CC-BY-ND license[15], the "ND" denomination stands for "No Derivatives". This can be misleading as the license allows the creation of derivatives works but not their distribution.

3.5 Patent License

Some "open-source" licenses which are used mostly in relation with software and code, such as the Apache License or the General Public License, grant the user a right to modify content protected by patent claims from the original author.

A patent is another exclusive proprietary right that is granted to creators of innovative process and may be attached to some software.

3.6 Right to Grant Sub-Licenses

The copyright owner can grant licenses to third parties and allow them in turn to grant sub-licenses to others so that the content can be wider spread.

In the context of "open-source" research, this ability to sub-license is also crucial as it would allow users to license the content to third parties.

4. Restrictions on Redistribution

The licenses we studied balance the rights that we detailed above with certain obligations that bear on the licensees when dealing with the content.

Therefore, in this section, we will detail the restrictions that are used in "open-source" licenses and that we gathered in

[13] https://cdla.dev/permissive-1-0/

[14] https://catalog.ldc.upenn.edu/license/ldc-non-members-agreement.pdf

[15] https://creativecommons.org/licenses/by-nd/4.0/

the "Requirements on redistribution and publications" category of our metadata schema.

4.1 Attribution Requirement

This condition is one of the most often used conditions in open-source licenses. The best-known form of this requirement is the "BY" designation in Creative Commons licenses[16]. This requirement compels the user to attribute the original creator of the work when reusing his content either in derivative work or whenever the content is reused in any way. This is done by reproducing a statement inserted by the original author with its work and comes with a sentence such as "[Title] by [Author] licensed under CC-BY 4.0".

4.2 Documentation of Modifications

Licensees can also be compelled to document modifications they bring to the original content.

This condition is not based upon any traditional category of rights granted by copyright law. It is specific to software development where documentation is needed especially when a version of a software changes. For example, some GNU-GPL licenses (GPL 3.0 as for the latest version)[17] provide that any new version must carry notices that the content has been modified.

Indeed, this documentation can give essential information on code changes that might change the performance of a piece of software and its features and how they interact together with earlier versions.

Therefore, we thought it was mandatory for us to include this condition as it is essential in reusing or redeveloping software upon available content.

4.3 Retention of Copyright Notice

The retention of the copyright notice means that all derivative works shall keep the attribution notice and full license text from the original works. This retention can also be required for subsequent redistribution of content containing the original work when made by a licensee.

This condition provides that a user inserting content made available under a license providing for this condition must reproduce and retain the copyright notice that is attached to the original content. This is done mainly to remind subsequent users that the original content is available with copyright restrictions and nudges subsequent users to keep their contributions available under such conditions.

4.4 Share-Alike Requirement

As its name suggests, this requirement mandates users of content shared under licenses containing this condition to share any derivative content that they may produce under the same license as the original content.

This is mainly done to keep some form of control over the usage of the content and to maintain the reusability of the work.

By sharing the derived content under the same license as the original content the copyright owner ensures that knowledge can continuously flow under the same licensing scheme.

4.5 Copyleft Requirement

The Copyleft philosophy bears similarities with the ShareAlike requirement. However, the former differs from the latter in the sense that the licensee is required to license the derived content under the same license or a compatible license. The licensee must not impose conditions that may impair the redistribution of the original works afterwards.

The best-known example is the GNU-GPL License that requires users to license the modified works under the same license as the original work.

5. Requirement on Reuse

In addition to the restriction on redistribution of original or derivative work, some of the licenses we studied for this task also provide for some obligations on how the derivative content can be reused by licensees.

5.1 Grant of Commercial Use License

As previously mentioned in Section 3, the original copyright is granted with a set of rights that they can exploit either for free or commercially.

Therefore, when making content available under an open-source license, copyright owners can also decide to allow third parties to make profit from redistribution of the original or derived content. This may be especially useful for developers of commercial applications relying on open-source content while maintaining the underlying content available to all interested users.

One major exception is the Creative Commons CC-BY-NC license[18] which forbids the sharing of data for monetary compensation or commercial advantage.

5.2 Reuse of Content for Specific Activities

This category is not usually mentioned literally in open licenses but due to the focus on research activities of the ELG platform we identified some metadata items that are linked to the reusability of content.

In this section we will detail the different items that fall within this category:

- **Evaluation Use**

This item refers to the possibility of academic or commercial stakeholders to use the resource for the evaluation of technologies. This evaluation can allow to ensure that a resource is suitable for certain purposes. It can also allow to evaluate a language tool in the light of certain measurements.

- **Academic Use and Research Use**

We thought it useful to clearly notify users whether a resource is usable only in academic settings and differentiate them from research use by all types of users.

Even though we can understand them as similar restrictions, Research Use can also cover research and

[16] https://creativecommons.org/licenses/by/4.0

[17] https://www.gnu.org/licenses/gpl-3.0.html

[18] https://creativecommons.org/licenses/by-nc/4.0

development activities undertaken by private enterprises as well as academic research.

- **Language Engineering Research Use**

In addition to the previous category, we thought that it would also be necessary to properly identify research in the Language Engineering field. Indeed, the ELG is a platform that is dedicated to language resources and tools and that helps foster a European innovation space for European Languages.

Therefore, we inferred this condition from the exploitation rights granted by the license. The Computational Use of Data Agreement[19] provides that the content must be used for Computational Use which could imply Language Engineering.

- **Machine Learning Training Use**

Recently, we saw the emergence of language models as being now the primary use of language resources. The enhancement of methods relying on neural networks and artificial intelligence results in a further need for legal certainty on these use cases.

During our study, we considered that the right to create derivatives includes the right to train models with resources, as we believe that a model is derived from the training performed thanks to the resources.

6. Use of Rights for Searching Licenses

The analysis of licenses has produced a long list of rights. Although they are important for understanding the requirements set for users when using an LRT, not all of them are necessary for discoverability purposes. Thus, for the facet "condition of use", we have used only a carefully selected subset of them, to ensure that they cover the most usual user queries.

Similar facets are used in the CLARIN VLO[20] with the facet "Availability" with the CLARIN license categories[21] (Kelli et al. 2018) and the Google dataset search engine[22], where the "usage rights" has only two values: whether commercial use is allowed or not. We have, therefore, restricted the list of conditions to six values, namely: *no conditions*, *commercial use not allowed*, *derivatives not allowed*, *redistribution use not allowed*, *research use allowed*. All rights that are not included in the facet are mapped to the value "other specific restrictions".

7. Conclusion

In this paper we have detailed the various items that we identified during our investigation of licenses and turned into metadata items to help build a "legal search" feature in the ELG platform search engine.

This feature was identified as crucial from the beginning to make sure that the rights of creators are respected and to help reuse and bring legal certainty to all stakeholders.

8. Acknowledgements

We would like to acknowledge the European Language Grid Project which has received funding from the European Union's Horizon 2020 research and innovation programme under grant agreement n° 825627.

9. References

9.1 Bibliographical References

Choukri K., Piperidis S., Tsiavos P., Patrikakos T., Gavrilidou M., Weitzmann J.H. (2012). META-SHARE: Licenses, Legal, IPR and Licensing issues. Deliverable D6.1.3. In T4ME Net (META-NET) project. 24 February 2012.

Kelli A., Lindén K., Vider K., Labropoulou P., Ketzan E., Kamocki P. & Stranák P. (2018). Implementation of an Open Science Policy in the context of management of CLARIN language resources: a need for changes? Linköping Electronic Conference Proceedings, 147, 102-111.

Labropoulou, P., Gkirtzou, K., Gavriilidou, M., Deligiannis, M., Galanis, D., Piperidis, S., Rehm, G., Berger, M., Mapelli, V., Rigault, M., Arranz, V., Choukri, K., Backfried, G., Pérez, J. M. G., and Garcia-Silva, A. (2020). Making Metadata Fit for Next Generation Language Technology Platforms: The Metadata Schema of the European Language Grid. In Nicoletta Calzolari, et al., editors, Proceedings of the 12th Language Resources and Evaluation Conference (LREC 2020), Marseille, France, 5. European Language Resources Association (ELRA).

Piperidis, S. (2012). The META-SHARE Language Resources Sharing Infrastructure: Principles, Challenges, Solutions. In Nicoletta Calzolari (Conference Chair), et al., editors, Proceedings of the Eight International Conference on Language Resources and Evaluation (LREC'12), Istanbul, Turkey, May. European Language Resources Association (ELRA).

Piperidis, S., Harris P., Spurk C., Rehm G., Choukri K., Hamon O., Calzolari N., del Gratta R., Magnini B., and Girardi C.(2014). META-SHARE: One year after. In: In Nicoletta Calzolari (Conference Chair), et al., editors, Proceedings of the 9th Language Resources and Evaluation Conference (LREC 2014). European Language Resources Association (ELRA), pp. 1532–1538.

Rehm G., Berger M., Elsholz E., Hegele S., Kintzel F., Marheinecke K., Piperidis S., Deligiannis M., Galanis D., Gkirtzou K., Labropoulou P., Bontcheva K., Jones D., Roberts I., Hajic J., Hamrlová J., Kačena L., Choukri K., Arranz V., Vasiļjevs A., Anvari O., Lagzdiņš A., Meļņika J., Backfried G., Dikici E., Janosik M., Prinz K., Prinz C., Stampler S., Thomas-Aniola D., Pérez J. M. G., Silva A. G., Berrío C., Germann U., Renals S., and Klejch O. (2020). European Language Grid: An Overview. In Nicoletta Calzolari, et al., editors, Proceedings of the 12th Language Resources and Evaluation Conference (LREC 2020), Marseille, France, 5. European Language Resources Association (ELRA).

[19] https://spdx.org/licenses/C-UDA-1.0.html

[20] https://vlo.clarin.eu

[21] https://www.clarin.eu/content/licenses-and-clarin-categories

[22] https://datasetsearch.research.google.com/

Rodriguez-Doncel V. and Labropoulou P. 2015. RDF Representation of Licenses for Language Resources. In Proceedings of the 4th Workshop on Linked Data in Linguistics: Resources and Applications, pages 49–58, Beijing, China. Association for Computational Linguistics.

Wilkinson, MD., Dumontier, M., Aalbersberg, I.J., Appleton, G., Axton, M., Baak, A., Blomberg, N., Boiten, J.W., da Silva Santos, L.B., Bourne, P.E., Bouwman, J., Brookes, A.J., Clark, T., Crosas, M., Dillo, I., Dumon, O., Edmunds, S., Evelo, C.T., Finkers, R., Gonzalez-Beltran, A., Gray, A.J., Growth, P., Goble, C., Grethe, J.S., Heringa, J., 't Hoen, P.A., Hooft, R., Kuhn, T., Kok, R., Kok, J., Lusher, S.J., Martone, M.E., Mons, A., Packer, A.L., Persson, B., Rocca-Serra, P., Roos, M., van Schaik, R., Sansone, S.A., Schultes, E,, Sengstag, T., Slater, T., Strawn, G., Swertz, M.A., Thompson, M., van der Lei, J., van Mulligen, E., Velterop, J., Waagmeester, A., Wittenburg, P., Wolstencroft, K., Zhao, J., Mons, B. The FAIR Guiding Principles for Scientific Data Management and Stewardship. *Sci Data* **3,** 160018 (2016). https://doi.org/10.1038/sdata.2016.18

9.2 Related works

(License wizards, terms & conditions with licenses):

- https://joinup.ec.europa.eu/collection/eupl/solution/joinup-licensing-assistant/jla-find-and-compare-software-licenses
- https://ufal.github.io/public-license-selector/
- https://tldrlegal.com/
- http://licentia.inria.fr/
- RDF representation of licenses: Rodriguez-Doncel and Labropoulou 2015

The Legal and Ethical issues Workshop @LREC2022, pages 27–37
Marseille, 20 June 2022

About Migration Flows and Sentiment Analysis on Twitter Data: Building the Bridge Between Technical and Legal approaches to data protection

Thilo Gottschalk, Francesca Pichierri
FIZ Karlsruhe - Leibniz-Institute for Information Infrastructure
Hermann-von-Helmholtz-Platz 1, 76344 Eggenstein-Leopoldshafen

{francesca.pichierri, thilo.gottschalk }@fiz-karlsruhe.de

Abstract

Sentiment analysis has always been an important driver of political decisions and campaigns across all fields. Novel technologies allow automatizing analysis of sentiments on a big scale and hence provide allegedly more accurate outcomes. With user numbers in the billions and their increasingly important role in societal discussions, social media platforms become a glaring data source for these types of analysis. Due to its public availability, the relative ease of access and the sheer amount of available data, the Twitter API has become a particularly important source to researchers and data analysts alike. Despite the evident value of these data sources, the analysis of such data comes with legal, ethical and societal risks that should be taken into consideration when analysing data from Twitter. This paper describes these risks along the technical processing pipeline and proposes related mitigation measures.

Keywords: sentiment analysis, data protection, privacy

1. Introduction

Social media data are commonly processed for analysing and predicting social phenomena. They are relatively easy to obtain, cheap and contain a lot of valuable and diverse information - ranging from factual to subjective (Pereira-Kohatsu et al., 2019; Ligthart et al., 2021). Tweets are particularly popular among researchers due to their accessibility, actuality and ease of processing (Ligthart et al., 2021; Goritz et al., 2019). One particular field that shows strong interest in the use of such data is the field of migration studies and border security as can be observed by public funding directed towards research in this area[1], by research activities in general (Carammia et al., 2022), as well as by Frontex strategical-analysis documents[2] and public tenders (Frontex, 2019). In the field of migration studies, Twitter data analysis is considered very useful for a series of purposes such as measuring and predicting migration flows, providing necessary support to vulnerable groups/migrants/refugees, assessing the integration of migrants in destination countries or evaluating public opinion towards migration (Righi, 2019; Mijatović, 2021). The importance of such approaches was most recently highlighted in the context of the Ukraine war where social media intelligence (SOCINT) played an important role (Engelhaupt, 2022).

Despite the practical and analytical advantages, the processing of Twitter data can raise concerns regarding the right to data protection and privacy of Twitter users as well as affected third parties. Linkage of different datasets can produce a clearer picture of global migration flows but also raise risks for unwanted and inappropriate negative societal effects, e.g. for migrants and refugees.

Given these contrasting effects, it is crucial to design and implement analytical models and approaches in a way that balance technical and data protection requirements without undermining compliance with the legal framework, such as the General Data Protection Regulation (GDPR), nor the purposes of the data analysis. This alignment proves to be difficult especially for data scientists with no deeper understanding of the legal frameworks they conduct their work in. At the same time, legal experts often lack sufficient understanding of the technical approaches and the possible risks linked to them. This often results either in overregulation or in non-compliance of the processing.

Where risks and potential negative consequences towards users are identified at an early stage, it is possible to adopt mitigation measures to address these risks and foster compliance with the data protection by design and data protection by default principle, enshrined in Article 25 GDPR. That being said, compelling approaches require interdisciplinary efforts involving legal experts as well as developers and data scientists to find a common language that is intelligible to all parties and to break down the knowledge barriers between different fields of expertise.

On these grounds, this paper aims to provide a foundation for structured approaches towards privacy preservation in the analysis of Twitter data and aims to build a bridge between technical and legal data protection approaches in Twitter data driven sentiment analysis. In-

[1] See e.g. the EU project ITFLOWS: `https://www.itflows.eu/`; the project METICOS:`https://meticos-project.eu/`; and EFFECTOR:`https://www.effector-project.eu/`.

[2] `https://frontex.europa.eu/we-know/situational-awareness-and-monitoring/strategic-analysis/`.

spired by the analytical work conducted in the project ITFLOWS (IT tools and methods for managing migrations FLOWS)[3], this paper focuses on the use of Twitter data to detect risks of tensions related to migration and it directs the attention towards sentiment analysis performed on such data. On the context of migration research we explain legal and societal impacts of sentiment analysis on Twitter data, providing insights and guidance on common risks of technical approaches and how to mitigate them. While a variety of approaches have been discussed and proposed to ensure privacy of data subjects in data analysis, these approaches often either refer to structured data or neglect the technical pipeline of such approaches.

Such discussions are hence often difficult to follow for technical personnel, are not always suitable for unstructured social media content (such as textual Twitter data) and do not reflect the technical reality when processing personal data. In line with this, it can be observed that many existing research papers and approaches pose considerable risks to the data subject (e.g. simple re-identification, annotation) and correlating liability risks to the data controller. A very common problem are publicly available annotated datasets that contain not only analytical outcomes but the Tweet-ID as well. This, one the one hand, makes the research reproducible. On the other hand, it also allows easy identification of the Twitter user together with potentially sensitive information (e.g. sentiments towards specific topics). Such data can easily be used to identify and target members of certain groups for political advertisements, making the abstract data protection risk a concrete problem.[4] Neither the researchers, nor the affected data subjects are usually aware of this risk. With this paper we strive to highlight such risks and mitigation measures linked to the technical steps that typically compose the *sentiment analysis*.

While it is impossible to cover all existing analytical methods and techniques in the field of sentiment analysis, the paper aims to provide a starting point that can be used to develop a compelling *privacy aware* approach on a case-by-case basis for data driven sentiment analysis. It provides contextual and technical guidance and applicable substance to the more generic legal requirements imposed by the GDPR. The proposed structure can be used to validate research/processing approaches and thereby aims to foster legal and ethical sustainability within and beyond research approaches.

The paper starts by presenting the necessary background data protection concepts as laid down by the GDPR (Section 2). A data scientist in the role of controller needs to take proactive actions to ensure and demonstrate compliance with the obligations set by the GDPR, from the beginning to the end of processing. Therefore, particular attention will be directed towards the explanation of accountability-based mechanisms, such as the principles of data protection by design and by default under Article 25 GDPR and Data Protection Impact Assessments (DPIAs) under Article 35 GDPR. Secondly, the analysis moves towards a description of the general technical approach of Sentiment Analysis in the context of Twitter data (Section 3). Sentiment analysis can be conducted on Tweets by means of different techniques (Thakkar and Patel, 2015; Saberi and Saad, 2017). While there is no standard solution to the processing of social media data for the purpose of sentiment analysis, there are multiple (linked) processing steps that tend to play an important role and which regularly appear in one or another form in sentiment analysis methodologies. Such technical steps provide the structure for the analysis conducted in this paper. In principle, each step in the technical pipeline can raise risks but also provides a potential leverage point to mitigate overall risks (see Section 4) to data protection and privacy.

The paper hence addresses legal researchers and data scientists alike. We aim to provide understandable technical insights to legal scholars and foster the understanding of the data protection implications and technical solutions for data scientists/developers. The analysis invites data scientists to rethink their technical processes in favor of a privacy preserving perspective, provides a source for acknowledged and feasible mitigation measures and aims to strengthen the legal and technical capability to communicate the respective needs by providing recommendations for the identified analytical/processing steps.

2. Data Protection obligations

The GDPR imposes obligations onto data scientists when processing information through which it is possible to identify a natural person (personal data).

Under the GDPR, processing means 'any operation or set of operations which is performed on personal data or on sets of personal data' (Art. 4 (2) GDPR). It includes collection, recording, storage, alteration, use, dissemination, combination or erasure - in principle, the definition includes any possible operation that could be performed on personal data.

Data scientists could process personal data in the role of controllers when determining, alone or jointly with others, the purposes and the means of the processing (Art. 4 (7) GDPR) or they could do it in the role of processors when processing personal data on behalf of the controller(s). Data controllers are the primary bear-

[3]The goal of the ITFLOWS project is to provide accurate predictions and adequate management solutions of migration flows in the European Union. The project develops precise models which lay the foundation of the EUMigraTool (EMT), a software platform that will provide to relevant stakeholders a set of tools enabling simulations and predictions. The EMT has two main functions: predicting migration flows and detecting risks of tensions related to migration, `https://www.itflows.eu/`.

[4]Most of publicly available Twitter datasets contain TweetIDs, we hence refrain from referencing a specific one here.

ers of the obligations set by the regulation towards the person whose data is processed (data subjects), while data processors faces a limited number of obligations (see e.g. Art. 30 and Art. 32 GDPR). By nature, social media data usually have at least some relation to the publishing user. Contrary to wide believe (especially among data scientists), public availability must not be mistaken for consent to be freely used in any other context.

2.1. Data Protection Principles

When processing personal data, both controllers and processors need to comply with the general data protection principles listed in Art. 5 GDPR.

2.1.1. Lawfulness

Processing must be lawful, i.e. it must respect all applicable legal requirements. The core conditions for processing to be lawful are listed in Art. 6 GDPR. Processing is lawful only if and to the extent that at least one of the conditions listed applies, such as, for example, consent of the data subject, necessity for the performance of a task carried out in the public interest, necessity for the purposes of the legitimate interests pursued by the controller or a third party, if such interests are not overridden by the interests or rights and freedoms of the data subject (Art. 6 (1) GDPR). Furthermore, in Art. 9 the GDPR identifies some types of personal data which are particularly sensitive and merit enhanced protection, such as those revealing racial or ethnic origin, political opinions, religious or philosophical beliefs, trade union membership, those concerning health or sexual life or sexual orientation, genetic data and biometric data processed for the purpose of uniquely identifying a natural person. The processing of such sensitive data, in principle, is prohibited pursuant to Art. 9 (1) GDPR, unless one of the exemptions in Art. 9 (2) GDPR applies. Exemptions include situations where the data subject has given consent, where processing relates to personal data which are manifestly made public by the data subject; where processing is necessary for archiving purposes in the public interest, scientific or historical research purposes or statistical purposes in accordance with Art. 89 (1) GDPR. The latter often arguably provides a legal foundation for the processing, however, the Article particularly requires that the processing must be subject to appropriate safeguards, in accordance with the GDPR, for the rights and freedoms of the data subjects.

2.1.2. Fairness

Processing must be fair and conducted in an ethical manner. For example, data must not be obtained through unfair means, such as by deceiving data subjects or by acting without their knowledge.

2.1.3. Transparency

Processing must be transparent to the data subject concerned. The controller is obliged to take any appropriate measures to keep data subjects informed regarding the processing of their personal data before and during the processing activities and also in regard to a request of access. Information should be easily accessible and easy to understand. Elements concerning content and quality of the information duty are subject of Art. 12-15 GDPR.

2.1.4. Purpose limitation

Data must be collected for specified, explicit and legitimate purposes and not further processed in a manner incompatible with those purposes. The purpose of processing must be determined before processing is started and it must be unambiguous and clearly expressed. Furthermore, the purpose must be balanced between the rights and interests of the controller and the ones of the data subject. Each new purpose for data processing which is incompatible with the initial one must have its own specific legal basis. Exceptions to this rule are considered for archiving purposes in the public interest, scientific or historical research purposes or statistical purposes (Art. 5 (1) (b) GDPR), with the application of appropriate safeguards (Art. 6 (4) GDPR; Recital 50 GDPR).

2.1.5. Data Minimization

Processed personal data must be adequate, relevant and limited to what is necessary in relation to the purposes specified. Instead of a "process everything approach", such principle promotes a selective method which begins prior to collection and concerns not only the quantity but also the quality of personal data. It also requires to ensure that the period for which personal data are stored is limited to a strict minimum (Recital 29 GDPR). This principle also remains applicable under the research exemptions as laid down in Art. 89 GDPR.

2.1.6. Accuracy

Personal data must be accurate and kept up to date. In every processing activity, the controller must take every reasonable step to ensure respect to this principle. All inaccurate personal data should be erased or rectified without delay.

2.1.7. Storage Limitation

Personal data must be stored in a form which permits identification of data subjects for no longer than is necessary for the purposes for which the personal data are processed. Personal data must be deleted or anonymised as soon as they are no longer needed. Controllers are encouraged to establish time limits for erasure or for a periodic review (Recital 39). The storage limitation principle permits the storage of personal data for longer periods if it is processed exclusively for archiving purposes in the public interest, scientific or historical research purposes or statistical purposes in accordance with Art. 89 (1) GDPR and it is subject to implementation of the appropriate technical and organizational measures in order to safeguard the rights and freedoms of individuals.

2.1.8. Integrity and Confidentiality

Personal data must be processed in a way that ensures its appropriate security, integrity and confidentiality, including protection against unauthorized or unlawful processing, against accidental loss, damage or destruction. To ensure this, appropriate technical and organizational measures need to be implemented. Chapter IV of the GDPR (from Art. 24 to Art. 43) provides guidance to controllers and processors on how to adequately fulfill such principle.

2.1.9. Accountability

The controller is responsible for, and must be able to demonstrate compliance with, all the previous principles listed. Such requirement is further developed in Art. 24 GDPR.

2.2. Ensuring compliance with the obligations

In addition to the data protection principles listed above, the controller has to implement mechanisms to comply with the rights of the data subject laid down in Chapter III of the GDPR (from Art. 12 to Art. 23 GDPR).

The controller needs to take proactive actions to ensure and demonstrate compliance with the obligations set by the GDPR, from the beginning to the end of processing. To this purpose, appropriate and effective technical and organizational measures must be implemented; additionally, they need to be reviewed and updated where deemed necessary (Art. 24 GDPR). The determination of the measures to be taken depends on the processing being carried out, the types of data processed and the level of risk to data subjects. Ways to facilitate compliance include ensuring Data Protection by Design and by Default (Art. 25 GDPR) and conducting a Data Protection Impact Assessment (Art. 35 GDPR).

2.2.1. Data Protection by Design and by Default

Addressing data protection issues at a very early stage, when designing and setting up processing strategies and activities is crucial. Data Protection by Design means embedding data protection principles and safeguards in the design and development of data processing models, therefore ensuring protection of privacy-related interests right from the start (when the means for processing are determined). This requires that, conceptually, the relevant measures are defined prior to the system being set up, rather than implementing measures ex post.

By making data protection an important element of the core functionality of an analytical model, the controller is facilitated in ensuring a privacy compliant solution, allowing the processing to meet data protection requirements and ensure protection of data subjects´rights. Art. 25 (1) GDPR requires the implementation of appropriate technical and organisational measures (e.g. pseudonymisation) taking into account the state of the art, the cost of implementation and the nature, scope, context and purposes of processing as well as the risks to data subjects.

Data Protection by Default requires the controller to ensure that, by default, only personal data which are necessary to achieve a specific purpose of the processing are processed. This applies to the amount of personal data collected, the extent of their processing, the period of their storage and their accessibility. This would also mean for example avoiding using technical solutions that collect more personal data than are strictly necessary for a specific functionality or which do not ensure confidentiality.

Processors are not obliged to assist controller with data protection by design and default obligations (unlike with security measures under Art. 32 GDPR). However, controllers must select processors that provide sufficient guarantees to meet the GDPR´s obligations (Art. 28 GDPR). Breach of Art. 25 GDPR may result in the imposition of sanctions (Art. 83 (4) GDPR).

2.2.2. Data Protection Impact Assessment

The Data Protection Impact Assessment, DPIA, is a requirement provided by Art. 35 GDPR. The DPIA´s objective is to evaluate the impact of the planned processing activities on the protection of personal data and it must be carried out by the controller prior to processing. The assessment should contain at least:

(a) a systematic description of the data processing and the purposes of the processing and where applicable – the legitimate interests of the controller;

(b) an assessment of the necessity and proportionality of the data processing on the basis of the specified purpose;

(c) an assessment of the risks to the data subjects rights and freedoms (e.g. likelihood and severity)[5]

(d) measures proposed to address these risks, including safeguards, security measures, mechanisms to ensure personal data protection and to demonstrate compliance with the Regulation (see Article 35 (7) GDPR).

The DPIA is both an "accountability measure" as well as a "warning system" (Kuner et al., 2020, p. 699). The outcome of the assessment is helpful in the determination of "appropriate measures" to be carried out in order to demonstrate compliance with data protection principles and obligations.[6] Through the DPIA, risks and potential negative consequences of processing activities to data subjects can be identified at an early

[5]According to Recital 76 GDPR, "The likelihood and severity of the risk to the rights and freedoms of the data subject should be determined by reference to the nature, scope, context and purposes of the processing. Risk should be evaluated on the basis of an objective assessment by which it is established whether data processing operations involve a risk or a high risk".

[6]See Recital 84 GDPR.

stage. The controller can evaluate and propose mitigation measures to address the risks identified and significantly limit the probability of negative outcomes. This identification and evaluation exercise supports compliance with the data protection by design and default principle. Although the regulation specifies that the DPIA must be carried out before the processing starts, it is advisable controllers see the DPIA as a process where data processing operations, risks and measures put in place are managed and reviewed continuously.

The DPIA is required in cases where a data processing operation is likely to result in high-risk to the rights and freedoms of individuals, in particular if it makes use of new technologies. According to Recital 75 GDPR, the risk "may result from personal data processing which could lead to physical, material or non-material damage". For example, the processing may give rise to discrimination, identity theft, financial loss, damage to reputation, economic or social disadvantage. Art. 35 (3) GDPR provides a non-exhaustive lists of processing likely to result in high risk (Datenschutzkonferenz (DSK), 2018). These include cases where special categories of data, e.g. information on racial or ethnic origin, political opinions, religious or philosophical belief, is being processed on a large scale[7]. Recital 75 GDPR mentions cases where personal aspects are evaluated in order to create or use personal profiles, e.g. when aspects concerning personal preferences, behaviour, location, movement are analysed or predicted; it also mentions cases where personal data of vulnerable natural persons are processed. Data protection authorities in part provide examples of processing scenarios that by default do or do not result in a DPIA obligation (Brink and Wolff, 2021, *Hansen*, Art. 35 Rn. 13). In addition, the WP29 DPIA guidelines lay out a list of criteria which can be taken into account when establishing whether processing activities are "likely to result in high risk" (Article 29 Working Party, 2017, p. 8-11).

DPIAs are not mandatory for all data processing activities as the obligation is tied to the existence of a likely high risk. However, it has been pointed out that, in practice, a controller needs to always conduct a preliminary assessment of the processing activities to identify whether the latter are likely to result in a high risk and therefore in need of a DPIA (Kuner et al., 2020, p. 671). Furthermore, in general it may be prudent to conduct DPIAs, whether or not the high-risk standard is met, or in doubt of it. The DPIA is, in fact, a very useful tool that helps controllers to comply with data protection law, ensure best practices and minimize liability (Article 29 Working Party, 2017, p. 9).

There is no specific DPIA template, although there are some valuable suggested formats that can be taken into consideration (e.g. (Information Commissioners Office (ICO), 2017; Commission Nationale de l'Informatique et des Libertés (CNIL),)). Controllers may also develop their own templates. When carrying out a DPIA, controllers can seek the advice of the Data Protection Advisor where designated.[8] Furthermore, they do not necessarily need to conduct the assessment on their own but can also outsource the DPIA to third parties (Brink and Wolff, 2021, *Hansen*, Art. 35 Rn. 11).

[7]Article 35 (3) (b) GDPR.

3. Sentiment Analysis

Processing in Sentiment Analysis, especially on social media data, often results in high risk for the data subjects. In the case of Twitter, every single Tweet is at least related to the author of the Tweet and can be related to an undefined number of natural persons. As sentiment analysis is often linked to sensitive topics, there is a high risk that special categories of data (Art. 9 GDPR) are processed. In consequence, it becomes particularly important to mitigate data protection risks in all processing steps.

3.1. Definition of Sentiment Analysis

"Sentiment Analysis is the review of written or other forms of communication or qualitative data to determine a quantifiable and comparable measure of some form of feeling in the communication or data" (Peslak, 2017, p. 38). In other words, it is a computational study of people´s affective states in relation to a particular entity, such as a topic or event, which aims to create "actionable knowledge" (Ligthart et al., 2021, p. 4998). Sentiment analysis is a complex process that usually consists of numerous tasks, such as subjectivity classification and sentiment orientation (Saberi and Saad, 2017; Ligthart et al., 2021). Information related to sentiments or opinions concerning a specific topic are mined from a word, sentence or document (level of analysis) and, in a simple approach, sentiments are classified into positive (denoting the state of happiness, satisfaction etc.), negative (denoting the state of discontent, anger etc.) and in a few cases also into neutral (when no sentiment has been detected). Factual information are discarded as SA is directed towards subjective sentences (Saberi and Saad, 2017) but can play a role in the interpretation of the analysis.

Datasets for SA are usually user-generated textual content. To this end, social media data proved to be a particularly valuable source of data as it is highly subjective and full of informal language, i.e. textual content. In this context, Tweets are particular popular as they are easily obtained, contain real-time/recent[9] information on topics and they have a similar format (Ligthart et al., 2021).

[8]Article 35 (2) GDPR; see also Recital 84 GDPR.

[9]the currentness of the data depends on the TwitterAPI. E.g. the Firehose API provides real-time access to all tweets, standard access limits access to a certain time-window, research access is limited to historical data but not to a specific time-window.

3.2. Technical Approach to Sentiment Analysis

Sentiment Analysis is an umbrella term and can be conducted by means of different techniques and approaches. In the context of Twitter, the analysis is usually based on textual data of tweets. To this end, the technical approaches usually rely on various forms of natural language processing paired with additional methods aligned in a processing pipeline (Thakkar and Patel, 2015; Saberi and Saad, 2017; Ligthart et al., 2021). The design of a processing pipeline, i.e. the linked methods and concepts, to conduct sentiment analysis on the available Twitter data can be manifold. While there is no standard order to the processing of social media data for the purpose of sentiment analysis, there are multiple (linked) processing steps that tend to play an important role and regularly appear in one or another form in sentiment analysis. The order and the relevance of the steps is driven by various factors such as the available data, purpose of the analysis, expertise and available tools. We hence describe common processing steps in a logical, yet not obligatory, order. Such steps can be broken down into

1. *Source Identification* (3.2.1),
2. *Data Collection* (3.2.2),
3. *Data Cleansing* (3.2.3),
4. *Data Analysis* (3.2.4).

For each of these steps there are uncountable options to conduct the necessary tasks. A task can be conducted by means of complex machine learning (ML) based approaches (which can be unsupervised, supervised and semi-supervised), semantic-based analysis or hybrid/combined approaches but also by more simplistic processing approaches (e.g. counting Tweets). For the purposes of this paper we will depict selected exemplary approaches in each step in order to shed light on common approaches and - in combination with Section 4 - provide insights on the legal implications, risks and potential mitigation measures that need to be considered when planning to conduct data driven sentiment analysis.

For example, Topic Modelling can be used for purposes of data cleansing (Section 3.2.3) as well as for the actual analysis of data with regard to sentiments. The goal is hence not to investigate one specific approach in a specific context but rather to emphasize the importance to acknowledge where and why a certain approach was chosen. Further research on specific legal implications in a given context would be desirable but are out of the scope of this paper.

3.2.1. Source identification

Prior to the actual analysis, a feasible data source and appropriate data selection/extraction methods need to be defined. Both steps are of utmost importance and need to be aligned with the purpose of the research. To do so, the research question must be clearly defined and narrow enough to provide a proper definition of the processing purpose. Where available, different sources should be taken into consideration and there should be reasonable explanation for the chosen data source. For Twitter data, valid sources can be the Twitter API itself, but also (pre-processed) sources[10] such as Knowledge Bases (e.g. TweetsKB (Fafalios et al., 2018) or MigrationsKB (Chen et al., 2021b)).

Recommendation: Sources should be identified not only by accessibility and volume but also lawfulness of their creation, legal (e.g. Terms of Use, domestic law) and practical limitations (e.g. difficult data cleansing; re-identification possibilities). A reasoning for the chosen source and the weighing of interest has to be provided.

3.2.2. Data Collection

Rule-based content extraction is the most straight forward approach to limit extraction of data to relevant topics. All major social media platform allow access to user-generated content through APIs and thereby (usually) allow extraction of data based on keywords (i.e. only a certain topic, such as *migration*) or metadata (i.e. only data from June-August) or other queries (Calisir and Brambilla, 2018, p. 116). However, as already pointed out by Calisir and Brambilla (2018), such traditional approach often lacks specificity and results in noisy outcomes, two shortcomings that could, among other, clash with the GDPR demands regarding data quality, (sufficient) data minimization and/or purpose limitation.

Twitter provides an API to access tweets in a structured manner. The Twitter API provides access to *Tweets, Users, Direct Messages, Lists, Trends, Media, Places* and currently consists of two versions and multiple tiers (Twitter API v2; Standard v1.1; Premium v1.1 Enterprise). The tiers provide different but overlapping features. From a data protection perspective, the used tier should be driven by the underlying question/purpose of the processing. The respective API functionality is further limited by context of processing (currently *Standard Project, Academic Research Project*). In the context of academic research, Twitter allows access to the full-archive endpoints (Tweet counts, Tweet search). However, in the EU framework the access to the archives is additionally governed by the GDPR and the granted contractual access by Twitter must not be mistaken for a hall pass to process Twitter data without limits.

In addition to general legal requirements (e.g. GPDR), the use of Twitter data is governed by private agreements such as the Twitter Developer Policy[11] in which Twitter imposed their own privacy and data protec-

[10](e.g. http://www.sentiment140.com/)

[11]`https://developer.twitter.com/en/developer-terms/policy`.

tion principles on the users. In addition to the Developer Policy, Twitter provides governance through various rule sets (e.g. *Automation Rules, Display Requirements, API restricted Uses Rules, Twitter Rules, Twitter Brand Resources, Periscope Community Guidelines, Periscope Trademark Guidelines, Batch compliance*) which are not examined within this article but constitute private agreements between the data user and Twitter. These private agreements are partly reflecting GDPR requirements but are also logically governed by Twitter's economic interests and liability considerations rather than fundamental rights aspects and shift liability towards the end user. To a great extent the ToU limit access to Twitter data to what is lawful under the applicable legal frameworks, but sometime also excess legal requirements. However, - in contrast to popular believe - the ToU, provision of data through the Twitter API or even signed contracts *do not* automatically result in the lawfulness of the processing to the data but solely limit Twitter´s liability through shifting responsibility to the developers. Lawfulness from a data protection perspective is, hence, solely driven by the factual circumstances of the processing as laid down in the GDPR. Twitter *expects* the developers to comply with the national and international regulations on their own, although the Twitter API and access restrictions are designed to support developers in their endeavour to act lawful.

Beyond the contractual agreement between Twitter and the developers/controllers, additional rules are imposed on the data controller through generally applicable legal instruments such as the GDPR. These *general* obligations are often referred to in the contractual agreements and compliance with them is subject to contractual obligations. However, the obligation to comply with general requirements does not stem from contracts but rather from the law itself (i.e. these obligations exist independently, with or without reference in the ToU). Failure to comply with general data protection obligations results in an unlawful infringement of the data subjects rights to data protection and privacy and a contractual breach in relation to Twitter.

Recommendation: The collection of data should be conducted with the lowest privacy impact possible for the specific approach. Targeted collection is preferable to ex-post data cleansing. To this end, the respective API documentations (where available) should be checked and a reasoning for the chosen approach in the light of the purposes of the analysis has to be provided. This encompasses limitations in the volume (e.g. timeframes) as well as content-limitations (e.g. exclude Hashtags, Usernames)

3.2.3. Data Cleansing

For most data analysts, data cleansing is a technically relevant step to make the analysis efficient. However, it should also be seen as a way to ensure compliance with the principle of data minimisation as laid down in Art. 5 (1) (c) GDPR and which requires removal of any personal data that is not required for the analysis.

The chosen cleansing approach often depends on the used libraries (e.g. in python NLTK, re, spaCy, gensim, scikit, TensorFlow, or MITIE, text2vec, Moses in C++). Libraries can be described as a toolbox that can be used in various scenarios with multiple different tools (or methods) that can be applied alone or in conjunction depending on the specific needs. In consequence, there are uncountable different approaches to conduct the primary analysis. To reduce impacts on fundamental rights and interests it is important to choose a) the correct libraries b) the right tools (c.f. 4). Some libraries (e.g. NLTK) provide specific guidance/documentation how to use Twitter data (Bird and Tan,), however, due to the myriads of applications of NLP, general discussions or descriptions of anonymization methodologies are usually not provided. GDPR compliant pre-processing/preparation of data hence remains in the hands of the data scientists using these tools. Prior to any analysis, sensitive pieces of text need to be identified and then masked via suppression or generalization approaches (Hassan et al., 2021, p. 1).

Which information has to be filtered out depends on the specific purpose of the processing. Accordingly, the *why* and *how* of the chosen cleaning methods should be clearly explainable. Data controllers should be able to provide proper reasoning as to why certain tools or methodologies for data cleansing are used. For example, Tweets can filtered/cleaned using tools such as *Presidio* (Microsoft, 2022) to identify and exclude personal data from text or erasing geo-data, by relying on filtering of specific keywords or through application of topic modelling approaches. In the given example, a valid reason could be that, while extracting tweets based on the keyword "migrant", tweets concerning "migrant birds" (far away from the topic of migration flows and border control) can also be included, whereas detection of Tweets through topic modelling becomes more precise (Chen et al., 2021b) (Chen et al., 2021a).

In addition to the principle of data minimisation, the principle of data accuracy (Art. 5 (1) (d) GDPR) can impose further requirements on the data controller. To this end, Twitter provides an API endpoint to check offline data against the status of the Twitter database. This endpoint is intended to help controllers/developers to identify if the Twitter content (and hence the underlying intent of the Twitter user) may have changed. To achieve this, the respective dataset with each line containing either the Tweet IDs or the user IDs can be uploaded to the endpoint. Twitter will internally compare the dataset against the internal Twitter data and provide the developer with a set of JSON objects relating to a specific Tweet providing information if the *Tweet or account was deleted, Tweet or account was deactivated, geo data was removed, account is protected or account was suspended*. This compliance check should be conducted on a regular basis and prior to any major analytical approaches. Failure to test the own dataset against Twitter data can result in inaccurate data and infringed not only Twitter´s ToU but more importantly the GDPR principle of data accuracy laid down in Article 5 (1) (d) GDPR.

The foundation of the sentiment analysis can usually broken down to a NLP task. To this end, the processing of data consists of *Tokenization* and data cleaning. Tokenization breaks down textual data into smaller 'pieces' (i.e. tokens). Tokens are often single words but can also be hashtags, emoticons, multiple words or other information embedded in textual data received from the Twitter data. In an additional step, these special characters and stop words are usually removed from the dataset to make processing more efficient and then accessible (e.g. in an array) for further analytical steps in the processing pipeline. To this end, it should be specified which methodology was used for Tokenization and why. In addition, it needs to be acknowledged that Tokenization becomes more difficult for some languages. This can direct the focus towards English tweets due to relative ease of Tokenization of English language with "out-of-the-box" solutions. As a consequence Tokenization can shift sentiment analysis to certain user groups which can generate unforeseen bias in the outputs and should be properly reflected in the interpretation of SA outcomes.

Pursuant to Art. 5 (1) (d) GDPR, the data controller needs to ensure that the stored data reflects the user intent and the current state of content on Twitter. In consequence, an additional pre-processing/cleansing step should be layered on top of the traditional cleansing steps for NLP. To ease this, Twitter provides data controller with a *Batch compliance*[12] procedure, which is unfortunately not very openly communicated and hence often unknown to data users.

Recommendation: Presumed compliance with the ToU does **not** automatically constitute legal compliance under the applicable law - especially in international contexts. The driving factor when designing data processing approaches should be the applicable legislation (e.g. GDPR and national specifications). Existing approaches to foster data accuracy, such as Twitter´s Batch Compliance procedure should be used unless more efficient approaches are available. Tokenization should not only be seen as a necessary preparatory step for the analysis but also as a step to remove personal information from the dataset.

3.2.4. Analysis

As mentioned above, the analysis is strongly dependent on the purpose of the processing, the available skills and tools. Accordingly, analytical approaches cannot be comprehensively covered within a single paper but require contextual analysis and research. Regularly used approaches in the context of Twitter data, for example, make use of *Metadata extraction, Topic Modelling, Entity linking* – to name a few. In discussions between legal and technical personnel the focus often lies on the analysis only, neglecting impacts of the preparatory steps described above.

Sentiment analysis is a text categorization task with the goal to extract a positive or negative orientation that text expresses toward some object based on features of the data (i.e. in the unstructured Tweet text). In principle, is a classification task that - in its simplest form - can be described as multi step approach based on classification of words in a sentence (positive +1; negative -1; neutral 0) that results in a calculation of the final score of the sentence to detect the sentiment to an object. An object in this sense can be anything (e.g. a movie, a book, migrants or a political party). In a simple approach, sentiment analysis can be a binary classification task that simply checks for certain words that are considered either positive (excellent, great) or negative (awful, ridiculous). However, the ruleset for such a simplistic approach has its limits when classification tasks becomes more complex. More refined and complex approaches hence become increasingly important and, for example, rely on supervised or unsupervised machine learning approaches not only linked to single words but contextual information (e.g. reflected through ngrams, topics). Usually the algorithm should learn to return a predicted class for new/unknown documents. Despite complex rulesets, outcomes will usually provide a probability that a document belongs to class (i.e. reflects a positive or negative sentiment). From a legal perspective, the key component that needs to be assessed is the underlying classifier and the used ruleset. For example, it can be distinguished between *generative* (e.g. naive Bayes) and *discriminative* (e.g. logistic regression) classifiers. Generative classifiers build a model how a class (e.g. sentiment) would generates input data (e.g. document). Provided an observation, i.e. an unknown Tweet, the classifier can identify which class would most likely generate such an observation. In the context of sentiment analysis, Topic Modelling – for example – can be useful to identify topics represented in Tweets, to detect negatively connoted Tweets. Equally, topic modelling can also be used to identify relevant tweets as part of the data cleansing (Section 3.2.3).

Topic modeling techniques can be used to extract and categorize "hidden semantic structures" in a textual data, such as a tweet; in simple terms, word frequency and patterns are detected and grouped in order to identify topics (Chen et al., 2021b). This procedure can easily be conducted over hundreds of thousands of Tweets and/or other sources. This means that instead of using a whole bag of words, the words that reflect a certain topic are identified. A topic, in this case, not nec-

[12] `https://developer.twitter.com/en/docs/twitter-api/compliance/batch-compliance/quick-start`.

essarily reflects the "human" understanding of a topic but can be used to detect subjective information such as opinions, attitudes, and feelings expressed in text (Lin and He, 2009; Onan et al., 2016). From a data protection perspective, the data controller should be able to provide a valid reasoning why a specific approach was chosen from the available options (e.g.e.g. Latent Dirichlet Allocation (LDA) (Blei et al., 2003), Biterm Topic Model (BTM) (Yan et al., 2013), Latent Semantic Analysis (LSA) (Deerwester et al., 1990), Non Negative Matrix Factorization (NMF), Parallel Latent Dirichlet Allocation (PLDA), Pachinko Allocation Model (PAM)). Similarly, there are many different approaches for extraction and classification (e.g. unsupervised, semi-supervised, supervised techniques) and diversity can be found in datasets, area of interest and language used (Rana et al., 2016). Where classifications rulesets are generated by a machine-learning approach, their underlying concept should be subject to a legal and ethical assessment prior to the use of such approach. Depending on the training methods, the ruleset can contain information that is not interpretable by humans. If the methodology (here: ruleset) cannot be assessed by a natural person, it should be acknowledged that, in principle, it can result in unforeseen or unwanted (although mathematically correct) outcomes.

Among others, possible reasons for a decision towards a specific approach can be the efficiency of the approach, necessity of extraction of implicit or explicit topics, lawfulness of underlying datasets and their quality. With regard to the latter, a challenge can be, for example, the lack of consensus on a definition of "hate-speech" that contributes to the problem of finding reliably annotated data (Kovács et al., 2021; Zhang and Luo, 2019). This becomes particularly important where rules to determine sentiment are driven by supervised machine learning and the supervised classifier is trained on documents d that have been hand-labeled with a class c (i.e. positive or negative). For example, BERT (Bidirectional Encoder Representations from Transformers) is a machine learning model used for NLP tasks (Devlin et al., 2018) that enables processing of each token (e.g. word) of input text in the full context of all tokens before and after. In addition, models are usually pre-trained on a large corpus of text and then fine-tuned for specific task (transfer learning). Shortcomings in annotated data hence have to be considered by the data controller, especially if data can be linked to natural persons during or after the analysis (e.g. false-positive identification of hate-speech linked to an identifiable individual). In consequence, such approaches should only be used on properly cleaned data sets to avoid any linkage with personal data. In addition, various methodologies may raise a general risk to reinforce biases or misunderstandings. The data controller should hence be sufficiently skilled to compare different approaches, evaluate the pros and cons not only from a technical but also from a legal and ethical perspective. This is also the case where the analysis relies on publicly available libraries. Such libraries may benefit from community inputs – however, their output and/or correctness should not be assumed and the risk of perpetuating biased or faulty concepts underlying the library should be assessed and acknowledged. When analysis outputs are intended to be reused or published (e.g. research articles) or made available in data collections (e.g. Knowledge Bases or Knowledge Graphs (Fafalios et al., 2018; Mendes et al., 2012)) that enable further analysis and/or research with the data, the aforementioned risks are multiplied. Such activities can hence result in an infringement of data subjects rights to privacy and data protection and generate liability concerns for the data controller (i.e. the data scientist). In consequence, it is recommended enforce access restrictions to such data – even though it may seem undesirable in research context at first glance.

Recommendation: The analytical approaches are usually driven by the underlying research question, respective expertise and practical limitations (e.g. computational power). Nevertheless, the shortcomings of the chosen approaches and implications for further analysis should be made transparent and also be included where data sets or results are shared/published.

4. Legal, Ethical and Societal Implications

As shown above, sentiment analysis comes with various risks and challenges that can be addressed on multiple levels. In general, the data controller should be aware that mitigation measures can and have to be applied during the planning, pre-processing, analysis and subsequent use (e.g. publication) of data. In all of these phases, technical and organizational mitigation measures have to be taken into consideration. If mitigation of risks is not possible in an early phase, the corresponding risk has to be addressed and mitigated later in the process. This could, for example, mean that the analysis itself is lawfully possible but research outcomes could not be published because the data could not be cleaned properly in the pre-processing (or later on). The illicit publication of personal data results in liability risks for the data controller, but also generates broader ethical and societal risks (e.g. misuse of research outcomes for political advertisements).

Beyond the technical mitigation measures in the respective steps, it is the task of the data controller to transparently communicate remaining risks and what further measures might be taken to reduce legal, ethical and societal risks especially when data is reused. Especially in the area of research, it should be carefully considered who will have access to the method itself and/or the outputs of the data. Indiscriminate access to generated datasets bear a high risk for misinterpretation and/or misuse especially if the shortcomings and mitigation measures implemented in the pre-processing and/or analysis are not properly addressed. Mitigation of these risks could, for example, require the usage of a data trustee as envisioned in the novel Data Governance Act (DGA) to enable third parties access to the (research) data. To date, research in sentiment analysis is widely focused on the "efficiency" of a method in comparison to other approaches. While this approach is compelling from a mere research perspective it would be desirable to accompany these research aspects with legal, ethical and societal risks and how they can be addressed within the respective pipeline/approach. Such discussions, currently only take place in a very limited scope and data scientists often see such risks as hindering rather than guiding for their own research.

(Hassan et al., 2021, p. 3) point out that the detection of personal information in unstructured textual data suffers from severe limitations as current approaches a) often fail to detect identifying phrases, b) detect natural entities (NE) that should not be suppressed from the analysis (e.g. references to countries) and c) only detect NE that they have been trained to use. While these shortcomings are true, these approaches still provide a feasible anonymization solution in some contexts. However, the data controller needs to be aware of the respective shortcomings and should be able to provide a reasoning why a certain library, tool or approach was used.

During and after the analysis it is important to acknowledge the risk of error manifestation, depending on the analytical method. Sentiment analysis approaches that are based on topic modelling hence have to be subject to regular evaluation and usage of such approaches in operational contexts should be subject to human review. Correctness should not be taken as granted (e.g. specific terms have been identified as hate-speech/negative in 2020 but the same term has a different connotation a few years later). Published outcomes and/or datasets (e.g. Knowledge Bases) should hence properly depict the underlying methodology as well as the measures to ensure privacy of the data subjects as well as correctness of the outcomes. Such information should be manifested not only in accompanying publications but rather linked with data directly in form of metadata. Where personal information remains in the data (e.g. because data cleansing is not possible), it is particularly relevant to acknowledge and address risks in the accuracy of analysis. Risks can be connected, for example, to the "simple" fact that people express sentiments in complex ways (e.g. the use of irony, sarcasm, humor)(Saberi and Saad, 2017, p. 1664), and often texts contain slangs, abbreviations, typos, incomplete information and implicit language which challenge basic classification (Ligthart et al., 2021, p. 5031). At the same time, the categorization of sentiments into two or three groups (positive, negative and neutral) inevitably oversimplifies the complexity of sentiments´ affective qualities and this has to be always kept in mind. Depending on the social context, application of sentiment analysis further bears a specific risk for misinterpretation. To this end, the analysis as well as the interpretation of sentiment analysis should acknowledge different meanings/sentiments depending on the region and context of use (e.g. the word *cunt* has very different meanings reaching from very negative to positive in GB, AUS while in Canada the very same word is seen exclusively negative and offending). Where outcomes are published - e.g in a Knowledge Base -, they should reflect these social and contextual differences (Kovács et al., 2021). Given the technical difficulty in representing societal differences at least the user/researcher needs to be aware of them and address them when building upon a KB.

In a broader picture, opinion and sentiment mining can contribute to a "chilling effect" or "self-censorship effect" that should be countered with transparent processing approaches, lawful processing (i.e. proper data cleansing) as well as open discussion about risks and shortcomings of the used approaches (Manokha, 2018; Kennedy, 2012).

All of the aforementioned steps and mitigation measures require further research both on the legal and technical level. To this end, it would be desirable to further foster interdisciplinary efforts in both realms.

5. Acknowledgements

This work has received funding from the European Union's Horizon 2020 research and innovation programme under grant agreement No. 882986.

6. Bibliographical References

Article 29 Working Party. (2017). Guidelines on data protection impact assessment (dpia) and determining whether processing is "likely to result in high risk" for the purposes of regulation 2016/679, wp 248 rev.01, brussels, 4 october 2017.

Bird, S. and Tan, L.). Nltk - twitter howto.

Blei, D. M., Ng, A. Y., and Jordan, M. I. (2003). Latent dirichlet allocation. *Journal of machine Learning research*, 3(Jan):993–1022.

Brink, S. and Wolff, H. A. (2021). BeckOK DatenschutzR.

Calisir, E. and Brambilla, M. (2018). The problem of data cleaning for knowledge extraction from social media. In Cesare Pautasso, et al., editors, *Current Trends in Web Engineering*, pages 115–125, Cham. Springer International Publishing.

Carammia, M., Iacus, S. M., and Wilkin, T. (2022). Forecasting asylum-related migration flows with machine learning and data at scale. *Scientific Reports*, 12(1):1–16.

Chen, Y., Gesese, G. A., Sack, H., and Alam, M. (2021a). Temporal evolution of the migration-related topics on social media.

Chen, Y., Sack, H., and Alam, M. (2021b). Migrationskb: A knowledge base of public attitudes towards migrations and their driving factors. *CoRR*, abs/2108.07593.

Commission Nationale de l'Informatique et des Libertés (CNIL).). Privacy impact assessment.

Datenschutzkonferenz (DSK). (2018). List of processing activities for which a DPIA is to be carried out.

Deerwester, S., Dumais, S. T., Furnas, G. W., Landauer, T. K., and Harshman, R. (1990). Indexing by latent semantic analysis. *Journal of the American society for information science*, 41(6):391–407.

Devlin, J., Chang, M.-W., Lee, K., and Toutanova, K. (2018). Bert: Pre-training of deep bidirectional transformers for language understanding. *arXiv preprint arXiv:1810.04805*.

Engelhaupt, E. (2022). Social media crackdowns during the war in ukraine make the internet less global. *ScienceNews*.

Fafalios, P., Iosifidis, V., Ntoutsi, E., and Dietze, S. (2018). Tweetskb: A public and large-scale rdf corpus of annotated tweets. In *European Semantic Web Conference*, pages 177–190. Springer.

Frontex. (2019). Service Contract for the Provision of Social Media Analysis Services Concerning Irregular Migration Trends and Forecasts (as part of Prewarning Mechanism) - Frontex/OP/534/2019/DT. accessed 12-October-2021.

Goritz, A., Kolleck, N., and Jörgens, H. (2019). *Analyzing Twitter data: Advantages and challenges in the study of UN climate negotiations*. SAGE Publications Ltd.

Hassan, F., Sanchez, D., and Domingo-Ferrer, J. (2021). Utility-preserving privacy protection of textual documents via word embeddings. *IEEE Transactions on Knowledge and Data Engineering*, pages 1–1.

Information Commissioners Office (ICO). (2017). What is a dpia?

Kennedy, H. (2012). Perspectives on sentiment analysis. *Journal of Broadcasting & Electronic Media*, 56(4):435–450.

Kovács, G., Alonso, P., and Saini, R. (2021). Challenges of hate speech detection in social media. *SN Computer Science*, 2(2):1–15.

Kuner, C., Bygrave, L., Docksey, C., and Drechsler, L. (2020). *The EU General Data Protection Regulation: A Commentary*. Oxford University Press. Available at: https://global. oup. com/academic ....

Ligthart, A., Catal, C., and Tekinerdogan, B. (2021). Systematic reviews in sentiment analysis: a tertiary study. *Artificial Intelligence Review*, pages 1–57.

Lin, C. and He, Y. (2009). Joint sentiment/topic model for sentiment analysis. In *Proceedings of the 18th ACM conference on Information and knowledge management*, pages 375–384.

Manokha, I. (2018). Surveillance, panopticism, and self-discipline in the digital age. *Surveillance & Society*, 16(2):219–237.

Mendes, P. N., Jakob, M., and Bizer, C. (2012). Dbpedia: A multilingual cross-domain knowledge base.

Microsoft. (2022). Presidio - data protection and anonymization api.

Mijatović, D. (2021). COE - Commissioner for Human Rights: A distress call for human rights. The widening gap in migrant protection in the Mediterranean".

Onan, A., Korukoglu, S., and Bulut, H. (2016). Lda-based topic modelling in text sentiment classification: An empirical analysis. *Int. J. Comput. Linguistics Appl.*, 7(1):101–119.

Pereira-Kohatsu, J. C., Quijano-Sánchez, L., Liberatore, F., and Camacho-Collados, M. (2019). Detecting and monitoring hate speech in twitter. *Sensors*, 19(21):4654.

Peslak, A. (2017). Sentiment analysis and opinion mining: current state of the art and review of google and yahoo search engines' privacy policies. *Journal of Information Systems Applied Research*, 10(3):38.

Rana, T. A., Cheah, Y.-N., and Letchmunan, S. (2016). Topic modeling in sentiment analysis: A systematic review. *Journal of ICT Research & Applications*, 10(1).

Righi, A. (2019). Assessing migration through social media: a review. *Mathematical Population Studies*, 26(2):80–91.

Saberi, B. and Saad, S. (2017). Sentiment analysis or opinion mining: a review. *International Journal of Advanced Science Engineering Information Technology*, 7:1660–1667.

Thakkar, H. and Patel, D. (2015). Approaches for sentiment analysis on twitter: A state-of-art study. *arXiv preprint arXiv:1512.01043*.

Yan, X., Guo, J., Lan, Y., and Cheng, X. (2013). A biterm topic model for short texts. In *Proceedings of the 22nd international conference on World Wide Web*, pages 1445–1456.

Zhang, Z. and Luo, L. (2019). Hate speech detection: A solved problem? the challenging case of long tail on twitter. *Semantic Web*, 10(5):925–945.

The Legal and Ethical issues Workshop @LREC2022, pages 38–43
Marseille, 20 June 2022

Transparency and Explainability of a Machine Learning Model in the Context of Human Resource Management

Sebastien Delecraz[1], Loukman Eltarr[1], Olivier Oullier[2,3,4]
[1]Gojob AI Lab, Aix-en-Provence, France
[2]Inclusive Brains & BRAINS4, Marseille, France
[3]Aix-Marseille University, CNRS, Cognitive Psychology Laboratory (UMR 7290), Marseille, France
[4]Optivio Inc, Boston, Massachusetts, USA
sebastien.delecraz@gojob.com, loukman@gojob.com, olivier@inclusive-brains.com

Abstract

We introduce how the proprietary machine learning algorithms developed by Gojob, an HR Tech company, to match candidates to a job offer are as transparent and explainable as possible to users (i.e., our recruiters) and our clients (e.g. companies looking to fill jobs). We detail how our matching algorithm (which identifies the best candidates for a job offer) controls the fairness of its outcome. We have described the steps we have taken to ensure that the decisions made by our mathematical models not only inform but improve the performance of our recruiters.

Keywords: Fairness, Trust, Human Resources Technologies, Artificial Intelligence, Equal Opportunity Framework

1. Introduction

Human Language Technologies had a significant impact on the business of Human Resource Management (HRM) over the past twenty years. Human Resources Technologies (HR Tech), for instance, have leveraged mathematical models to improve (job) recruitment-related tasks. There are now very efficient models to execute Natural Language Processing (NLP) tasks. These are well suited to process and make sense of the wealth of data (CV, resume, emails, text messages, spoken conversations) that is being exchanged between candidates and employers, including when a recruiter or a recruitment agency acts as an enabler. If one takes the example of data found in resumes, unless guidelines are given to the candidates by the employer or the recruitment agency/platform, most of the time the content to process is not structured. Depending on regulatory constraints (e.g., data protection and privacy laws) in the country in which the recruitment process takes place, as well as the agreement signed by the job candidate prior to sharing data as part of his/her job application, the content of the resume can or cannot belong to the private domain. Regardless of this data being considered private or not, its analyses as part of HRM processes must meet several criteria including (but not limited to):

- an ethical, fair, non-discriminatory and inclusive job selection process;
- transparency and explainability of the mathematical models and non-algorithmic processes employed to assist with decisions;
- compliance to legal and regulatory constraints related to data privacy and protection.

Machine Learning (ML) algorithms have become a key part of decision-making solutions across a great variety of research and business sectors where large amounts of structured or unstructured data need to be processed and make sense of to inform the choices to be made. Today, the way the most efficient ML models (like deep learning or gradient boosting) function is often difficult to monitor. It is also challenging to understand how the algorithm(s) at play make decisions.

If one take the example of gradient boosting algorithms, they are quite opaque, to say the least, in the way they operate. An important issue in the research and business sector leveraging ML is therefore to understand the decision processes and outcomes of the mathematical models at play and which covariates are really acting as discriminators. The challenge of understanding the "algorithmic ghost in the machine" has been picked up by a consortium of multidisciplinary scientists from various country who founded the field of machine behavior: an approach consisting of using rigorous behavioral analytics and metrics to track the behavior of algorithms in order to identify how they make decisions (Rahwan et al., 2019).

In the context of job recruitment, the decisions made by ML models must be controlled, adapted and consistent with the different challenges and objectives of the individuals and/or organizations using them, as well as complying with legal and regulatory constraints. In the HR tech business, the outcomes of ML algorithms must be aligned with the business sector's best practices. This bears a legitimate question of trust and understanding, when compromise between interpretability and performance is too often the name of game. This constitutes a serious issue when, at least in theory, no compromise should be made when it comes to clarity of the data analysis process, ethics, and compliance.

As a temporary recruitment agency leveraging Artificial Intelligence (AI) to optimize its job matching services, Gojob developed a proprietary job matching machine learning solution consisting in a scoring algorithm able to identify the most relevant temporary workers for a request made by one of its clients (i.e., a job offer). Our algorithms are a tool for recruiters to help them staff specific HR needs as fast and as accurately as possible. It is therefore essential for our recruiters to (i) know why a candidate's profile is put forward in (and by) the learning mathematical model, (ii) to understand on which characteristics the recommendation decision is being based, and (iii) to make sure that ML algorithms operate in an ethical, inclusive and therefore non-discriminatory fashion. These are a must-have for the recruiter to trust the ML-powered tools (s)he uses on a daily basis to assist with the decisions to be made to deliver on his/her job. In addition, the recruiter has to be able to justify to the job candidate and to the client (i.e., the possible future employer of the candidate) why a person is deemed fit or not for the position to be filled.

An algorithm should only be considered in light of its performance and results according to a given set of (more or less standard) metrics, but also while taking into account the context in which the data processing it operates (i.e., the decision it makes) happens. This is why, here, in the first section, we introduce some of the safeguards we put in place to ensure that our algorithms, at the core of the daily jobs of our recruiters, do not provide predictions containing ethical and discriminatory biases. In the second section, we show how we used a tool based on the concept of the Shapley values (Shapley, 1953) to reach an acceptable level of accuracy and explainability of the behavior of our Machine Learning models with respect to the different features we use for it to deliver, and keep learning.

2. Ethics and Social Artificial Intelligence

The mission of our company is to provide access to employment to those who are seeking a job, and to offer them the ability to thrive by learning new skills, regardless of their age, gender, origin, education, or level of professional experience. It is also our mission to provide our clients with the best job applicants for the positions they need to fill. Non-discrimination and limited opportunities to learn are major issues blue collar workers face on a daily basis. To date, there is no satisfactory solution available to address this issue, either in Europe or in the US, where Gojob is located. This is what lead to our strategic business decision to have a specific focus on young individuals who are Neither in Employment nor in Education or Training (NEET) in the retail, logistics, and manufacturing industries. There are unfortunately over 2 million people referred to as NEET in France, 10 million in the United States of America (OCDE, 2017). We use our technology to ensure a successful first work experience (or return to work) with our client (i.e., future employer) through training, mentoring, mobility and financial services, while measuring the results after six months based on a set of given criteria: namely the NEET has worked more than sixty days over a period, has signed a contract for a temporary job that lasts more than thirty days, has created their own job or is in training. In 2021, our company has staffed 43% of NEET people as part of temporary job missions, out of approximately fifteen thousand temporary workers (who work on average 5% more hours than other temporary workers).

Given this context, we want to ensure that no particular group is discriminated by our mathematical models and algorithms. Our proprietary database is constituted of applications made by temporary workers in France who are voluntarily and willingly applying for jobs. The atomic item is composed by the set of attributes related to a temporary worker, the set of information related to the job description to which the candidate could (or would) apply for and a label which describes the outcome of the application.

For example, our hypothesis is that applicants who need a residence permit to be allowed to work are more likely to be negatively affected by the model because of a possible bias in our database. The same thing goes for other sensitive attributes (age, gender, nationality, etc.). Therefore, we use dummy variables to categorize, detailed in previous works (Delecraz et al., 2022), what we assume would be a group of candidates that would be "favored" by the algorithm, as opposed to the group that would be "discriminated" by:

- **gender**: male or female;
- **nationality**: French nationality or not;
- **place of birth**: born in France or not;
- **education**: has declared an education level or not;
- **residence permit (RP) requirement**: can work without a residence permit or need to have one;
- **age**: four age groups (18–25, 25–35, 35–45, 45-55) that we consider independently of each other (given a group, we compare those who belong to it against the rest of the population). We stop our ages groups at 55 years old because the number of candidates in our database older than 55 years is way too low (mostly because this age group is generally not seeking temporary jobs) to conduct a qualitative analysis.

We conducted an analysis across these sensitive attributes to assess the fairness of the outcomes provided by our ML model (based on regularizing gradient boosting using XGBoost, an optimized distributed gradient boosting library) using the FairLearn toolkit (Bird et al., 2020), an open-source project which provides which proposes many methods of fairness analysis for machine learning models. We examined how the model performs based on the Equal Opportunity fairness definition; a metric considered in the specific scientific literature (Hardt et al., 2016) to be the more relevant one to address this question. If $\hat{Y}$ is a binary predictor of the outcome of a worker application and Y the associated ground truth, we consider the class 1 as the preferred outcome in the classification task (the worker was recruited). Given a sensitive attribute A indicating the belonging to a group considered as discriminated and $\bar{A}$ the belonging to the favored group, $\hat{Y}$ is considered equal opportunity with respect to sensitive attribute A if:

$$\mathbf{P}\left(\hat{Y}=1 \mid Y=1, A\right)=\mathbf{P}\left(\hat{Y}=1 \mid Y=1, \bar{A}\right) \tag{1}$$

Before implementing a fair algorithm, we analyzed the data to observe possible biases towards and/or under-representation of some categories. We observed that the distribution of the label is not the same across sensitive attributes. All the work related to this subject is detailed in a previous article (Delecraz et al., 2022). Our analysis shows that our model never exceeds the 5% True Positive Rate Parity (which is the absolute value of the difference between the two probabilities in equation 1). Of course there is no threshold that defines if a model is fair or not. In the literature, depending on the application, we find references to thresholds ranging from 5% to 20%. In our case, we take these first scores as a starting point and of course aim at a score of 0%.

3. Explainability of the Outcomes of Machine Learning Model

Machine learning models are designed and used to optimize a metric or a cost function. In the case of our ML-based solution to assist in job recruitment tasks, knowing that our model considers a candidate as relevant to a given offer is not enough. We need to give the recruiter a minimum amount of insights and information when (s)he reviews the profile of a job candidate, in order to understand which variables were particularly discriminating, either locally or overall. Our intent is to actually understand the rules the algorithm has generated, not just how the algorithm functions. Understanding a model consists in analyzing how it works as a whole, in a given context, that is to say through the input data, the algorithm itself, the output predictions, the weights the model gives to different features, the distributions of different variables and the effect the model gives each one.

It is therefore important to know the "why" of a prediction and to identify the instances where the model is flawed. In particular, the model can make (rightly or wrongly) unexpected decisions, and it is therefore essential to understand what has influenced the prediction in one direction and what could have influenced it to go the other way. A better understanding of the model can sometimes lead to a better understanding of the problem (or question to answer) and to the discovery of new subtleties. Molnar (2020) give a good explanation and broader vision of the explainability issues at play.

Machine Learning techniques are destined to become more and more widespread and to intervene very regularly in decision-making processes in professional and personal settings. Today, the most efficient models are not easy to interpret and there is a lack of visibility on how their decision processes operate. For example, gradient boosting algorithms are quite opaque. An important issue is to understand the decisions output of our model and which covariates are really discriminating. In a context focused on recruitment, the decisions made by the model must be controlled, adapted and consistent with the different challenges. It should be noted that the decisions must be aligned with the business knowledge. This is a true question of trust and understanding, and the compromise between interpretability and performance is not always obvious. We used the SHAP library toolkit (Lundberg and Lee, 2017; Lundberg et al., 2018; Lundberg et al., 2020), based on the concept of Shapley values (Shapley, 1953). This tool allows one to have a local and global vision of the decisions of the model in an agnostic way. The SHAP value measure the participation of a feature to the prediction. For each prediction of our model, we compute the SHAP value for each of its feature.

3.1. Global and Local View

We have adopted two different observation positions to try to explain the decisions of our model. A close up view explanation can provide a clear view. In particular, a global view can give the impression of complex dependencies on a given covariance, whereas a local view can show simpler and clearer interactions. This allows one to see what might change in the output if the input changes slightly. Yet, a helicopter view allows one to access aggregated information as well as to get an idea of how the model works on a group rather than an individual. It is possible to group instances according to the granularity we want to consider.

3.1.1. Global view

The global view allows us to quickly understand which features matter when the model makes a decision. The set of features we use in our model is designed to capture the different characteristics that allow us to evaluate the suitability of a temp for a job offer. The SHAP library provides a tool to examine global model behavior. We report the SHAP importance compute for each feature in Table 1. A SHAP value is computed for all feature for each prediction. Given a feature, we compute its importance by doing the average of the absolute values of the SHAP values overall the predictions. These values allow us to identify the features that, overall, have the most impact. Features meaning and name have been deliberately hidden for reasons of confidentiality.

Features	SHAP importance
Feature 13	0.85489
Feature 2	0.78975
Feature 7	0.48765
Feature 3	0.25791
Feature 12	0.24747
Feature 8	0.16531
Feature 0	0.16264
Feature 1	0.15541
Feature 5	0.05532
Feature 9	0.03777
Feature 11	0.02633
Feature 4	0.02554
Feature 10	0.01142
Feature 6	0.00768

Table 1: SHAP importance for each feature used by the model.

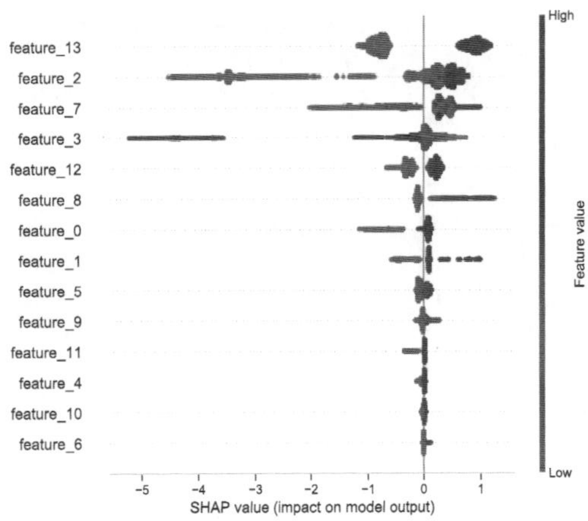

Figure 1: Feature importance with SHAP values. For each dot, vertical position depict the feature, horizontal position indicates whether the effect of that value caused a higher or lower prediction and the color describes the value taken in that dot.

The explainability that results from these first figures in this global view is more useful to the teams that design the model than to the end users, namely our recruiters. However, further analysis allows us to learn more about the different features, especially those that have a low importance in decision-making. For example, we can deduce that features with a very low SHAP value do not capture well enough what can be decisive for a recruitment and that they should either be improved or removed from the model. However, we can also observe one of the weaknesses of the SHAP tool, namely the existence of correlation between features. For example here, we have calculated that on our corpus of data, Feature 10 and Feature 13 have a correlation score of 0.6. The model (remember that it is an XGboost) could therefore have identified this correlation and decided not to give importance to Feature 10, as Feature 13 would allow it to obtain more or less the same decisions.

In Figure 1 we can identify the SHAP values for each variable. On the x-axis we can see their impact (on the right if the impact on the prediction is positive, on the left if it is negative). On the y-axis are printed the different variables and ordered by the total magnitude of their SHAP values. The color code indicates the value of the variable (the closer the color is to red, the higher the value, conversely blue symbolizes low values). Note that when several points are aligned horizontally but scattered vertically, they represent points that have been impacted similarly. Whereas points that are horizontally distant but have the same color represent instances that have been impacted differently for similar values of the variable concerned. This last case means in particular that there was an interaction with other variables.

By reading the feature importance in Figure 1, we can first notice the monotonic effects that the model has learned for every feature. Feature 13 has the biggest weight here and its effect is quite unequivocal. The fact that the points are located in two small clusters show little interaction with other features and a strong homogeneous effect. The Feature 2 shows a more uneven effect. Its high values have a similar impact on the model, but the low values are more spread out. Some latter have a more or less neutral impact, but some others have a quite strong negative impact and take a wide range. The Feature 2 strong importance is likely to come from these instances rather than a really global effect. Feature 3 has a similar behavior to the Feature 2. However, it differentiates itself because of its negative monotony and also because some really high values endure a negative impact that is really far from the one on the other points. In contrast, Feature 4, 10 and 6 are meaningless for the model. The model ignores those features, and we can say that they have little effect on the model decisions.

We could go further in the plot reading, and it really is a wealthy source of information. One only has to get a good understanding of the global effects. It is possible to discern whether a feature effect is global or focused on some instances only. Moreover, a very important aspect is to challenge these effects and make sure they are aligned with the business logic. Depending on the case a model should not base its decision on one feature only but rather on interactions and non-linear effects. This action permits us to find undesirable effects and debug the model.

3.1.2. Local view

We also analyze the insights on local prediction and visualize the effect of the different variables. In the Appendix A, we provide a couple of examples we randomly chose in the data. In the Figures 2a we will zoom in on some predictions. The red color indicates positive impact and the blue color indicates a negative impact. Each time we can see the value of the concerned feature. We also see the output value (negative value means the model gave the negative class to the instance x).

If we compare Figure 2a with Figure 2b we can see that the outputs are appreciably similar but the reasons are totally different. Both instances have been given the negative class by the model. In the Figure 2a the feature that contributes the most is Feature 7 followed by Feature 13 and 8. Here the negative impact was carried by three features only. The other variables had a mild positive impact. To extend the reflection conducted in the global view part, Feature 2 (which had an increasing effect on the model) has a positive impact with a value of 0.229. This value can seem low, but the model estimated that it had a positive impact. Therefore, a worker corresponding to this instance should increase his value for the Feature 2 and also for Feature 7 if he wants to be classified as positive the next time. In the Figure 2b, the most important feature was Feature 13 as it was in the previous example. However, other features have been reversed as Feature 12, 7 and 2. One can see that according to these two examples, turning Feature 7 from 0.025 to 0.245 has a stronger impact than turning Feature 2 from 0.229 to 0.005.

In Figure 2c, we can see that the profile was supported by the model because of the high values for both of features 13 and 7. In the three examples Feature 8 was low and brought a really mild negative impact. To go further we could explore the distribution of this variable and in what scenarios it has a positive impact eventually.

With this type of representation, we can quickly explain to the recruiters which features have the most impact on the model's decision. In case of rejection, our recruiters have the possibility to send feedback to the candidate to explain the reason, or the actions that the candidate can do to quickly increase his chances to be qualified for the job offer. In case of acceptance, the recruiter has explanations about the decision-making which improves his confidence in the model. He can also provide a detailed explanation to the client on the relevance of the candidate to the job offer.

4. Conclusion

The study in this article shows the control we maintain over our Machine Learning algorithms as a social impact company. While no final hiring decision is made by a machine alone, the choices the matching algorithm makes must be fair and explainable to our recruiters for them to make the final call. This is why we have built into our AI-based automation process algorithmic safeguards that signal possible biases (theory) and measured biases (outcomes) as well as ways to visualize and understand what sources of information the model's decisions are based on. We strongly believe that safeguards algorithms to minimize biases and discrimination should become the norm when artificial intelligence is used in job recruitment processes.

5. Bibliographical References

Bird, S., Dudík, M., Edgar, R., Horn, B., Lutz, R., Milan, V., Sameki, M., Wallach, H., and Walker, K. (2020). Fairlearn: A toolkit for assessing and improving fairness in AI. Technical Report MSR-TR-2020-32, Microsoft, May.

Delecraz, S., Eltarr, L., Becuwe, M., Bouxin, H., Boutin, N., and Oullier, O. (2022). Making recruitment more inclusive: Unfairness monitoring for a job matching machine learning algorithm. In *International Workshop on Equitable Data and Technology (Fairware'22)*, pages 364–372, Pittsburgh, Pennsylvania, USA, 5.

Hardt, M., Price, E., and Srebro, N. (2016). Equality of opportunity in supervised learning. In *Proceedings of the 30th International Conference on Neural Information Processing Systems*, NIPS'16, page 3323–3331, Red Hook, NY, USA. Curran Associates Inc.

Lundberg, S. M. and Lee, S.-I. (2017). A unified approach to interpreting model predictions. In *Proceedings of the 31st International Conference on Neural Information Processing Systems*, NIPS'17, page 4768–4777, Red Hook, NY, USA. Curran Associates Inc.

Lundberg, S. M., Nair, B., Vavilala, M. S., Horibe, M., Eisses, M. J., Adams, T., Liston, D. E., Low, D. K.-W., Newman, S.-F., Kim, J., et al. (2018). Explainable machine-learning predictions for the prevention of hypoxaemia during surgery. *Nature Biomedical Engineering*, 2(10):749.

Lundberg, S. M., Erion, G., Chen, H., DeGrave, A., Prutkin, J. M., Nair, B., Katz, R., Himmelfarb, J., Bansal, N., and Lee, S.-I. (2020). From local explanations to global understanding with explainable ai for trees. *Nature Machine Intelligence*, 2(1):2522–5839.

Molnar, C. (2020). *Interpretable machine learning*. Lulu.com.

OCDE. (2017). Youth not in employment, education or training (neet).

Rahwan, I., Cebrian, M., Obradovich, N., Bongard, J., Bonnefon, J.-F., Breazeal, C., Crandall, J. W., Christakis, N. A., Couzin, I. D., Jackson, M. O., et al. (2019). Machine behaviour. *Nature*, 568(7753):477–486.

Shapley, L. S., (1953). *A Value for n-Person Games*, volume 2, chapter 17, pages 307–318. Princeton University Press.

A. Example of SHAP value decomposition for predictions

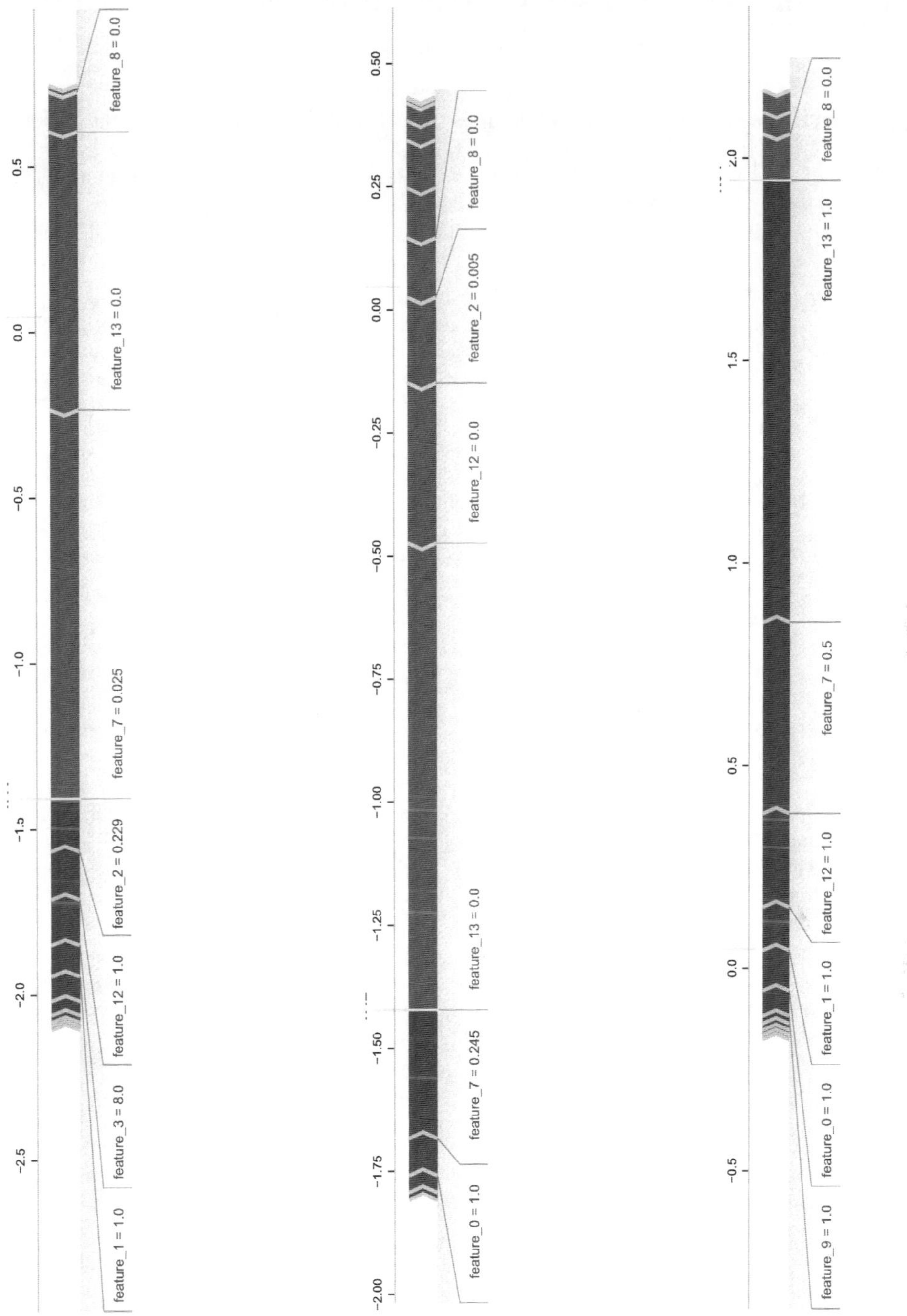

(a) Prediction 1 (b) Prediction 2 (c) Prediction 3

Figure 2: Decomposition of two negative and one positive prediction showing each feature impact with SHAP values.

The Legal and Ethical issues Workshop @LREC2022, pages 44–47
Marseille, 20 June 2022

Public Interactions with Voice Assistant – Discussion of Different One-Shot Solutions to Preserve Speaker Privacy

Ingo Siegert[1], Yamini Sinha[1], Gino Winkelmann[1], Oliver Jokisch[2], Andreas Wendemuth[3]
[1]Mobile Dialog Systems, Otto von Guericke University Magdeburg, Germany
[2]Cybersecurity and Data Management, HSF University, Meissen, Germany
[3]Cognitive Systems, Otto von Guericke University Magdeburg, Germany
siegert@ovgu.de, yamini.sinha@ovgu.de, gino.winkelmann@st.ovgu.de, oliver.jokisch@hsf.sachsen.de

Abstract

In recent years, the use of voice assistants has rapidly grown. Hereby, above all, the user's speech data is stored and processed on a cloud platform, being the decisive factor for a good performance in speech processing and understanding. Although usually, they can be found in private households, a lot of business cases are also employed using voice assistants for public places, be it as an information service, a tour guide, or a booking system. As long as the systems are used in private spaces, it could be argued that the usage is voluntary and that the user itself is responsible for what is processed by the voice assistant system. When leaving the private space, the voluntary use is not the case anymore, as users may be made aware that their voice is processed in the cloud and background voices can be unintendedly recorded and processed as well. Thus, the usage of voice assistants in public environments raises a lot of privacy concerns. In this contribution, we discuss possible anonymization solutions to hide the speakers' identity, thus allowing a safe cloud processing of speech data. Thereby, we promote the public use of voice assistants.
Keywords: voice assistant, public recordings, speaker anonymization

1. Introduction

The topic of data protection is becoming increasingly important today. In the field of voice assistants, there have been many discussions in recent years dealing with the protection of personal data (Schönherr et al., 2020; Siegert et al., 2021). Most current applications of voice assistants focus on the use of own assistant systems in private environments, but there are many applications possible where voice assistants can be employed in public spaces (i.e., museum guides, self-shopping support, etc (Porcheron et al., 2018; Lopatovska and Oropeza, 2018; Steven et al., 2017). In this context, the discussion is intensified on the one hand, as speech applications have rapidly grown and by their convenience of use along with outstanding speech understanding even in difficult acoustic environments. On the other hand, by the fact that for the first time, technical systems not just process personal data that can be used to identify users but directly use the voice as personal (biometric) data for the interaction. Furthermore, when using voice assistants, users are getting aware (often for the first time) that their data is processed in the cloud. The implications of a privacy breach in regard to speech data and possible solutions are extensively presented in (Tomashenko et al., 2021; Siegert et al., 2020a).
From a legal perspective, the protection of personal data is often limited to the country or jurisdiction in which the person lives. Other jurisdictions may have incompatible privacy policies which forbid to transfer any private data between them (Nautsch et al., 2019). In recent years, attempts have been made to draft agreements and decisions between the European Union and the United States of America in the field of data protection. The goal of each of these negotiations has been to reach an agreement on how to securely transfer personal data of citizens of European member states to the United States of America, based on the European Data Protection Directive. The resolutions negotiated to date have been progressively declared unworkable (European Court of Justice (Grand Chamber), 2020).
Especially, the aim of the GDPR to "enhance individuals' control and rights over their personal data and to simplify the regulatory environment" could cause practical implications on the use of voice assistants for public applications. Regarding the processing of the content of the transmitted data itself, this may not be crucial (at least) for information-providing systems, as users can be informed beforehand that their request will be processed and no personal data should be given. Recent field studies using a public voice assistant service showed that users do not tend to disclose private information (Siegert, 2020). But, in terms of the voice data itself, this is not possible, as users can be clearly identified by their voice, and a (recognizable) voice profile can be created. Thus, it could be possible to not only identify users based on their voice profile, but also to carry out additional voice analyses, such as the current mood or affect, which are shown to have an influence on the shopping experience.
A possible solution to prevent the identification of users by their voice is to rely on anonymization techniques. Anonymization has the advantage that truly anonymized data are not subject to the GDPR and as such can in principle be freely processed. But according to the GPDR, anonymization should take into account two parts, 1) that it is irreversible and 2) that it is done in such a way that it is impossible (or extremely impractical) to identify the data subject (WP29 (Article 29 Data Protection

Working Party), 2014). What does that imply for the use of voice assistants in public spaces? To answer that question, we formulated several assumptions:

- Users usually make only a few requests to the voice assistant.
- The anonymization should work regardless of the speaker's language, accent, sex, or gender.
- The anonymization should be fast, i.e., without a distracting delay in the interaction.
- The anonymization should run locally, independently of the voice assistant, and should also provide an audio stream.

In the following, three anonymization techniques are presented and their implication and outcomes are discussed. Hereby, we limit the utilized methods to work without a training phase, as we identified that as the most critical issue during the interaction with voice assistants. We believe that for a satisfying speech-based interaction, one-shot anonymization should be aimed so that the users can directly utter their commands which will be anonymized "on-the-fly".

2. Utilized Anonymization Techniques

2.1. McAdams coefficient

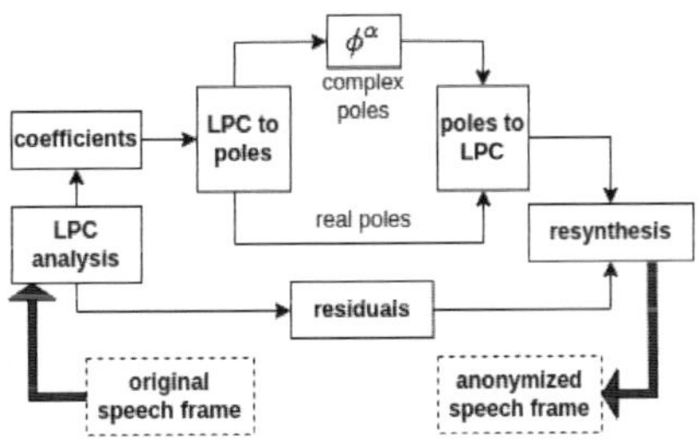

Figure 1: Pipeline of McAdams coefficient-based speaker anonymization, taken from (Patino et al., 2020). The angle ϕ of non-zero imaginary poles are raised to the power of McAdams coefficient α.

The anonymization technique using the McAdams coefficient (α) adjusts the timbre or spectral envelope, by frame-wise shifting the formant positions (Patino et al., 2020). Formats describe the spectral maximum resulting from an acoustic maximum of the human vocal tract and their location defines the peculiarity of specific phonemes (i.e. a unit of sound that distinguish words, as letters would do for written language). Due to anatomic differences in the vocal tract of humans, the formants for the same phoneme of different humans underlie specific variations. Therefore, slight variations to the formant positions obscure the speaker characteristics but preserve the produced sound, cf. (Siegert, 2015). Therefore, the formant positions have to be estimated from the original's speaker formants (i.e. speech analysis), then the formant shift has to be applied and afterwards, the speech including the shifted formants has to be re-produced (i.e. speech synthesis).

To get an estimation of the source (i.e. residuals) and filter (i.e. representation of the formants) coefficients, a Linear Predictive Coding (LPC) is utilized. The filter coefficients are used to determine the shift in the non-zero imaginary terms of the poles (determined by α) and then converted back to LPC coefficients and together with the residual used to resynthesize the new anonymized speech frame in the time domain. This drafted approach requires neither training nor large amounts of training data. It simply alters the original speech using signal processing techniques to change the voice impressions of the speaker (Sinha and Siegert, 2022).

2.2. Real-time voice changer

A Real-time voice changer is usually a device or software, which can change the impression of a voice by changing the tone or pitch of a voice, adding distortions to the user's voice, or combining the previous methods in various ways. During the current analyses, we relied on Voxal from NHC software offering good usability. Besides the amplification or attenuation of some frequency components, high and low passes are often used as pre-configuration in voice changers. As high-pass filters had a very high fundamental frequency when being applied to female voices, we observed some problems for male voices using the same setup. Consequently, male speakers are very difficult to understand, since important fundamental frequencies are no longer present. The opposite case led to similarly poor results. Thus, to have an anonymization technique that works for several speakers without having to manually tune it individually, a very careful approach in setting the various filter options is necessary.

2.3. TTS-based anonymization

For comparison, we also included a TTS-based anonymization and relied on eSpeak. eSpeak is a compact open-source speech synthesizer. It uses a "formant synthesis" method, allowing many languages to be provided in a small size (Phutak et al., 2019). The speech is clear, and can be used at high speaking rates, but is not as natural or smooth as larger synthesizers which are based on human speech recordings. The advantage of formant synthesis is that it needs less computation and generates reliably intelligent speech output even at very high speeds with small memory footprint for the engine and its voice data and can therefore be easily included in IoT devices without huge performance loss. In the current contribution, the main purpose of the TTS anonymization is to serve as a ground truth to evaluate the anonymization success of the McAdams and real-time voice changer.

3. Experimental Setup

3.1. Dataset

We used spontaneous interactions between humans and a voice-assistant from the "Voice Assistant Conversation Corpus" (VACC), cf. (Siegert, 2020). It consists of high-quality device-directed and human-directed German spontaneous speech, recorded by 13 male and 14 female speakers of a mean age of 24 ± 3.32 years. The recordings took place in a living room-like surrounding so that the participants could get into a more informal communication atmosphere compared to a laboratory setting. In this analysis, we only used the device-directed speech, which comprise approximately 3,800 utterances with an average length of 2.3s (min: 0.02s and max: 6.09s).

3.2. Anonymization Ability

A pre-trained speaker recognition model (VGGVox) was used to test the identification ability of the anonymized speech samples. It is based on a VGG-M architecture and adapts a deep-CNN architecture, cf. (Nagrani et al., 2017). The model was trained on a large-scale dataset called VoxCeleb1, consisting of over 140,000 utterances by 1,251 celebrities with a wide range of different ages, accents, nationality, etc. Ergo, the model learns speaker-specific cues and prosody mannerisms comprehensively. Furthermore, we use the missrate or false negative rate (FNR), i.e., the number of times the predicted speaker is not the same as the actual speaker. A euclidean distance is used to classify the speaker ID by comparing the speech feature vectors from the test speech, here anonymized speech, with all the enrolled speakers' speech feature vectors. A score of 0 or 1 is assigned according to the speaker ID prediction to refute or confirm the test speaker, respectively.

3.3. ASR Performance

In order to evaluate the degradation in intelligibility caused due to anonymization is measured by Word Error Rate (WER). We used a popular ASR, by Google, that performs well to recognize spontaneous speech, as identified in previous studies (Silber-Varod et al., 2021; Siegert et al., 2020b). The recognized ASR transcription is compared with a reference text to calculate the WER by counting the number of substituted (S), deleted (D) and inserted (I) words against the total number of words (N) in the reference text. In previous experiments, we identified a WER for the original dataset of 0.09 in average (Siegert et al., 2020b).

4. Results

Using device-directed utterances from the 27 speakers of VACC, we generated anonymized speech using: i) McAdams coefficient and ii) eSpeak TTS synthesizer, and iii) Voxal voice changer. In the first method, the McAdams coefficient α is set to 0.8, achieving a good compromise between anonymity and ASR performance, identified in previous experiments (Sinha et al., 2022). Whereas for eSpeak, synthesized speech samples are simply generated by providing the transcription of each speech sample. For Voxal, a specific general configuration consisting of a pitch shifters and amplifiers was utilized. The in such a way altered speech is the anonymized speech, which is then used to further evaluate the success of anonymity and degradation in ASR performance.

Table 1: Anonymization ability and ASR performance of the analyzed techniques.

Anonymization technique	Missrate (in %)	WER
McAdams ($\alpha = 0.8$)	38.72	0.18
eSpeak	83.21	0.68
Voxal	70.11	0.30

We evaluated speaker anonymization and the ASR performance. The overall results regarding ASR intelligibility, measured as WER, and performance in anonymization, measured as missrate, are given in Table 1. Regarding the WER it can be seen that all anonymization techniques result in a worse WER than the original samples. Hereby eSpeak results in a quite high WER and thus a very low ASR intelligibility. The best WER can be observed with the McAdams technique. Regarding male and female speakers, no difference in the WER is observable.

Regarding the missrate, in first sight Voxal and eSpeak result in a better anonymization, but this is due to the much lower ASR intelligibility. When distinguishing male and female speakers it is apparent that for male speakers the missrate is significantly lower than for female speakers, i.e. female speakers achieve a better anonymity, see Fig 2. For the TTS-based system, we are a bit surprised that such a large amount of TTS-voices can fool the automatic speaker verification at all, as the listening impression of the generated voice is quite different from the original sample. Furthermore, it could be assumed that a TTS-voice which is obviously not one of the original speakers will never be identified as one of the known speakers. We assume that this observation is connected to the way the voice samples and the previously trained voiceprints are compared (distance-based similarity measure). The differences in the miss-rate between male and female speakers could be just partly explained by the fact, that we use a male TTS-voice, as also Voxal and the McAdams coefficient show a similar gender bias. It seems as for female speakers a higher anonymization could be achieved. With original, i.e. non-anonymized data, the speaker identification model does not show this behavior. Therefore, we assume that during the anonymization specific female speaker characteristics are changed, while being left unchanged for male speaker. But additional experiments are needed to test thy hypothesis.

5. Conclusion

In this contribution, we discuss several possibilities to allow a fast anonymization without a speaker adaption phase, usable for one-shot speaker anonymization while interacting with public voice assistants. We compared a formant shift algorithm and a real-time voice changer, for comparison we also included a TTS system. To evaluate the success of the anonymization, we measured the

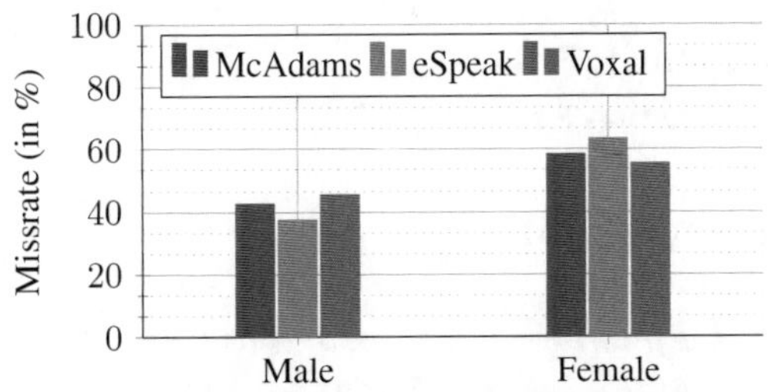

Figure 2: Comparison of miss-rate performance.

anonymization ability using a pre-trained speaker recognition model and the corresponding data. Furthermore, we evaluated the ASR performance using a state-of-the-art cloud based ASR-service. Regarding the anonymization, we could show that for the selected techniques, anonymization ability and ASR performance are connected. With this actual available one-shot anonymization techniques, it is not possible to achieve both a good ASR performance and a good speaker anonymity, so far. This approach maybe suitable for short interactions and many users. Especially, if the speech content itself does not contain personal information, which is often the case for public voice assistant interactions for information purposes, cf. (Kisser and Siegert, 2022).

6. Acknowledgements

This research has been funded by the Federal Ministry of Education and Research of Germany in the project Emonymous (project number S21060A).

7. Bibliographical References

European Court of Justice (Grand Chamber). (2020). Judgment of 16 July 2020, ECLI:EU:C:2020:559. ECLI:EU:C:2020:559.

Kisser, L. and Siegert, I. (2022). Erroneous reactions of voice assistants "in the wild" — first analyses. In *Elektronische Sprachsignalverarbeitung 2022. Tagungsband der 33. Konferenz*, volume 103 of *Studientexte zur Sprachkommunikation*, pages 113–120, Sonderborg, Denmark. TUDpress.

Lopatovska, I. and Oropeza, H. (2018). User interactions with "alexa" in public academic space. *Proceedings of the Association for Information Science and Technology*, (55):309–318.

Nagrani, A., Chung, J. S., and Zisserman, A. (2017). Voxceleb: a large-scale speaker identification dataset. *arXiv preprint arXiv:1706.08612*.

Nautsch, A., Jasserand, C., Kindt, E., Todisco, M., Trancoso, I., and Evans, N. (2019). The GDPR & Speech Data: Reflections of Legal and Technology Communities, First Steps Towards a Common Understanding. In *Proc. Interspeech 2019*, pages 3695–3699.

Patino, J., Tomashenko, N., Todisco, M., Nautsch, A., and Evans, N. (2020). Speaker anonymisation using the mcadams coefficient. *arXiv preprint arXiv:2011.01130*.

Phutak, V., Kamble, R., Gore, S., Alave, M., and Kulkarni, R. (2019). Text to speech conversion using raspberry-pi. *International Journal of Innovative Science and Research Technology*, 4(2).

Porcheron, M., Fischer, J. E., Reeves, S., and Sharples, S. (2018). Voice interfaces in everyday life. In *Proc. of the 2018 CHI Conference on Human Factors in Computing Systems*, CHI '18, page 1–12.

Schönherr, L., Golla, M., Eisenhofer, T., Wiele, J., Kolossa, D., and Holz, T. (2020). Unacceptable, where is my privacy? exploring accidental triggers of smart speakers.

Siegert, I., V.Silber-Varod, Carmi, N., and Kamocki, P. (2020a). Personal data protection and academia: Gdpr issues and multi-modal data-collections "in the wild". *The Online Journal of Applied Knowledge Management: OJAKM*, 8:16 – 31.

Siegert, I., Sinha, Y., Jokisch, O., and Wendemuth, A. (2020b). Recognition performance of selected speech recognition apis – a longitudinal study. In *Speech and Computer*, pages 520–529, Cham. Springer.

Siegert, I., Weißkirchen, N., Krüger, J., Akhtiamov, O., and Wendemuth, A. (2021). Admitting the addressee detection faultiness of voice assistants to improve the activation performance using a continuous learning framework. *Cognitive Systems Research*, 70:65–79.

Siegert, I. (2015). *Emotional and user-specific cues for improved analysis of naturalistic interactions*. Ph.D. thesis, Otto von Guericke University Magdeburg.

Siegert, I. (2020). "Alexa in the wild" – Collecting Unconstrained Conversations with a Modern Voice Assistant in a Public Environment. In *Proc. of the 12th LREC*, pages 608–612, Marseille, France. ELRA.

Silber-Varod, V., Siegert, I., Jokisch, O., Sinha, Y., and Geri, N. (2021). A cross-language study of selected speech recognition systems. *The Online Journal of Applied Knowledge Management: OJAKM*, 9:1 – 15.

Sinha, Y. and Siegert, I. (2022). Performance and quality evaluation of a mcadams speaker anonymization for spontaneous german speech. In *Fortschritte der Akustik - DAGA 2022*, pages 1185–1188, Stuttgart, Germany.

Sinha, Y., Wendemuth, A., and Siegert, I. (2022). Emotion preservation for one-shot speaker anonymization using mcadams. In *Elektronische Sprachsignalverarbeitung 2022*, pages 235–242, Sonderborg, Denmark.

Steven, M., Pan, D., and Engineer, M. (2017). A case study on using voice technology to assist the museum visitor. In *MW17: Museums and the Web 2017*.

Tomashenko, N., Wang, X., Vincent, E., Patino, J., Srivastava, B. M. L., Noé, P.-G., Nautsch, A., Evans, N., Yamagishi, J., O'Brien, B., et al. (2021). The voiceprivacy 2020 challenge: Results and findings. *arXiv preprint arXiv:2109.00648*.

WP29 (Article 29 Data Protection Working Party). (2014). Opinion 05/2014 on anonymisation techniques.

The Legal and Ethical issues Workshop @LREC2022, page 48
Marseille, 20 June 2022

Brij Mohan Lal Srivastava, PhD
Co-founder of Nijta at Inria Startup Studio, Lille

Voice Anonymization and the GDPR

Keynote Speech for the Joint Workshop on Legal and Ethical Issues in Human Language Technologies and Multilingual De-Identification of Sensitive Language Resources, LREC 2022, Marseille, 24 June 2022

Large-scale centralized storage of speech data poses severe privacy threats to the speakers. Indeed, the emergence and widespread usage of voice interfaces starting from telephone to mobile applications, and now digital assistants have enabled easier communication between the customers and the service providers. Massive speech data collection allows its users, for instance researchers, to develop tools for human convenience, like voice passwords for banking, personalized smart speakers, etc. However, centralized storage is vulnerable to cybersecurity threats which, when combined with advanced speech technologies like voice cloning, speaker recognition, and spoofing, may endow a malicious entity with the capability to re-identify speakers and breach their privacy by gaining access to their sensitive biometric characteristics, emotional states, personality attributes, pathological conditions, etc. Individuals and the members of civil society worldwide, and especially in Europe, are getting aware of this threat. With firm backing by the GDPR, several initiatives are being launched, including the publication of white papers and guidelines, to spread mass awareness and to regulate voice data so that the citizens' privacy is protected.

In this talk, I will present our startup project Nijta and its timely efforts to bolster such initiatives. Nijta proposes solutions to remove the biometric identity of speakers from speech signals, thereby rendering them useless for re-identifying the speakers who spoke them. Besides the goal of protecting the speaker's identity from malicious access, the underlying algorithm aims to do so without degrading the usefulness of speech. The output is a high-quality speech signal that is usable for publication and a variety of downstream tasks. The algorithm was subjected to a rigorous evaluation protocol which was designed by us to realistically measure voice privacy and fulfill the criteria laid down by the European Data Protection Board. This protocol led to the finding that the previous approaches do not effectively protect the privacy and thereby directly inspired the VoicePrivacy initiative which is an effort to gather individuals, industry, and the scientific community to participate in building a robust anonymization scheme. Finally, I present a methodology to remove the residual speaker identity from the anonymized speech signal using the techniques inspired by differential privacy. Such techniques provide provable analytical guarantees to the proposed anonymization algorithm and open up promising perspectives for future research.

In practice, the tools developed by Nijta are an essential component to build trust in any software ecosystem where voice data is stored, transmitted, processed, or published. They aim to help the organizations to comply with the rules mandated by civil governments and give a choice to individuals who wish to exercise their right to privacy.

Nijta

The Legal and Ethical issues Workshop @LREC2022, pages 49–52
Marseille, 20 June 2022

Cross-Clinic De-Identification of Swedish Electronic Health Records: Nuances and Caveats

Olle Bridal*, Thomas Vakili, Marina Santini*****
*Linköping University,**DSV, Stockholm University, ***RISE Research Institutes of Sweden
ollbr616@student.liu.se, thomas.vakili@dsv.su.se, marina.santini@ri.se

Abstract

Privacy preservation of sensitive information is one of the main concerns in clinical text mining. Due to the inherent privacy risks of handling clinical data, the clinical corpora used to create the clinical Named Entity Recognition (NER) models underlying clinical de-identification systems cannot be shared. This situation implies that clinical NER models are trained and tested on data originating from the same institution since it is rarely possible to evaluate them on data belonging to a different organization. These restrictions on sharing make it very difficult to assess whether a clinical NER model has overfitted the data or if it has learned any undetected biases. This paper presents the results of the first-ever cross-institution evaluation of a Swedish de-identification system on Swedish clinical data. Alongside the encouraging results, we discuss differences and similarities across EHR naming conventions and NER tagsets.

Keywords: de-identification, clinical NLP, NER, electronic health records, cross-clinic evaluation

1. Introduction

Clinical text mining is a subfield of Natural Language Processing (NLP). Current NLP state of the art is based on pre-trained language models, which are typically trained on gigabytes – or even terabytes – of data (Devlin et al., 2019; Smith et al., 2022). Since any manual inspection or fine-grained annotation of sensitive data of this size would be unthinkable, there is a risk of leaking sensitive information about persons mentioned in the datasets (Carlini et al., 2020). The privacy-breaching risks of models trained on sensitive data are especially problematic in the clinical domain, where training corpora often consist of sensitive electronic health records (EHR). While general-purpose datasets *can* contain sensitive documents, nearly *all* EHRs contain sensitive data to some degree. One source of concern is the prevalence of *Protected Health Information* (PHI) in the data, such as names and other identifiers.

De-identification of PHI can be addressed using Named Entity Recognition (NER), a prolific subfield of NLP. Removing a PHI or replacing it with a surrogate value is called *automatic de-identification*. Due to the privacy regulations of the GDPR[1], the datasets containing PHI used to train clinical NER systems cannot be shared. Typically only researchers who have signed a confidentiality agreement have access to the source EHRs. Because of this restriction, clinical NER systems are trained and tested on data from the same institution. Furthermore, it is rarely possible to evaluate a de-identification system on data from outside the institution that trained the model. In these cases, it is impossible to assess whether a NER system has overfitted to the particular ways that the sources of the electronic health records have been written.

Since we have the rare opportunity to test a clinical NER model trained on EHRs from one hospital on EHRs from a different hospital, we present the results of such an evaluation together with a discussion about differences and similarities across EHR naming conventions and NER tagsets. Specifically, we evaluate a de-identification system pre-trained on a dataset based on EHRs from Karolinska University Hospital (Region Stockholm)[2] on a test set built on the EHRs from Linköping University Hospital (Region Östergötland). All of the EHRs are written in Swedish. The EHRs used for pre-training the de-identification model belong to the *Health Bank* (Dalianis et al., 2015), while the EHRs used for testing[3] come from the *LIU-Hospital-EMRs-collection* (Jerdhaf et al., 2021).

Our results are encouraging. However, they also show an urgent need to harmonize annotation standards, since many institutions and regions in Sweden follow different naming conventions and thus require different NER tagsets.

2. Related Work

Certain tasks, such as de-identifying EHRs, have significant ethical implications. Thus, it is extra important that benchmark results for such problems are not only *internally* valid but also generalize to the problem more broadly. However, internal (or intrinsic) evaluation is the norm in machine learning or deep learning. Normally, intrinsic evaluation is "self-asserted", as pointed out by Liao et al. (2021), who examine the reliance on benchmarking as the primary evaluation

[1]The General Data Protection Regulation (GDPR) is a regulation of data protection and privacy in the European Union (EU) and the European Economic Area (EEA).

[2]This research has been approved by the Swedish Ethical Review Authority under permission nr. 2019-05679.

[3]The research has been approved by the Swedish Ethical Review Authority (Etikprövningsmyndigheten), authorization nr.: 2021-00890.

method for machine learning research. They argue that benchmarking, in which a model is trained on a subset of the available data and evaluated on a held-out dataset (Gareth et al., 2013), mainly focuses on confirming the *internal validity* of a model. The validity of the results relies on the assumption that the held-out dataset is representative of the problem that the benchmark aims to model. However, this assumption is rarely stated explicitly, nor is the problem that the benchmark is meant to represent always clearly defined.

When building a NER system to detect PHIs, the training data typically originates from a small set of related clinics located in a limited geographical area. The commonly used MIMIC and i2b2 datasets (Johnson et al., 2016; Johnson et al., 2020; Stubbs and Uzuner, 2015) share this trait. A de-identification system, however, should also be useful to users in other locations and settings than the creators of the system. The sensitive nature of clinical data, however, prohibits the free dissemination of training data which makes it difficult to assess how representative the data are in reality.

Yang et al. (2019) build a de-identifier using LSTM-CRFs trained using i2b2 data and evaluate it new data created by annotating EHRs from other clinics. Their evaluation shows that the performance of their de-identifier drops slightly when evaluating on data from other clinics. They suggest that de-identification systems be customized for a target clinic and their results highlight the importance of evaluating the cross-clinic validity of systems.

Since we have the rare opportunity to test a clinical NER model trained on EHRs from one hospital on EHRs from a different hospital, we start filling this gap with the findings presented in this paper.

3. Data and Datasets

3.1. Stockholm Health Bank EHRs

The NER dataset used for fine-tuning was the *Stockholm EPR PHI Corpus*. This corpus contains 4,480 manually annotated PHI entities spanning nine PHI classes and a total of 380,000 tokens (Dalianis and Velupillai, 2010). The annotated texts are from the aforementioned *Health Bank* and are EHRs from Stockholm hospitals that were written between 2006 and the first half of 2008. The annotators processed 100 EHRs sampled equally from five clinics in the following specializations: neurology, orthopaedics, oral surgery, infectious diseases and clinical nutrition.

3.2. LIU Test Set

The sample of EHRs used for testing come from the *LIU-Hospital-EMRs-collection* (Jerdhaf et al., 2021). This collection contains EHRs from three clinics, i.e. cardiology, neurology and orthopaedics (two locations). The size and the chronology of the collections are shown in Table 1. From each of the clinics, 1,000 sentences were randomly sampled, amounting to a total of 3,000 sentences. This sample set was pre-annotated using the Swedish BERT-NER model (Malmsten et al., 2020) fine-tuned on the SUC 3.0 dataset[4]. The pre-annotated sentences were then presented to an annotator who manually validated the tags and fixed the errors. The distribution of the NER tags in the test set are shown in Table 2, where PER stands for Person Name, LOC for location and ORG for Organization.

4. Experiments

4.1. NER with a Clinical BERT Model

A new clinical Swedish NER model was created using data from the *Health Bank*. This model is based on the SweDeClin-BERT model that is described and evaluated in Vakili et al. (2022). SweDeClin-BERT is based on the Swedish KB-BERT model (Malmsten et al., 2020) that has been adapted to the clinical domain through *continued pre-training* using de-identified data from the Health Bank (Dalianis et al., 2015).

The fine-tuned model – SweDeClin-BERT NER – was trained for three epochs using the *Stockholm EPR PHI Corpus* (described in section 3.1) and evaluated on a held-out test set containing 10% of the dataset. Table 4 shows the fine-tuned model's recall and precision for each of the PHI classes in the held-out test data.

4.2. Evaluation on LIU Test Set

The *Stockholm EPR PHI Corpus* used to create SweDeClin-BERT NER uses a different and more fine-grained NER tagset than the tagset employed by KB-BERT-NER on which the LIU test set has been based upon. Because of this difference, the output of SweDeClin-BERT NER needed to be mapped to the tags used for the LIU test set. Mapping First names and Last names to Person names was rather straightforward. However, the existence of the Health Care Unit-class in the SweDeClin-BERT NER tagset rendered the evaluation on the entities Person and Location somewhat problematic. Some of the entities tagged as Locations and Organizations in the LIU testset were flagged as health care units by the SweDeClin model, thus being counted as false negatives. It was, however, deemed that the Health Care Unit-class was suitable in some of these cases. The classes Location and Organization were therefore evaluated on a case-by-case.

The KB-BERT-NER model (Malmsten et al., 2020) used to pre-annotate the LIU test set was used as a baseline classifier. Both models were evaluated on the LIU test set. The recall, precision and F_1 scores of both models are shown in Table 4 where we can observe an increase of precision and a drop in recall compared to the baseline model and an overall better F_1 for Person. We can also observe a steep increase of precision and a similarly steep drop of recall for the Location-class resulting in an unchanged F_1. The SweDeClin-NER model did not tag any entities as Organizations, which is why there is no precision score. However, the model

[4]https://spraakbanken.gu.se/en/resources/suc3

Clinics	Size (MB)	Raw Words	EMRs	Time Span
Cardiology	543.278	52 610 553	664 821	2013-2019
Neurology	294.745	29 622 531	314 669	2013-2019
Orthopaedics US	332.414	35 835 451	481 902	2015-2020
Orthopaedics ViN	280.130	29 791 200	361 097	2013-2020
Total	1450.567	147 859 735	1 822 489	5-7 years

Table 1: Clinics, size and chronology of *LIU-Hospital-EMRs-collection*

Clinic	PER	LOC	ORG
Cardiology	99	33	5
Neurology	95	10	7
Orthopedics	89	14	12
Total	283	57	24

Table 2: Distribution of entities in the test set.

PHI Class	Recall	Precision	F1
Age	100%	100%	1.0
First Name	97%	98%	0.97
Last Name	96%	97%	0.96
Partial Date	99%	98%	0.98
Full Date	87%	91%	0.89
Phone Number	93%	89%	0.91
Health Care Unit	89%	88%	0.97
Location	89%	81%	0.85
Organization	29%	80%	0.43

Table 3: SweDeClin-BERT NER's recall and precision for each PHI class are displayed and were calculated on the test data from Dalianis and Velupillai (2010).

tagged 59 % of the Organization entities as Health Care Units.

5. Discussion

The results of our evaluation are informative and highlight a number of issues that are currently uncharted. We focus on two influential factors, namely non-standardized NER tagsets and differing naming conventions across institutions.

5.1. NER Tagsets

There is no consensus on what NER-tags to use for automatic de-identification, and all configurations come with advantages and drawbacks. The *Stockholm EPR PHI Corpus* departs from the standard set of HIPAA categories that frequently serve as a starting point.

For example, while HIPAA only considers *names*, *Stockholm EPR PHI Corpus* and SweDeClin-BERT NER classifies first and last names separately. This finer-grained label has the advantage that it allows for higher-quality surrogate replacement, since a de-identification system can maintain separate word lists for the different types of names. On the other hand, the sets of names overlap and this introduces ambiguity when determining whether a classification was correct or not. In contrast, the LIU test set is closer to the HIPAA definition of PHIs as it considers all names equal by including both in the *Person* label.

Merging the first and last names into a single class is trivial, making the mapping between the labels of the datasets easy. However, we also discovered a discrepancy regarding *titles*. The *Stockholm EPR PHI Corpus* does not consider a persons title as part of the name, but the Linköping dataset includes the title in their definition of the *Person* entity.

Other classes are ambiguous in more subtle ways. The *Stockholm EPR PHI Corpus* treats *Locations*, *Organizations* and *Heath Care Units* as separate classes while the Linköping dataset only distinguishes between *Locations* and *Organizations*. Whether or not a health care unit should be considered as an organization or a location is not obvious. In fact, the entity can fill both functions depending on the context. For example, a patient can be *treated by* a clinic (organization) or be *physically at* a clinic (location).

Similarly, sometimes a hospital will only be referred to by its geographical location. For example, the Linköping University Hospital may be referred to simply as *Linköping* because the rest is obvious from the context. In such cases, the correct entity might be *Organization* even though the word is only referring to a Location.

5.2. Cross-Institutional Research Challenges

This cross-institutional study is, to the best of our knowledge, the first study measuring the generalizability of a Swedish de-identification system. Considerable efforts were made to lessen the impacts of the legal hurdles that arise from complying with privacy laws.

The restrictions arising from the sensitive nature of the data made it challenging to interpret the results. For example, the co-authors could not look at each others classifications across institutions. This made the error analysis data more challenging than it had otherwise been. Any nuances in annotation standards, such as the lack of titles in the *Stockholm EPR PHI Corpus*, had to be discovered on the results without context.

5.3. Conclusions and Future Work

In this exploratory study, we cross the institutional boundaries and test a BERT-based Swedish clinical

PHI Class	KB-BERT NER			SweDeClin-BERT NER		
	Recall	Precision	F_1	Recall	Precision	F_1
Person	97%	72%	0.83	85%	98%	0.91
Location	94%	68%	0.79	67%	95%	0.79
Organization	50%	54%	0.51	59%	0%	-

Table 4: The recall, precision, and F_1 for the PHI classes labeled in the LIU test set. Metrics for KB-BERT NER are shown on the left while the metrics for SweDeClin-BERT NER are shown on the right.

NER model pre-trained on EHRs from Stockholm on the EHRs from clinics in Linköping. Results are encouraging and highlight nuances and caveats that we had not foreseen, such as the difficulty of mapping different NER tagsets. Future work includes retagging the LIU test set using Stockholm tagset, using SweDeClin-BERT to create pre-annotations. This would yield a more detailed gold-standard for that would be useful for anonymization. Moreover, harmonizing the NER tagset would facilitate the evaluation of NER models across institutions.

Acknowledgements

Research funded by *Vinnova* (Sweden's innovation agency), *Grant*: 2021-0169 and by the *DataLEASH* project.

Bibliographical References

Carlini, N., Tramer, F., Wallace, E., Jagielski, M., Herbert-Voss, A., Lee, K., Roberts, A., Brown, T., Song, D., Erlingsson, U., Oprea, A., and Raffel, C. (2020). Extracting Training Data from Large Language Models. *arXiv:2012.07805 [cs]*, December. arXiv: 2012.07805.

Dalianis, H. and Velupillai, S. (2010). De-identifying Swedish clinical text - refinement of a gold standard and experiments with Conditional random fields. *Journal of Biomedical Semantics*, 1(1):6, April.

Dalianis, H., Henriksson, A., Kvist, M., Velupillai, S., and Weegar, R. (2015). HEALTH BANK- A Workbench for Data Science Applications in Healthcare. *CEUR Workshop Proceedings Industry Track Workshop*, pages 1–18, January.

Devlin, J., Chang, M.-W., Lee, K., and Toutanova, K. (2019). BERT: Pre-training of deep bidirectional transformers for language understanding. In *Proceedings of the 2019 Conference of the North American Chapter of the Association for Computational Linguistics: Human Language Technologies, Volume 1 (Long and Short Papers)*, pages 4171–4186.

Gareth, J., Sohil, F., Sohali, M. U., Shabbir, J., Witten, D., Hastie, T., and Tibshirani, R., (2013). *An introduction to statistical learning with applications in R*, page 198. Springer Science and Business Media, New York.

Jerdhaf, O., Santini, M., Lundberg, P., Karlsson, A., and Jönsson, A. (2021). Implant term extraction from swedish medical records–phase 1: Lessons learned. In *Swedish Language Technology Conference and NLP4CALL*, pages 35–49.

Johnson, A. E. W., Pollard, T. J., Shen, L., Lehman, L.-W. H., Feng, M., Ghassemi, M., Moody, B., Szolovits, P., Celi, L. A., and Mark, R. G. (2016). Mimic-iii, a freely accessible critical care database. *Scientific data*, 3(1):1–9.

Johnson, A., Bulgarelli, L., Pollard, T., Horng, S., Celi, L., and Mark, R. (2020). Mimic-iv (version 1.0).

Liao, T., Taori, R., Raji, I. D., and Schmidt, L. (2021). Are We Learning Yet? A Meta-Review of Evaluation Failures Across Machine Learning.

Malmsten, M., Börjeson, L., and Haffenden, C. (2020). Playing with words at the national library of Sweden–making a Swedish BERT. *arXiv preprint arXiv:2007.01658*.

Smith, S., Patwary, M., Norick, B., LeGresley, P., Rajbhandari, S., Casper, J., Liu, Z., Prabhumoye, S., Zerveas, G., Korthikanti, V., Zhang, E., Child, R., Aminabadi, R. Y., Bernauer, J., Song, X., Shoeybi, M., He, Y., Houston, M., Tiwary, S., and Catanzaro, B. (2022). Using DeepSpeed and Megatron to Train Megatron-Turing NLG 530B, A Large-Scale Generative Language Model. *arXiv:2201.11990 [cs]*, February. arXiv: 2201.11990.

Stubbs, A. and Uzuner, (2015). Annotating longitudinal clinical narratives for de-identification: The 2014 i2b2/UTHealth corpus. *Journal of Biomedical Informatics*, 58:S20–S29, December.

Vakili, T., Lamproudis, A., Henriksson, A., and Dalianis, H. (2022). Downstream Task Performance of BERT Models Pre-Trained Using Automatically De-Identified Clinical Data. (Accepted to LREC 2022).

Yang, X., Lyu, T., Li, Q., Lee, C.-Y., Bian, J., Hogan, W. R., and Wu, Y. (2019). A study of deep learning methods for de-identification of clinical notes in cross-institute settings. *BMC medical informatics and decision making*, 19(Suppl 5):232, December.

The Legal and Ethical issues Workshop @LREC2022, pages 53–63
Marseille, 20 June 2022

Generating Realistic Synthetic Curricula Vitae for Machine Learning Applications under Differential Privacy

Andrea Bruera[1,3*], **Francesco Aldà**[2], **Francesco Di Cerbo**[3]
[1]Queen Mary University of London, [2]SAP SE, [3]SAP Security Research
a.bruera@qmul.ac.uk, francesco.alda@sap.com, francesco.di.cerbo@sap.com

Abstract

Applications involving machine learning in Human Resources (HR, the management of human talent in order to accomplish organizational goals) must respect the privacy of the individuals whose data is being used. This is a difficult aim, given the extremely personal nature of text data handled by HR departments, such as Curricula Vitae (CVs). We present a methodology for the generation of synthetic CVs which reflect real-world distributions of candidate attributes while providing strong privacy guarantees. These synthetic CVs can be used for training machine learning models instead of (or together with) the original data. Also, our methodology may be adapted to similar types of documents, requiring the generation of a mixture of structured data and natural language. We employ a Bayesian network to model the conditional dependencies between the candidate attributes. The structure of the underlying graph and the conditional probability distributions are learnt under differential privacy from an existing dataset. Then, we generate synthetic CVs by guiding the text generation of a Transformer-based generative language model with a manually-prepared set of prompts where the attributes sampled from the Bayesian network are plugged in. We show by way of both intrinsic (based on linguistic properties) and extrinsic (based on training a model for a classification task using the synthetic CVs) measures that our methodology can be successfully used for machine learning applications in HR, where anonymization is fundamental.

Keywords: Synthetic Data, Differential Privacy, Bayesian Network, Generative Language Model

1. Introduction

In Human Resources (HR) settings, Artificial Intelligence (AI) and Natural Language Processing (NLP) have the potential of offloading time-consuming tasks, such as selecting candidates for a position, understanding the skill set of the workforce, planning training and learning activities, from humans onto machine learning models (Ore and Sposato, 2021; Eubanks, 2022). However, machine learning models require training data; and textual data for HR applications, such as Curricula Vitae (CVs, or resumes), contain extremely sensitive pieces of personal data. These have to be protected, by means of anonymization techniques, against misuses due to the risk of identification of the individuals (Silva et al., 2020) described in the original CV dataset, making it compliant with data protection regulations active in multiple countries around the world.

With respect to anonymization, we adopt the definition provided by the General Data Protection Regulation - GDPR (Voigt and Von dem Bussche, 2017) - of the European Union, which describes anonymous information as "information which does not relate to an identified or identifiable natural person or to personal data rendered anonymous in such a manner that the data subject is not or no longer identifiable" (GDPR Recital 26). In our case, this means that a CV can be considered anonymized when it is not possible to re-identify the subject that it describes.

Some of the information contained in CVs - 'direct identifiers' - can be easily spotted and made anonymous by way of pre-trained Named Entity Recognition - NER (Nasar et al., 2021) - models or pattern-based (Paccosi and Aprosio, 2021) approaches (e.g. for emails, phone numbers).

However, a second type of information, called 'indirect identifiers', appear in textual data, which may lead to the re-identification of the individuals involved despite the absence of direct identifiers (Tucker et al., 2016). These can be especially understood in terms of the interaction of multiple pieces of information which, by themselves, would not allow re-identification, but that instead would do so when taken together, as an interconnected network. For instance, it is not easy to re-identify a male individual by simply knowing that he served as President of the United States of America. But it becomes much easier if it is known that he was born in Hawaii and obtained an undergraduate degree from Columbia University.

It is important to anonymize training datasets because the trained AI models with personal information may retain certain glimpses of personal data that can later be inferred using attacks like membership inference (Shejwalkar et al., 2021) leading to re-identification of individuals. One may argue that AI models can still be lawfully trained and used by the responsible entity for data collection and processing (the so-called Data Controller, in GDPR terms). But then these models must be subject to all requirements coming from data protection regulations (Francopoulo and Schaub, 2020).

If an individual requests the deletion of his personal information according to GDPR Article 17 "right to be forgotten", a Data Controller has to find a way to deal

*Work carried out at SAP Security Research

with a text classification model trained also on that individual's data. Retraining the model for each and every deletion request would be a waste of resources in terms of time, energy and money. Anonymization allows to protect trained models from such situations.

We present an approach to avoid these issues, which consists of generating realistic synthetic CVs to be used for machine learning applications in HR. The point is not to generate CVs whose textual form would make it hard for a human reader to tell whether it was created by a computer or not; but rather, to generate CVs which capture relevant statistical properties of the attributes of the candidates, containing enough noise to ensure that re-identification is not possible, but sufficient signal to be used for machine learning applications.

This approach is increasingly common in disparate machine learning fields (Nikolenko and others, 2021), and the closest example to our case is that of healthcare and medicine (Chen et al., 2021), where data anonymization is of paramount importance. Notice that our work, despite being specific to CVs, may be in principle adapted to other kinds of documents where a mixture of structured data and raw text needs to be generated while ensuring de-identification.

An additional benefit of generating training data is that the resulting size can be as big as needed: this feature is fundamental especially for deep learning models, which require huge amounts of training data in order to learn effectively.

In our approach, we start from real samples, from which relevant attributes are extracted, and whose conditional dependencies and distributions across candidates are modelled through a Bayesian network (BN) (Niedermayer, 2008). Since the structure and the conditional probability distributions are learnt from real samples which may contain sensitive information, we make use of a differential privacy (DP) mechanism known as PrivBayes (Dwork et al., 2006; Zhang et al., 2017). This ensures that the re-identification risk for individuals can be controlled and mitigated as required.

As an intermediate step, we generate synthetic candidates in the form of sets of attributes, whose conditional distributions are close enough to those of real world candidates, yet providing DP. Finally, these results are plugged into a set of linguistic prompts (Radford et al., 2019), which are presented to a generative language model that will generate each section of the synthetic CV (Schick and Schütze, 2021). We validate our approach in two ways: first, with a set of intrinsic measures (Gatt and Krahmer, 2018), looking at various linguistic properties of our generated text; secondly, with an extrinsic measurement - a candidate role classification task - where we show that our synthetic CVs, which avoid the risks of re-identification, can be successfully used as training data instead of the original, real-world, identifiable CVs, with limited loss of performance.

2. Related Work

2.1. NLP For HR

NLP is increasingly being used in HR applications, but its use for this specific aim is still considered to be limited (Strohmeier, 2022). Some examples are CV (or resume) parsing (Sinha et al., 2021), which focuses specifically on the task of extracting information about candidates from raw text data in the form of CVs; automatized procedures for candidate rating, ranking (Freire and de Castro, 2021) and selection (Kmail et al., 2015), or algorithms to match CVs and job posts (Jain et al., 2021). Notice that these approaches focus exclusively on getting the best results for each application. They do not take into consideration how to mitigate the re-identification risk involving training data independently of the task, which is instead the main interest of our work.

2.2. Differential Privacy And NLP

In recent years, differential privacy has become the de-facto standard for privacy-preserving statistical data analysis and machine learning. It provides strong, formal anonymization guarantees by enforcing that the output distribution of a randomized algorithm is not affected by small changes in its input, namely the addition (or removal) of a single data point (Dwork et al., 2006). Given its effectiveness, it has increasingly been used in NLP as a framework for anonymization (Lyu et al., 2020; Igamberdiev and Habernal, 2021).
A somewhat related approach to ours is that of Krishna et al. (2021), where the authors transform a raw text dataset by adding noise to the latent representation of a language model, before using it for a text classification application. However, Habernal (2021) shows that the sensitivity of the privacy mechanism was underestimated thus leading to an incorrect privacy analysis. In our case, instead, DP is guaranteed by the usage of PrivBayes (Zhang et al., 2017), whose robustness has been formally and empirically demonstrated, and has been adopted in other works (Ping et al., 2017).

2.3. Generation Of Synthetic Training Data For NLP

Given that deep learning models, the state of the art in most NLP tasks (Lauriola et al., 2022), require a big amount of data, which for certain linguistic phenomena can be hard to gather, recently it has become commonplace to either augment existing training data (Feng et al., 2021) with synthetic data, or employing a fully synthetic dataset, after having generated it from scratch (Schick and Schütze, 2021).
When the resulting dataset has to look like natural text, the generation process makes often use of the recently proposed generative language models based on the Transformer architecture (Vaswani et al., 2017), such as GPT (Radford et al., 2019) and CTRL (Keskar et al., 2019). These models are trained to generate realistic natural language text, word after word. The choice

of each new token is conditioned on the previous ones, with extremely realistic results.

3. Our Approach To Synthetic CV Generation

Our approach is composed of three steps: first, the extraction of candidate attributes from a dataset of real CVs, in fact transforming the CVs into structured data entries (Section 3.1); second, the creation of a differentially private Bayesian network representing the conditional dependencies between the selected attributes (Section 3.2); finally, the generation of a synthetic dataset of CVs (Section 3.3). This final stage, in turn, involves, for each CV to be generated, sampling a synthetic set of attributes for a candidate from the differentially private Bayesian network; inserting them in a series of ready-made prompts reflecting the structure of a CV; and finally feeding these filled prompts, sequentially, to the generative language model so as to create a coherent CV.

3.1. Information Extraction

The first step consists in the extraction of candidate attributes from a dataset of real CVs, in the form of raw text, using various techniques: NER and pattern heuristics to find the attributes, relation extraction (RE) to annotate the relationships holding between these attributes and the candidate (Silva et al., 2020; Paccosi and Aprosio, 2021). The output of this step is a structured dataset, containing the key attributes which constitute a candidate profile (e.g. Alma Mater, various features for education history and work experience, technical skills, spoken languages). While looking at the values of extracted attributes may still lead to the re-identification of an individual at this stage, the subsequent steps of the process will make the likelihood of such risk proportional to DP's ε. Importantly, direct personal identifiers (like name, surname, email address, social media accounts) are ignored and not included as candidate attributes.

Notice also that the goal of this phase is to retain only attributes over which distributions across candidates can be learnt, and that the breadth and scope of this phase of information extraction can vary according to each use case.

3.2. Ensuring De-Identification: Bayesian Networks

From this structured dataset of candidate attributes, we build a Bayesian network, a probabilistic graphical model which represents a set of variables and their conditional dependencies as a directed acyclic graph (Niedermayer, 2008). In our setting, the nodes of the graph are the candidate attributes and an edge between two attributes represents a cause-effect relationship between them. For example, the work experience of a candidate is naturally influenced by their education history, and edges between the corresponding attributes would represent this dependency. We provide the visualization of a possible Bayesian network for some simplified candidate attributes in Figure 1.

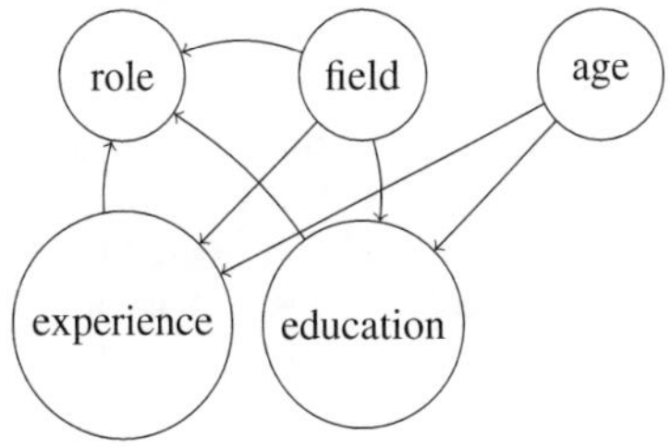

Figure 1: Toy example of a Bayesian network for candidate attributes.

Each node is associated with a function that takes as input the set of possible values for the node's parent variables, and gives as output the probability distribution on the node's values. This function constitutes a conditional probability distribution.

The structure of the graph can be learnt from data or built a priori, while the conditional probability distributions are usually learnt from data. In our case, we learn both from data. The structure of the network or the conditional probabilities may therefore leak some information on an individual in the training set. In order to provide strong privacy guarantees and minimize the re-identification risk, we leverage the notion of differential privacy.

Definition 1. *(Dwork et al., 2006) A randomized algorithm $\mathcal{M} : \mathcal{D} \to \mathcal{Z}$, i.e., the output of $\mathcal{M}$ is a random variable, is said to provide ε-differential privacy if for every $\varepsilon > 0$, for any pair of neighboring datasets $(X, X') \in \mathcal{D} \times \mathcal{D}$ that differ in one entry only, and for every measurable $Z \subseteq \mathcal{Z}$ the following holds*

$$\Pr[\mathcal{M}(X) \in Z] \leq e^{\varepsilon} \cdot \Pr[\mathcal{M}(X') \in Z]. \quad (1)$$

The privacy budget ε controls the anonymization level of the mechanism $\mathcal{M}$. The smaller the value of ε, the stronger the privacy guarantee provided, as the output distributions are pulled closer and closer.

A standard way of providing differential privacy to vector-valued functions is by adding Laplace-distributed noise to its output (Dwork et al., 2006). For functions that returns categorical values, the exponential mechanism is generally used instead (McSherry and Talwar, 2007).

These mechanisms are the main ingredients behind PrivBayes (Zhang et al., 2017), which provides a successful mechanism for learning the structure as well as the conditional probabilities of a Bayesian network under differential privacy. The following generation steps will be protected against the risks of re-identification due to the robustness of post-processing of any differentially private mechanism (Dwork et al., 2006).

Once the private Bayesian network is built, we can sample new values for all the nodes in the graph. These generated values follow the conditional dependencies of the attributes and preserve the consistency and statistical properties of the original dataset up to the noise addition which acts as a de-identification barrier. In our case, this means that we can generate a synthetic set of attributes for a realistic, but not real, candidate.

3.3. CV Generation Using Specialized Prompts And A Generative Language Model

The candidate attributes sampled from the Bayesian network together with the artificial personal details are then used to generate the text for each section of the synthetic CV.

We start from the hunch that CVs can be viewed through the lens of storytelling as strongly structured stories: in this sense, their structure, which is very similar across candidates, being relatively standardized, should reflect some degree of sequentiality, coherence and development (Popova, 2014). We therefore adapt methodologies proposed in story generation (Yao et al., 2019; Wang et al., 2020; Alhussain and Azmi, 2021) involving the use of pivotal bits of story structures. We employ them in the form of short, incomplete natural language sentences (prompts), that we provide as inputs to the generative model to direct it towards a coherent linguistic output similar to a CV.

In our approach, we exploit the attributes generated by the Bayesian network described in 3.2 as a way to control the text generation. The intuition is that the attributes will influence the probabilities of the words chosen by the model. Because of this, the resulting text will describe coherently the synthetic candidate, using a mixture of fixed attributes and real-looking text. To give an example, given two attributes {'University': 'Columbia'} and {Field of Study: 'Political Science'}, we guide the generative model to select words which are more probable when the words 'Columbia' and 'Political Science' are found in the previous context. Using a toy vocabulary {'international', 'beach', 'beer', 'law'}, higher probabilities should be assigned by the model to 'international' and 'law'.

As we were saying above, in order to make the model generate realistic text, before presenting the synthetic attributes to the generative model, we further plug them in a set of linguistic structures called prompts (Radford et al., 2019; Wang et al., 2020). Prompts are typical bits of sentences where the attribute would be found in a human language (e.g., 'I studied x at y', 'I worked as p at q for r'). Since CVs contain different sections, usually with the aim of resuming the candidate's past experience and skills in a sequentially coherent way, we previously define an ordered list of prompts, which will correspond to the various sections and will contain the relevant attributes. These prompts, with the attributes plugged in, are what will be actually presented, one after another, to the generative model as starting points for the generation of each section of the CV.

Importantly, the generation works in a cyclical fashion, in a feedback loop: at each step, the model receives as input the preceding text of the synthetic CV (including text generated by the model itself), followed by the next prompt in the list as input. Its task is to generate the following natural language section in the synthetic CV. Obviously, at the beginning there is no previously generated text, but only the first prompt.

In this way, at each section we direct the model towards the creation of a new section conditioned on the previous ones, to ensure sequential coherence.

4. Model Implementation

In order to evaluate our approach, we implement in a very simple use case the full pipeline we presented. The final aim is that of generating a dataset of synthetic CVs that can be used to train a machine learning model. Starting from an existing dataset of CVs (Jiechieu and Tsopze, 2021) annotated with the candidate roles (Section 4.1), we first extract a set of candidate attributes (universities, companies, years of experience; Section 4.2), then we learn the structure and conditional probabilities of a differentially private Bayesian network modelling the conditional dependencies between the extracted attributes (Section 4.3); in parallel, we manually create a set of prompts to be filled with candidate attributes generated with the BN, which we feed sequentially to GPT-2 (Radford et al., 2019), a public generative language model (Section 4.4).

4.1. Dataset

As a starting point, we use the dataset of real-world CVs presented in (Jiechieu and Tsopze, 2021). In it, direct identifiers had already been anonymized, leaving however all indirect identifiers (see Section 1) in the text. The dataset, made of around 28000 CVs in English, was collected online from a dedicated website [1]. Each CV was automatically annotated with the role(s) provided by each applicant, to be used as its label for classification tasks; for simplicity, in the case of multiple roles, we only employ the first one. This leaves us with a set of nine possible classification labels [2]. We do not apply any particular pre-processing to the text, except for the removal of HTML markup.

4.2. Attribute Extraction

In order to extract the attributes for the candidates, we use a mixture of NER and pattern-based approaches (Paccosi and Aprosio, 2021). As a NER model, we use Spacy's Transformers[3] pre-trained NER model (without fine-tuning it), which encodes the input using RoBERTa (Liu et al., 2019) pre-trained embeddings.

[1] `www.indeed.com`

[2] Software Developer, Project Manager, Java Developer, Python Developer, Web Developer, Software Developer, Front-End Developer, Systems Administrator, Database Administrator, Network Administrator, Security Analyst

[3] https://spacy.io/universe/project/spacy-transformers

We focus on three types of attributes: universities, companies, and years of work. For each sentence in a CV, we first extract the spans for the named entities using Spacy; then, we only keep the organizations (labelled 'ORG'), which we further add to the candidate's attributes as universities, if the word 'University' appears in the span, and as companies otherwise. We extract the years of experience with a simple heuristics, looking for the regular expression `"(\d+)\syears"`, considering only cases where the integers are inferior to 10 (otherwise, the expression would catch also the candidate age).

Ideally, each CV should contain mentions of both universities and companies - however, we find that this is not the case. Therefore, we filter the dataset keeping only the entries where we could find at least one university or one company, and one attribute for years of experience. This reduces the size of the dataset to around 7000 CVs. We further assume that the levels of education corresponding to each university follow gradually (one university: Bachelor's, two universities: Master's, three universities: Ph.D.), and we add these accordingly as attributes to the candidate profile.

An important issue is to keep only the essential amount of data points and attributes, in order to limit the computational strain when using the Bayesian network. To do so, first of all, we keep only the first three companies (and their matched years of experience) and universities.[4]

Then, to reduce the presence of attributes over which no generalization is possible, and to keep under control the time required to learn the Bayesian network, we set a frequency threshold for the extracted universities and companies. We only keep the original mentions for attributes appearing at least 5 times (leaving us with 792 universities and 1048 companies), and we substitute the entities filtered out with two generic spans ('Other University', 'Generic IT Company') just to use them as dummy features for the generation of CVs. Finally, we also include among the attributes the applicant role, extracted as described in Section 4.1.

Regarding direct identifiers (e.g., name, address, email, social media links, etc.), for each realistic candidate, we generate them as purely fake data using an existing Python library[5]: the aim is just that of providing realistic prompts to the generative language model. Since all these values are generated artificially and independently of the original dataset, no data privacy is compromised at this step.

Finally, for training the Bayesian network, we create a separate set, containing only the candidates having at least one company and one university, leaving us with a set of around 1500 CVs.

[4]When not enough years of work could be extracted, we randomly generated an integer, ranging between 0 and the minimum between 0 and the biggest number of extracted years of experience.

[5]https://faker.readthedocs.io

4.3. Bayesian Network

For the Bayesian network, we use the Python package developed by the authors of Ping et al. (2017). As introduced in 3.2, we consider the following attributes in our experiments: the applicant role; up to three universities and education titles; up to three job experiences, with their length in years; the total number of years of work. Regarding the conditional dependencies among the nodes, these are learnt under differential privacy using PrivBayes (Zhang et al., 2017; Ping et al., 2017), where we limit the maximum number of parent nodes to 3.

The conditional probabilities are learnt from the reduced set of around 1500 CVs described in Section 4.2, adding Laplace noise to ensure differential privacy, as described in Zhang et al. (2017). As presented in Section 3.2, the privacy budget ε controls the anonymization guarantees. The smaller the value of this parameter, the higher the noise injected and hence the privacy guarantees provided. When learning the Bayesian network, we experiment with different values of the privacy budget ε in order to investigate its effect on our downstream classification task: 0.1 (which, following Zhang et al. (2017), ensures strong DP); 1; 10; 10000.

4.4. Prompting The Generative Model

To generate the synthetic CVs with GPT-2, we manually define a template CV structure reflecting standard versions of CVs, consisting of:

1. An introductory fake personal information part (see Section 4.2), followed immediately by a short summary of the candidate's skills;
2. Education;
3. Work experience;
4. Linguistic skills;
5. Hobbies.

For each section, we write a set of two to five possible prompts to randomly sample from at generation time, so as to ensure variability. These prompts are common ways of introducing the corresponding CV sections (e.g. for education, 'I studied x at y', 'I attended y, where I studied x').

Notice that not all the sections involve attributes generated by the Bayesian network: in our case, only sections 1 (fake personal information, candidate role), 2 (universities and titles), 3 (companies and years of work) do. In the other cases, prompts are just generic bits of sentences (e.g. for hobbies, 'In my spare time, I') which are meant to nevertheless drive the generation towards a coherent profile. In the case of sections 2 and 3, where multiple universities and companies are present, prompts will be generated sequentially multiple times (i.e. first for the Bachelor's, then for the Master's, etc).

As per GPT-2 [6], we use the English pre-trained Medium model (Radford et al., 2019) available within Huggingface's Transformers library (Wolf et al., 2020). We chose English as the language for our experiments because this is the language of the dataset we used for the extrinsic task (see Sections 4.1 and 5.2). The generation, as discussed in section 3.3, works in a cyclical way, so as to enforce coherence among the various sections: generation starts from the prompt for section 1, and then is stopped after 30 words (slightly longer than the average length of a sentence in English (Sigurd et al., 2004)); the prompt for section 2 is appended to the result of the generation, and this whole text is fed back as a new prompt to GPT-2, which again generates no more than 30 words; and so on until the end of all the sections is reached, and the CV is ready.
We generate in this way a set of 4000 synthetic CVs, matching the training dataset of real CVs (see Section 5.2), that we will use in the following evaluation steps.

5. Empirical Evaluation

We evaluate both the linguistic quality of the CVs, using a set of dedicated metrics (Section 5.1), and their downstream usability for machine learning, through a classification task (Section 5.2). Results show that, despite some loss in terms of performance, the generated data which guarantee privacy can be successfully used for machine learning, opening to a wide range of HR applications.

5.1. Intrinsic Evaluation: Linguistic Features

Intrinsic evaluations of generated texts look at the linguistic properties of the results, independently of their effect on performance on a given NLP task (Gatt and Krahmer, 2018). A common way of evaluating generated text is to obtain a matched set of real sentences starting from the same input, comparing the two (an overview of such metrics can be found at Gatt and Krahmer (2018)) - but, in our case, this is not possible. Another one is that of asking humans to evaluate the generated texts on a range of criteria. However, this approach has been subject to scrutiny for its arbitrariness (Howcroft et al., 2020) and, most importantly, it does not apply to our case, since we are not interested in fooling people into believing that a synthetic CV is actually real. We nevertheless report some examples of CVs generated with our methodology in the Appendix. The approach we use here, instead, is that of defining a set of automatized ways of measuring intrinsic linguistic properties of the generated texts along a number of dimensions (Roemmele et al., 2017; See et al., 2019). In doing this, we exclusively want to investigate the quality of the generated by GPT-2 following our prompts. Therefore, we assume that the features produced by the Bayesian network should have no effect on this, and we report the intrinsic evaluation scores obtained from the training set for $\varepsilon = 0.1$, which ensures the highest level of differential privacy.
More specifically, we are interested in measuring, on the one hand, the lexical diversity and refinement of the generated texts, and on the other, their syntactic complexity. We want to do so because the prompts for the type of text we are generating, CVs, are less open-ended than prompts for other genres. We suspect that this may negatively impact the generation abilities of GPT-2, making it turn towards repetitive, oversimplified, shallow output.
We therefore adopt a set of measures from Roemmele et al. (2017). First, given that high-quality writing has been associated with the presence of more diverse words and phrases (Pitler and Nenkova, 2008), we report the **type-token ratio (TTR)**, both for bi-grams and uni-grams, computing it within each CVs and then averaging the results.
Second, since lower frequency words indicate a more advanced output (Crossley et al., 2011), we compute the **average word frequency** of the generated words, using as frequency estimates, token occurrencies from a dump of the English version of Wikipedia, considering only words appearing at least 10 times in the whole corpus (Roemmele et al., 2017).
Finally, we turn to noun phrases (NPs) and verb constructions as indicators of syntactic complexity, and therefore richer text (McNamara et al., 2010). We look at the **average ratio of NPs and verbs** over sentence length, and at the **average number of tokens contained in each type of phrase or construction** (in the case of verbs, we measure the length in tokens of the subtree in the dependency parse), again divided by sentence length. To single out NPs, verbs and their dependency parse subtrees, we use the pre-trained Spacy Transformers model.
To provide a comparison with real-world text, we compute the same metrics on a random sample of 4000 real CVs (that we call 'Real') taken from the dataset of (Jiechieu and Tsopze, 2021).
Results are reported in Table 1: in general, they indicate that the generated text mirrors closely enough the intrinsic linguistic properties of real world CVs, with a few trade-offs between the two.
GPT-2, through prompting, generates a higher number of token types (higher TTR uni-gram), but tends to repeat bi-grams (lower TTR bi-gram) slightly more often than real candidates do. In a parallel fashion, the NPs produced by GPT-2 are more frequent (higher NP ratio), but slightly shorter (smaller NP average length) than those of real CVs; and the opposite is true of verb constructions (verbs ratio), whose longer average length indicate higher complexity for GPT-2 than for real candidates. Finally, the average corpus token frequency of generated and real CVs are quite close, with GPT-2 preferring slightly more common words. This provides an initial sanity check of our approach to the

[6] We did not use GPT-3 (Brown et al., 2020), the most recent version of GPT, as its pretrained weights were not publicly available at the time of the work.

generation of synthetic CVs.

	Generated	Real
TTR uni-gram	0.071	0.043
TTR bi-gram	0.249	0.334
Average word frequency	11.42	11.03
NP ratio	0.296	0.249
NP average length	0.067	0.0827
Verbs ratio	0.085	0.093
Verb-subtree average length	0.582	0.411

Table 1: Results for the intrinsic evaluation tests

5.2. Extrinsic Evaluation: Applicant Role Classification

5.2.1. Methodology

To evaluate to what extent our synthetic CVs can be used for downstream machine learning in HR applications, we exploit the labeled dataset that we obtained at the end of the process described in Section 4.2.
Remember that each CV comes with the role of the candidate provided by the candidate themselves. This will be the label for our classification task, which we call **Candidate Role Classification**, and that can be considered as an automatized recruitment task, similarly to CV-job description matching or candidate recommender (Zaroor et al., 2017; Lamba et al., 2020). As introduced in Section 4.1, there are nine labels in total. We randomly split the 7000 real CVs containing at least either one university or one company, and one explicit mention of the years of work (see Section 4.2) into a train set of 4000 CVs and a test set of 1000 CVs (equivalent to a 80/20 split), leaving 2000 CVs on the side as a potential development set, that eventually we do not use.
We do not apply any pre-processing to the generated text, except for the removal of the direct identifiers - the fake personal information (cf. Section 4.2) - as they are just noise: they are purely random tokens and have no relation with the classification label.
Since the aim of our work is not obtaining the highest score possible, but rather validating our approach within a machine learning framework, we train and test two different general-purpose classifiers based on word embeddings, widely used in the field of NLP.
The first one is the **fastText** (Joulin et al., 2017) classifier, which builds upon the CBOW model of fastText (Bojanowski et al., 2017), employing both uni-grams and n-grams to efficiently learn to perform text classification. We train the model for 100 epochs using default parameters.
The second one is instead based on **BERT** (Devlin et al., 2019), a pre-trained contextualized language model which has been shown to excel at a wide range of NLP tasks (Rogers et al., 2020). We fine-tune the BERT large cased model for text classification with Huggingface's Transformers library, for 10 epochs, with default parameters.

5.2.2. Results

We report the results in Table 2. The table shows the weighted F1 scores obtained against the real CV test data using three different training data - real, generated, and augmented (merging generated and real) CVs.
The first case, that of real CVs, constitutes an upper bound on the classification performance, given that train and test have similar, human-generated, linguistic form. Instead, in the second case, where the training set is fully synthetic, the model faces a greater challenge, in that it has to learn to abstract from the surface form of the synthetic CVs, which is different from that of the real ones, in order to be able to learn.

	BERT	fastText
Real CVs		
	0.88	0.81
Generated		
$\varepsilon = 10000$	0.71	**0.75**
$\varepsilon = 10$	0.71	0.75
$\varepsilon = 1$	0.73	0.74
$\varepsilon = 0.1$	0.73	0.68
Augmented		
	0.89	0.81

Table 2: Results for the extrinsic evaluation on Candidate Role Classification

Despite a certain loss in performance against the upper bound, which is to be expected, CVs generated with our approach can provide good performance (remember that there are nine possible classes - random baselines, at around 0.11, are reported in Figures 3 and 4). Most importantly, they do so while providing differential privacy, which is an extremely important added value, if not a necessary requirement, in the case of HR applications for NLP models.
Also, augmenting the dataset of real CVs with synthetic CVs gives a marginal advantage to the model. This seems to suggest that our methodology for the creation of training data may be of particular interest in cases where a big training set needs to be bootstrapped from a small dataset of CVs, and where there are no strong constraints on differential privacy. In such cases, the real and the synthetic sources of training data can be used together.
By closely inspecting the results, however, no clear decreasing trend emerges as more noise is added through the ε parameter. This is surprising, as one would expect that the gradual addition of noise, pushing further apart the distributions of the attributes across training and test set, should negatively impact classification performance. We interpret this as suggesting that the lion's share of successful classification is due to the prompts and GPT-2, and not so much to the features generated by the Bayesian network - at least for our current clas-

sification task, and for the attributes we have chosen.

	BERT masked	**BERT random**
Real CVs		
	0.65 (-.23)	0.12
Generated		
$\varepsilon = 10000$	**0.55** (-.16)	0.11
$\varepsilon = 10$	0.56 (-.15)	0.1
$\varepsilon = 1$	0.54 (-.19)	0.09
$\varepsilon = 0.1$	0.57 (-.16)	0.08
Augmented		
	0.64 (-.25)	0.13

Table 3: Further analyses for Candidate Role Classification with BERT: providing an empirical random baseline, and measuring the effect of removing explicit mentions of the candidate roles in text. We report the scores, together with the loss in performance from the original setting within brackets.

	fastText masked	**fastText random**
Real CVs		
	0.75 (-.06)	0.11
Generated		
$\varepsilon = 10000$	0.58 (-.17)	0.1
$\varepsilon = 10$	0.58 (-.17)	0.18
$\varepsilon = 1$	0.55 (-.19)	0.13
$\varepsilon = 0.1$	**0.62** (-.06)	0.2
Augmented		
	0.71 (-.10)	0.12

Table 4: Further analyses for Candidate Role Classification with fastText (same table structure as Figure 3).

However, we reckon that if the overall generated text, and not simply the mentions of the attributes, is the most important part of the training procedure, classifier performance could be driven by simple heuristics, as is sometimes the case in NLP tasks (Rosenman et al., 2020). In our case, in particular, the models may be simply looking for explicit mention of the candidate role in the generated text.

In order to investigate whether this is the case, we perform an additional ablation-style analysis, where we first remove from the training set explicit mentions of a CV's label, and then re-run the classification. More specifically, we mask explicit mentions of a CV candidate role by a generic mention 'worker' in the generated training sets (e.g. instead of 'I was employed as a Java Developer at', the CV would appear as 'I was employed as a worker at'). Results are reported in Table 3 and Table 4, under the mention 'masked'.

To show that performance is well above chance, we also report empirical random baselines ('random' columns in Figures 3 and 4), which fluctuate around the theoretical random baseline of $1/9 = 0.11$. They were computed by averaging the results of 100 train/test runs obtained after randomly permuting the nine labels of the training set.

When masking mentions of candidate roles, scores decrease in all cases. This indicates that both BERT and fastText classification models make use of the explicit mention of the class. BERT is affected more (average -0.19). fastText, instead, seems to be slightly more robust to our ablation-style manipulation (overall average -.13). Despite this loss in performance, however, scores remain well above the random baseline reported.

This validates our approach: it confirms, by looking at the cases where the synthetic CVs are involved (Generated and Augmented), that our generation procedure can create training data which encodes semantic information which is coherent with the candidate profile and role. Also, the robustness of our approach with respect to the noise injected in the probability distributions seems to promise that strong privacy constraints can be respected.

6. Conclusion

We have presented and empirically validated a methodology for the generation of synthetic CVs which reflect real-world distributions of candidate attributes while providing anonymization.

Synthetic CVs are interesting from two points of view. First, they are relevant for developing HR applications in compliance with personal data protection regulations, especially when powered by machine learning models. Secondly, they are a type of document that, in order to be generated, requires both structured data and raw text: therefore we expect that work on the generation of CVs could be adapted in principle to other similar types of text.

Our approach makes use of three stages: application of NLP techniques to extract candidate attributes; using Bayesian networks in order to learn the conditional dependencies between the attributes under differential privacy; and finally generating synthetic CVs by driving the generation of a Transformer-based generative language model through a manually-prepared set of prompts where the attribute sampled from the Bayesian network are plugged.

Evaluations based on linguistic properties indicate that the generated CVs have good-enough linguistic quality, and a machine learning evaluation (training a model for a classification task using the synthetic CVs instead of the real ones) shows that our approach, which provides differential privacy and a potentially unlimited amount of training data, offers promising performances for machine learning applications in HR.

Acknowledgement

This work was partially funded by the European Union's Horizon 2020 research and innovation programme under project TESTABLE, grant agreement No 101019206.

Bibliographical References

Alhussain, A. I. and Azmi, A. M. (2021). Automatic story generation: a survey of approaches. *ACM Computing Surveys (CSUR)*, 54(5):1–38.

Bojanowski, P., Grave, E., Joulin, A., and Mikolov, T. (2017). Enriching word vectors with subword information. *Transactions of the association for computational linguistics*, 5:135–146.

Brown, T., Mann, B., Ryder, N., Subbiah, M., Kaplan, J. D., Dhariwal, P., Neelakantan, A., Shyam, P., Sastry, G., Askell, A., et al. (2020). Language models are few-shot learners. *Advances in neural information processing systems*, 33:1877–1901.

Chen, R. J., Lu, M. Y., Chen, T. Y., Williamson, D. F., and Mahmood, F. (2021). Synthetic data in machine learning for medicine and healthcare. *Nature Biomedical Engineering*, 5(6):493–497.

Crossley, S. A., Weston, J. L., McLain Sullivan, S. T., and McNamara, D. S. (2011). The development of writing proficiency as a function of grade level: A linguistic analysis. *Written Communication*, 28(3):282–311.

Devlin, J., Chang, M.-W., Lee, K., and Toutanova, K. (2019). Bert: Pre-training of deep bidirectional transformers for language understanding. In *Proceedings of the 2019 Conference of the North American Chapter of the Association for Computational Linguistics: Human Language Technologies, Volume 1 (Long and Short Papers)*, pages 4171–4186.

Dwork, C., McSherry, F., Nissim, K., and Smith, A. (2006). Calibrating noise to sensitivity in private data analysis. In *Theory of cryptography conference*, pages 265–284. Springer.

Eubanks, B. (2022). *Artificial intelligence for HR: Use AI to support and develop a successful workforce.* Kogan Page Publishers.

Feng, S. Y., Gangal, V., Wei, J., Chandar, S., Vosoughi, S., Mitamura, T., and Hovy, E. (2021). A survey of data augmentation approaches for nlp. In *Findings of the Association for Computational Linguistics: ACL-IJCNLP 2021*, pages 968–988.

Francopoulo, G. and Schaub, L.-P. (2020). Anonymization for the gdpr in the context of citizen and customer relationship management and nlp. In *workshop on Legal and Ethical Issues (Legal2020)*, pages 9–14. ELRA.

Freire, M. N. and de Castro, L. N. (2021). e-recruitment recommender systems: a systematic review. *Knowledge and Information Systems*, 63(1):1–20.

Gatt, A. and Krahmer, E. (2018). Survey of the state of the art in natural language generation: Core tasks, applications and evaluation. *Journal of Artificial Intelligence Research*, 61:65–170.

Habernal, I. (2021). When differential privacy meets nlp: The devil is in the detail. In *Proceedings of the 2021 Conference on Empirical Methods in Natural Language Processing*, pages 1522–1528.

Howcroft, D. M., Belz, A., Clinciu, M.-A., Gkatzia, D., Hasan, S. A., Mahamood, S., Mille, S., Van Miltenburg, E., Santhanam, S., and Rieser, V. (2020). Twenty years of confusion in human evaluation: Nlg needs evaluation sheets and standardised definitions. In *Proceedings of the 13th International Conference on Natural Language Generation*, pages 169–182.

Igamberdiev, T. and Habernal, I. (2021). Privacy-preserving graph convolutional networks for text classification. *arXiv preprint arXiv:2102.09604*.

Jain, L., Vardhan, H., Kathiresan, G., and Narayan, A. (2021). Optimizing people sourcing through semantic matching of job description documents and candidate profile using improved topic modelling techniques. In *Advances in Artificial Intelligence and Data Engineering*, pages 899–908. Springer.

Jiechieu, K. F. F. and Tsopze, N. (2021). Skills prediction based on multi-label resume classification using cnn with model predictions explanation. *Neural Computing and Applications*, 33(10):5069–5087.

Joulin, A., Grave, É., Bojanowski, P., and Mikolov, T. (2017). Bag of tricks for efficient text classification. In *Proceedings of the 15th Conference of the European Chapter of the Association for Computational Linguistics: Volume 2, Short Papers*, pages 427–431.

Keskar, N. S., McCann, B., Varshney, L. R., Xiong, C., and Socher, R. (2019). Ctrl: A conditional transformer language model for controllable generation. *arXiv preprint arXiv:1909.05858*.

Kmail, A. B., Maree, M., Belkhatir, M., and Alhashmi, S. M. (2015). An automatic online recruitment system based on exploiting multiple semantic resources and concept-relatedness measures. In *2015 IEEE 27th International Conference on Tools with Artificial Intelligence (ICTAI)*, pages 620–627. IEEE.

Krishna, S., Gupta, R., and Dupuy, C. (2021). Adept: Auto-encoder based differentially private text transformation. In *Proceedings of the 16th Conference of the European Chapter of the Association for Computational Linguistics: Main Volume*, pages 2435–2439.

Lamba, D., Goyal, S., Chitresh, V., and Gupta, N. (2020). An integrated system for occupational category classification based on resume and job matching. In *Proceedings of the International Conference on Innovative Computing & Communications (ICICC)*.

Lauriola, I., Lavelli, A., and Aiolli, F. (2022). An introduction to deep learning in natural language processing: models, techniques, and tools. *Neurocomputing*, 470:443–456.

Liu, Y., Ott, M., Goyal, N., Du, J., Joshi, M., Chen,

D., Levy, O., Lewis, M., Zettlemoyer, L., and Stoyanov, V. (2019). Roberta: A robustly optimized bert pretraining approach. *arXiv preprint arXiv:1907.11692*.

Lyu, L., He, X., and Li, Y. (2020). Differentially private representation for nlp: Formal guarantee and an empirical study on privacy and fairness. In *Findings of the Association for Computational Linguistics: EMNLP 2020*, pages 2355–2365.

McNamara, D. S., Crossley, S. A., and McCarthy, P. M. (2010). Linguistic features of writing quality. *Written communication*, 27(1):57–86.

McSherry, F. and Talwar, K. (2007). Mechanism design via differential privacy. In *48th Annual IEEE Symposium on Foundations of Computer Science (FOCS'07)*, pages 94–103. IEEE.

Nasar, Z., Jaffry, S. W., and Malik, M. K. (2021). Named entity recognition and relation extraction: State-of-the-art. *ACM Computing Surveys (CSUR)*, 54(1):1–39.

Niedermayer, D. (2008). An introduction to bayesian networks and their contemporary applications. In *Innovations in Bayesian networks*, pages 117–130. Springer.

Nikolenko, S. I. et al. (2021). *Synthetic data for deep learning*. Springer.

Ore, O. and Sposato, M. (2021). Opportunities and risks of artificial intelligence in recruitment and selection. *International Journal of Organizational Analysis*, pages 1–12.

Paccosi, T. and Aprosio, A. P. (2021). Redit: A tool and dataset for extraction of personal data in documents of the public administration domain. In *CLiC-it 2021 Italian Conference on Computational Linguistics*.

Ping, H., Stoyanovich, J., and Howe, B. (2017). Datasynthesizer: Privacy-preserving synthetic datasets. In *Proceedings of the 29th International Conference on Scientific and Statistical Database Management*, pages 1–5.

Pitler, E. and Nenkova, A. (2008). Revisiting readability: A unified framework for predicting text quality. In *Proceedings of the 2008 conference on empirical methods in natural language processing*, pages 186–195.

Popova, Y. B. (2014). Narrativity and enaction: the social nature of literary narrative understanding. *Frontiers in psychology*, 5:895.

Radford, A., Wu, J., Child, R., Luan, D., Amodei, D., Sutskever, I., et al. (2019). Language models are unsupervised multitask learners. *OpenAI blog*, 1(8):9.

Roemmele, M., Gordon, A. S., and Swanson, R. (2017). Evaluating story generation systems using automated linguistic analyses. In *SIGKDD 2017 Workshop on Machine Learning for Creativity*, pages 13–17.

Rogers, A., Kovaleva, O., and Rumshisky, A. (2020). A primer in bertology: What we know about how bert works. *Transactions of the Association for Computational Linguistics*, 8:842–866.

Rosenman, S., Jacovi, A., and Goldberg, Y. (2020). Exposing shallow heuristics of relation extraction models with challenge data. In *Proceedings of the 2020 Conference on Empirical Methods in Natural Language Processing (EMNLP)*, pages 3702–3710.

Schick, T. and Schütze, H. (2021). Generating datasets with pretrained language models. In *Proceedings of the 2021 Conference on Empirical Methods in Natural Language Processing*, pages 6943–6951.

See, A., Pappu, A., Saxena, R., Yerukola, A., and Manning, C. D. (2019). Do massively pretrained language models make better storytellers? In *Proceedings of the 23rd Conference on Computational Natural Language Learning (CoNLL)*, pages 843–861.

Shejwalkar, V., Inan, H. A., Houmansadr, A., and Sim, R. (2021). Membership inference attacks against nlp classification models. In *NeurIPS 2021 Workshop Privacy in Machine Learning*.

Sigurd, B., Eeg-Olofsson, M., and Van Weijer, J. (2004). Word length, sentence length and frequency–zipf revisited. *Studia linguistica*, 58(1):37–52.

Silva, P., Gonçalves, C., Godinho, C., Antunes, N., and Curado, M. (2020). Using nlp and machine learning to detect data privacy violations. In *IEEE INFOCOM 2020-IEEE Conference on Computer Communications Workshops (INFOCOM WKSHPS)*, pages 972–977. IEEE.

Sinha, A. K., Akhtar, A. K., Kumar, A., et al. (2021). Resume screening using natural language processing and machine learning: A systematic review. *Machine Learning and Information Processing*, pages 207–214.

Strohmeier, S. (2022). Artificial intelligence in human resources-an introduction. In *Handbook of Research on Artificial Intelligence in Human Resource Management*. Edward Elgar Publishing.

Tucker, K., Branson, J., Dilleen, M., Hollis, S., Loughlin, P., Nixon, M. J., and Williams, Z. (2016). Protecting patient privacy when sharing patient-level data from clinical trials. *BMC Medical Research Methodology*, 16(1):5–14.

Vaswani, A., Shazeer, N., Parmar, N., Uszkoreit, J., Jones, L., Gomez, A. N., Kaiser, Ł., and Polosukhin, I. (2017). Attention is all you need. *Advances in neural information processing systems*, 30.

Voigt, P. and Von dem Bussche, A. (2017). The eu general data protection regulation (gdpr). *A Practical Guide, 1st Ed., Cham: Springer International Publishing*, 10(3152676):10–5555.

Wang, S., Durrett, G., and Erk, K. (2020). Narrative interpolation for generating and understanding stories. *arXiv preprint arXiv:2008.07466*.

Wolf, T., Debut, L., Sanh, V., Chaumond, J., Delangue, C., Moi, A., Cistac, P., Rault, T., Louf, R., Funtowicz, M., et al. (2020). Transformers: State-of-the-art natural language processing. In *Proceedings of the 2020 conference on empirical methods in natural language processing: system demonstrations*, pages 38–45.

Yao, L., Peng, N., Weischedel, R., Knight, K., Zhao, D., and Yan, R. (2019). Plan-and-write: Towards better automatic storytelling. In *Proceedings of the AAAI Conference on Artificial Intelligence*, volume 33, pages 7378–7385.

Zaroor, A., Maree, M., and Sabha, M. (2017). Jrc: a job post and resume classification system for online recruitment. In *2017 IEEE 29th International Conference on Tools with Artificial Intelligence (ICTAI)*, pages 780–787. IEEE.

Zhang, J., Cormode, G., Procopiuc, C. M., Srivastava, D., and Xiao, X. (2017). Privbayes: Private data release via bayesian networks. *ACM Transactions on Database Systems (TODS)*, 42(4):1–41.

Appendix: Examples of Generated CVs

We report three examples of synthetic CVs, generated using the methodology described above. To distinguish them from the text generated by GPT-2, manually written prompts (see Section 3.3) are reported in grey italics. The CVs were generated using a value of $\varepsilon = 0.1$, which ensures the highest privacy guarantees (see Section 3.2).

1. *Personal Details Name: Mariola Keudel Nationality: DE Address: Holtstr. 4/9 78091 Sebnitz Country of residence: DE Phone number: 08775 002138 Email: mkeudel@hofmann.de Field of expertise: IT - current position: Java Developer*

   Summary Dedicated and focused Java Developer who excels at helping companies gain control of their data. Work Experience and Career In my role as Java Developer at SCCM, I have worked on a number of IT projects.

   Studies and Education In my Ph.D. in Computer Science at Texas A&M University I specialized in the analysis of network traffic to understand how clients use network resources.

   Computer and Technical Skills My technical skills include Java, Java EE, SQL, Java EE 7, Spring and Spring Database.

   Languages I speak several languages, including French, Dutch, German, Italian and English.

   Hobbies and Interests My interests include learning new things about programming and software development, being a fun geek and a role model, and my desire to live in a big city and help others with their coding and programming skills."

2. *Personal Details Name: Fidel Peiró Nationality: ES Address: Sahin-Kreusel-Allee 2/4 40411 Neustadtner Waldnaab Country of residence: DE Phone number: 0293336135 Email: fpeirŎ0f3@quiros.net Field of expertise: IT - current position: Database Administrator*

   Summary With 5 years of experience working as Database Administrator, I have worked at several companies, such as: Microsoft, IBM, HP, Dell and HP Zellers.

   Work Experience and Career My responsabilities as Database Administrator at IBM include: Provide troubleshooting for database backups.

   Studies and Education I pursued a B.A. in Computer Science at University of Cincinnati studying Computer Science and Engineering.

   Computer and Technical Skills I have experience with Windows 8 and Microsoft Office Suite 2015.

   Languages I speak several languages, including Spanish, Italian, French, German and Japanese.

   Hobbies and Interests When I am not working, I like to go fishing, hiking, spending time with my family, playing golf and listening to music.

3. *Personal Details Name: Christopher Carter Nationality: US Address: Pasadizo de María Del Carmen Terrón 9 Puerta 5 Palencia, 11174 Country of residence: ES Phone number: +34720 46 84 32 Email: christopher.carter@chandler-garcia.net Field of expertise: IT - current position: Java Developer*

   Summary Highly motivated Java Developer who enjoys writing, networking and programming.

   Work Experience and Career In my role as Java Developer at Citrix, I was responsible for the entire Java development cycle from the very early days until the early years of its release in Java EE 6.

   Studies and Education I pursued a B.A. in Computer Science at Cornell University studying System Administration and Computer Systems.

   Computer and Technical Skills My technical skills include: programming, assembly language, Linux, C and C++ programming, Java/Ruby scripting and web development.

   Languages Aside from my native language, I speak English and German.

   Hobbies and Interests I enjoy hiking, reading books about languages and exploring my environment.

The Legal and Ethical issues Workshop @LREC2022, pages 64–72
Marseille, 20 June 2022

MAPA Project: Ready-to-Go Open-Source Datasets and Deep Learning Technology to Remove Identifying Information from Text Documents

**Victoria Arranz,[1] Khalid Choukri,[1] Montse Cuadros,[2]
Aitor García-Pablos,[2] Lucie Gianola,[3] Cyril Grouin,[3]
Manuel Herranz,[4] Patrick Paroubek,[3] Pierre Zweigenbaum[3]**
[1]ELDA/ELRA, Paris, France; [2]Vicomtech Foundation, Basque Research and Technology Alliance (BRTA), Donostia,Spain [3]Université Paris-Saclay, CNRS, Laboratoire interdisciplinaire des sciences du numérique (LISN), 91405 Orsay, France; [4]Pangeanic – PangeaMT, Valencia, Spain
{arranz,choukri}@elda.org, {mcuadros,agarciap}@vicomtech.org,
{lucie.gianola,cyril.grouin,patrick.paroubek,pierre.zweigenbaum}@lisn.upsaclay.fr, manuel@pangeanic.com

Abstract

This paper presents the outcomes of the MAPA project, a set of annotated corpora for 24 languages of the European Union and an open-source customisable toolkit able to detect and substitute sensitive information in text documents from any domain, using state-of-the art, deep learning-based named entity recognition techniques. In the context of the project, the toolkit has been developed and tested on administrative, legal and medical documents, obtaining state-of-the-art results. As a result of the project, 24 dataset packages have been released and the de-identification toolkit is available as open source.

Keywords: anonymisation, de-identification, sensitive information, deep learning, BERT, NER, annotated data

1. Introduction

Computing Technology, Artificial Intelligence, and Machine Learning have made tremendous progress in recent years. However, a large part of the lore of electronic documents produced for work, administration, entertainment, public services, public communication or personal expression on social-media cannot be used and shared easily for research purposes: this is caused by the presence of sensitive information identifying individuals, like person names, phone numbers, etc. The laws and regulations that protect the private life of individuals[1] require anonymising a document if it is to be disclosed and shared. In many cases, this prevents researchers from using this document for their experiments. Performing such anonymisation task manually is costly. Besides, ever more documents are needed to train the algorithms of all kinds that are used nowadays to process documents automatically. This started a quest for automatic anonymisation, which starts by first addressing the detection and then the removal of any identifying information, a task called de-identifying a document. Anonymisation implies that not only identifying information is not present in a document anymore, but also that it is impossible to infer the identity of a person from the material preserved after the de-identification of the document.

Developing a language- and domain-independent system that detects information in text documents is already a challenge, because access to the full original document with its identifying information is needed as training data to feed machine-learning algorithms. Such algorithms currently provide state-of-the-art performance. What is expected more precisely is to reach the highest possible recall (detecting all that information that needs to be found in the document). Furthermore, de-identifying a document imposes the extra constraint that enough material of the original document should be preserved for the document to remain usable for research purposes. This requires to adopt methods that not only yield a high recall, but also a high precision, since too many false positive alerts would result in a document with insufficient material left for any research purpose.

1.1. The MAPA Project

MAPA[2] (Multilingual Anonymisation for Public Administrations) (Gianola et al., 2020) is an integration project aiming to introduce Natural Language Processing (NLP) tools to develop a toolkit for effective and reliable de-identification of documents in the medical and legal fields. It addresses all EU official languages, including under-resourced ones, such as Latvian, Lithuanian, Estonian, Slovenian and Croatian.

The project has built a deployable, docker-ready, open-source fully multilingual de-identification toolkit able to detect personal data (for instance: person names, addresses, emails, credit card numbers, bank accounts, etc.) as defined by deployment cases in different Member States. The open source toolkit and resources for 24 EU languages are intended to help public administrations to comply with both GDPR[3] and the PSI Di-

[1]General Data Protection Regulation (GDPR): `https://gdpr.eu/`

[2]`https://mapa-project.eu/`

[3]`https://eur-lex.europa.eu/legal-content/EN/TXT/PDF/?uri=CELEX:32016R0679`

rective[4], particularly in the health and legal fields. The toolkit contributes to the promotion of Public Administration data sharing that is fully de-identified and thus not traceable to personal details, making it GDPR compliant. As a result, data that now remains in vaults and cannot be shared will be able to be re-used in European initiatives such as *NEC TM*[5] (data coming from Public Administrations for translation whose source language contains personal details), *ELRC*[6] (Public Administrations can share data that otherwise they would not be able to), and potentially *eTranslation*[7] (offering anonymisation services as a separate service or embedding it as part of its translation service), etc. MAPA's toolkit is easily customisable as it has pre- and post-processing modules available in the form of an API-ready toolkit dockerised version. This will ease integration and deployment as an isolated I/O module not disturbing current digital infrastructures. Furthermore, adaptation to specific terminology or regulation/language specific entities is made easier by the existence of the entry point offered by these pre- and post-processing modules with an intuitive interface based on regular expressions and add-on lexical resources. The de-identification toolkit is based on state-of-the-art Named-Entity Recognition (NER) (Yadav and Bethard, 2018; Huang et al., 2021), applicable to 24 EU languages. It is not restricted to names and surnames of European origin but addresses those mostly common in all EU countries, and with eTranslation in view, irrespective of whether the text is monolingual, bilingual or a patchwork of languages.

The remaining of this article is organised as follows. Section 2 describes the type of sensitive information that MAPA is targetting, with the hierarchy of named entities defined. In Section 3, we describe the MAPA open-source toolkit. Section 4 details the data production efforts and Section 5 reports on the toolkit evaluation approaches and results.

2. Sensitive Information to be De-Identified

The objective of MAPA is to build a multilingual de-identification toolkit that can de-identify personal and sensitive data referring to some person. For that purpose, multilingual language data in all 24 EU languages covered by the project needed to be annotated with the named entities to be detected, thus providing material for the development and evaluation of the system.

2.1. Named Entity Hierachy

The underlying model of the Named Entity (NE) hierarchy has been defined bearing in mind the needs of the de-identification tool. The objective has been to define a rich hierarchy with the entities that may be found in the different documents that need to be processed. The design of this hierarchy has focused on the legal and medical fields in particular but also targeting a general domain that can accommodate the multi-disciplinary application of the system once developed.

The MAPA NE hierarchy has three levels (as illustrated in Figure 1):

- Level 1 entities (in orange): implicit entities that can be inferred from their annotated elements.
- Level 2 entities (in blue): either explicit or implicit entities that may comprise some level-3 components and types to be annotated. They are also semantic classifiers for the lower level elements.
- Level 3 entity components and types (in green): these are either components within an entity or types of entity.

Despite having such a detailed hierarchy, not all elements are annotated. We benefit from the inferring capacity of some of them to reduce the annotation load (see Section 2.2) .

2.2. Annotation Guidelines

MAPA's annotation guidelines[8] explain the entity structure, relations and annotation definitions in detail. Given that several entities can be fully inferred either from their lower-level entities or from their level-3 components/types, not all elements within the hierarchy are annotated. This would be repetitive and very time consuming.

The annotation task has been carried out with the *INCEpTION*[9] annotation platform (Klie et al., 2018), an open-source tool which allows for a rich and flexible annotation of the data. For instance, an entity may be annotated with elements from any of the 3 MAPA levels if this is allowed by the annotation schema.

A series of general principles are stated in the guidelines defining what needs to be annotated. Sometimes these followed ambiguities and discussions with the annotators themselves. Establishing annotation principles that covered several domains while addressing domain-specific entities to be de-identified turned out to be rather complex. For that reason, guidelines were fine tuned after several annotation tests and inter-domain discussions took place to coordinate this fine-tuning. Some examples of general principles are as follows:

[4] Public Sector Information Directivehttps://eur-lex.europa.eu/legal-content/EN/TXT/PDF/?uri=CELEX:32019L1024&from=EN

[5] https://www.nec-tm.eu/

[6] https://lr-coordination.eu/

[7] https://ec.europa.eu/info/resources-partners/machine-translation-public-administrations-etranslation_en

[8] http://www.elra.info/media/filer_public/2022/05/10/mapa_annotation-guidelines-v6.pdf

[9] https://inception-project.github.io/

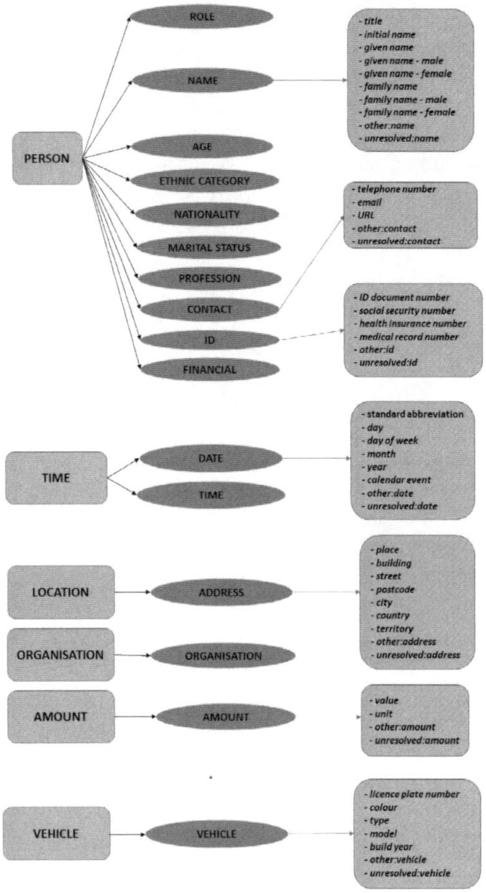

Figure 1: Named Entity Hierarchy

- Annotation needs to consider an entity's domain: for example, legal and administrative data contain many general references like Directives, Decisions, OJ numberings, etc. that will not be annotated.
- Annotation needs to consider an entity's nature: for instance, **Samsung** (referring to the organisation) should be annotated as ORGANISATION. However, **Samsung** (referring to a smartphone) will not be annotated ("phone" is not an entity type).
- The often-ambiguous distinction between **ROLE** and **PROFESSION** needs to consider the domain and the entity's function within a sentence (e.g., **judge** may indicate a ROLE if this refers to the judge taking care of some court ruling or to PROFESSION if the entity does not act as such in that context); etc.

Besides the general principles, annotation definitions are provided for annotators to understand some further entity cases and terminology in their annotation (e.g., how to deal with elements between entities, how to use the **other** and **unresolved** components, etc. Finally, specific instructions are provided for all entities defined within MAPA[10]

3. Open-Source Toolkit

MAPA is a de-identification toolkit for the detection and substitution of sensitive information in text. It is designed to work with potentially any language, provided it is trained/configured properly (Ajausks et al., 2020). In order to perform its task, MAPA relies on different components and approaches, which are configured and integrated into a simple web-service.

At its core, MAPA relies on Deep Learning, using Transformers based neural-networks, in particular BERT(Devlin et al., 2019). Since MAPA is meant to deal with multilingual content, it is developed using the multilingual pre-trained BERT model from Google. However, other BERT models (such as BETO(Cañete et al., 2020) for Spanish) can be used just by changing the name (file) of the base model when training, as long as the model to be used remains compatible with the Transformers library and follows the same "BERT" conventions (special BERT tokens, WordPiece tokenisation, etc.).

In order to achieve the anonymisation of the documents, MAPA performs two kind of tasks: sensitive entity detection/classification (cf. Section 3.1), and detected entities replacement. The latter can be of three types, depending on the user's needs (cf. Section 3.2).

3.1. Sensitive Entities Detection and Classification

The detection of sensitive entities is the task of selecting which entities bear the information that needs to be hidden, removed or replaced. Besides detection, the entities are classified into different types, since that information may help in later steps to perform the information removal/replacement.

The detection can be seen as a regular NERC (Named Entity Recognition and Classification) task, only that the targeted entities depend on your anonymisation use case. In MAPA, the provided datasets and models target a variety of entities, such as "PERSON", "ORGANISATION", "PROFESSION", "AGE", "GENDER", "DATES", "COUNTRIES", "CITIES", etc. (as seen in Section 2.1). These entities are arranged in a two-level hierarchy[11], to have more fine-grained entities if necessary (e.g. a mention of a PERSON containing a "first-name" and a "family-name"). The detection is performed by two different modules that complement each other.

3.1.1. Deep Learning Model Based Detection

The main technology used to provide the entity detection is based on a Transformers model. In MAPA we do

[10] Please refer to the guidelines for full details.

[11] The third level is inferred, as seen in Section 2.1.

provide several pre-trained models, for a few languages and domains, with different levels of performance. But MAPA also offers the capability to train new models provided that you have labelled data in a suitable format (cf Section 4).

3.1.2. Regular-Expression Based Detection

For certain entity types, it is easier to rely on patterns and regular expressions rather than on a Deep Learning based model. The Deep Learning detection can deal with everything provided enough training data is available, but there is no point in using it to detect entities such as phone-numbers, email addresses, URLs, or some identification numbers that can be easily matched using a regular expression. MAPA allows you to configure regular expressions and assign them a meaningful label. That label (entity-type) will be attached to any match occurred in the text.

3.2. Sensitive Entities Replacement

Once the relevant entities have been detected and classified, the anonymisation task requires one further step. The information is still there and needs to be removed or replaced. The simplest way to remove the information is by replacing the detected entities with a symbol like '*' (e.g. "The judge Robinson was in the room" becomes "The judge ******** was in the room"). However, depending on the intended usage for the resulting texts, this is not a suitable approach, because the texts become unnatural and hard to read. This is particularly a problem when intending to share the data for further processing by other systems.
MAPA allows to obfuscate the text with that simple approach, and allows to replace the information by other similar entities, leading to still-readable documents that no longer contain the original sensitive information (cf. Figure 2). For that, MAPA has different modules that complement each other.

3.2.1. Neural LM Based Replacement

The Neural Language Model replacement is based on a Deep Learning language model. Again the multilingual BERT model is used as the base, but any other BERT model could work. When using this approach, the words that form the sensitive entity are replaced using a neural language model to predict a suitable entity to fill the gap. There are several extra heuristics and filters applied to avoid getting the very same word that we want to have replaced, and to avoid sampling unsuitable words (like a word when it was a number and vice-versa).
Using the Neural LM replacement has some advantages. Firstly, no pre-compiled list of names needs to be used for replacement. Secondly, ideally the Neural LM should pick words that contextually fit better, for example to match the gender of the names, or to deal with morphological inflexion in certain languages. In any case, MAPA provides users with other two replacement types.

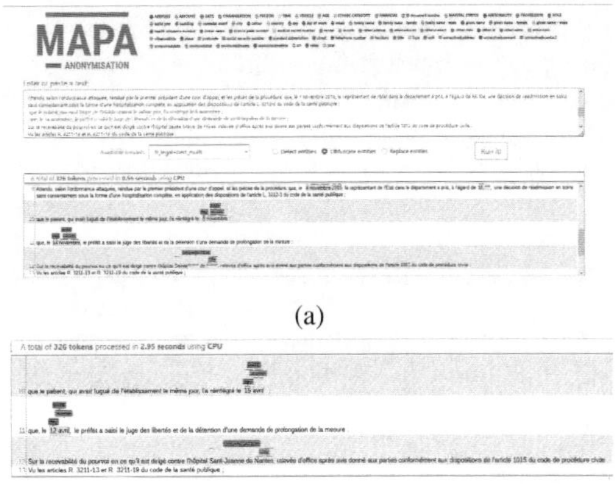

(a)

(b)

Figure 2: MAPA demo interface with obfuscation functionality (a) and enlarged view of the entity replacement (with a type plausible substitute) result on a sample legal text in French (b).

3.2.2. Random Character Replacement

This replacer is suitable for identifiers, number strings, or other arbitrary sequence of alpha-numerical characters. It simply replaces each character with another, randomly sampled, character of the same type (digit or letter). For example, an identification code such as X-6543-432 would become something like Z-3234-768.

3.2.3. Dictionary-Based Replacement

This is the classic replacement strategy, using a pre-compiled set of name lists, for the different entity types (people names, city names, etc.). When an entity of a certain type is found, a random name from the pairing list can be sampled as the replacement. This is simple, and for certain languages and domains it is effective. However, one needs to gather meaningful names for every entity type (and language). Further, nothing guarantees the coherence if the sampled entity does not match the context exactly (e.g., a female name in a context that requires a male name, or a French location name in a context that requires a German location name).
MAPA allows configuring specific replacement strategies for each entity type, and even for each language. So one can decide which kind of replacement is more suitable for which type of entity, or leave certain entity types untouched, without replacing them.

3.3. Integration and Deployment of the Toolkit

MAPA is an open source toolkit. That means that one can use it as-is, and also use it to plug one's own resources, including the training of new Deep Learning entity detection models.
The tool can be deployed as a web service. There is a configuration file that allows a fine-grained con-

trol over which models, which detection/replacement strategies and which resources are used when the tool is launched. The exposed web service receives texts of arbitrary length, and returns the list of detected entities, together with the resulting text, with the corresponding entity replacements applied.
The toolkit is offered with a ready-to-use Docker integration, so it is easy to deploy. Even without the Docker wrapping, the tool is based on Python, and uses pretty standard Python dependencies such as Pytorch and Transformers, so it should work on any environment.
The software produced by MAPA has been made available to the community through Gitlab[12].

4. MAPA Data Production

MAPA carried out the production of both Named-Entity (NE) annotated and unannotated datasets for all EU official languages. The objective was to produce (collect and annotate) relevant GDPR-compliant data in the 24 languages for system training, development, and evaluation. In addition, it also produced lists of person names for the 24 languages (cf. Section 4.5). Early stages of the project confirmed the great difficulty to obtain data with sensitive content (in both legal and medical domains) and a new strategy was defined that is further detailed in the sections below:

1. We would focus on other relevant NE rich data sources from related fields like administrative-legal (see Section 4.1).
2. We would enrich available medical data with named entities so as to use clinical documents with relevant sensitive information (cf. Section 4.2).
3. We would process already anonymised data by de-anonymising it first: this would allow us to work on real sensitive data with de-identification needs (cf. Section 4.3).
4. We would explore the production of synthetic data by translation means (cf. Section 4.4).

All annotated datasets, raw corpora and name lists produced within MAPA can be downloaded per language package through the ELRC-SHARE repository[13] and the ELRA Catalogue[14].

4.1. Data from other Relevant Sources

As part of the new strategy, MAPA produced the following resources:

- 24 corpora on the legal-administrative domain from EUR-LEX[15]: these comprised over 2000 sentences per language and the choice for this data was based on the availability of NE-relevant parallel texts. These texts were available for all languages except Irish[16]. The Irish version has been produced with the EC's eTranslation platform[17] and manually revised. All 24 datasets were annotated with MAPA's Named Entities for initial system development, providing good results and the output is a parallel NE annotated set in 24 languages.
- 24 1-Million sentence raw corpora were produced for potential further training, from the following sources and languages:
  - Court of Justice of the European Union[18] (CS, DA, DE, EL, EN, ET, FI, FR, IT, LT, LV, PL, PT, SV).
  - Spanish Council of State (ES)[19].
  - Malta Government Gazzette, Malta Law Courts online and EU documents (MT).
  - Wikipedia, news, web crawling and data augmentation (GA).
  - Wikipedia, news and web crawling (BG, HR, HU, NL, RO, SK, SL).

4.2. Medical Domain Datasets

For the clinical domain, since it was not possible to access real clinical data with sensitive content, we designed an alternative solution consisting in using a corpus of 485 clinical cases written in French from a larger dataset (Grabar et al., 2018; Grabar et al., 2019). We automatically reintroduced nominative data within the texts: to this end, we replaced some occurrences of pronouns or key phrases *("he", "she", "the patient")* by sequences of randomly selected first name and last name, and we also incorporated dates, and either full addresses (hospital name, street name, post code, city name) or basically only city names within sentences. The final corpus is composed of 2279 entities.[20] and

[12]https://gitlab.com/MAPA-EU-Project/mapa_project

[13]https://elrc-share.eu/repository/search/?q=MAPA

[14]http://www.elra.info/en/

[15]https://eur-lex.europa.eu/

[16]Although Irish became a full EU official language on 1 January 2007, EU institutions have profited from temporary derogations not to produce all acts in Irish on a transitional basis.

[17]https://ec.europa.eu/info/resources-partners/machine-translation-public-administrations-etranslation_en

[18]https://curia.europa.eu/

[19]For experiments on the Spanish legal and EUR-LEX data the reader can check (de Gibert et al., 2022).

[20]The final corpus is composed of 1019 person names, 539 dates, 524 ages, 62 organisations, 60 city names, 43 country names, 15 zip codes, 8 profession names, 7 addresses, and 2 places, for 485 files.

it has been manually revised to correct any wrong automatic replacement. This corpus has then been translated into the other 23 languages to be used in order to train the MAPA system in all languages (cf. Section 4.4). Even if clinical cases are not patient reports, they are composed of words belonging to the clinical domain.

4.3. Legal Domain Datasets

Obtaining legal text that could be annotated and used for system development and evaluation also proved to be a challenge. Some countries provide their court decisions as public data that can be used for language processing (this was the case for the Italian *Corte di Cassazione* [21]), but this is not the case for many Courts of Justice or Supreme Courts. As a consequence, we ventured into a task of de-anonymising to help us create and annotate legal data from the French *Cour de Cassation* and from the Greek Supreme Court *Areiospagos* [22]. The task consisted in identifying the elements that needed de-anonymising within the text (e.g., *à l'égard de M. X...*, and *de Mme X... Viviane, épouse Y..., actuellement hospitalisée à l'unité [...]-[...]*) and replacing them with the same type of entities from some available lists (containing person given names and family names, hospital names, addresses, etc.), and then, checking them to avoid any remaining wrong replacements. Once the data were de-anonymised, they were annotated with NEs and prepared for training, development and evaluation. Around 2,000 sentences were completed per language.

In addition to these court decision data, we also collected legal data from the Spanish Ministry of Justice, Court Cases from Maltese jurisprudence and we annotated some legal-administrative data from the ELRC-SHARE repository.

4.4. Synthetic Data

In order to increase the size of our annotated corpora, synthetic data were produced. All already annotated data was MT translated by exporting annotation first, translating raw text and then re-inserting annotation into the translated output. A pipeline was developed for that purpose and although it presented some drawbacks in terms of tag export and noise from MT, results were very interesting (cf. Section 5) and it is a path worth pursuing by tackling the detected shortcomings.

4.5. Lists of Person Names and Surnames

In addition to the annotated and raw corpora produced, lists of ~10,000 person names were built per language/country. These comprised commonly used names in the searched country, sometimes being of foreign origin too. In order to do so, first names and surnames were collected from different sources following availability. This was country and language dependent as some countries provide lists in their institutes of statistics or similar organisms and they are very helpful and willing to disseminate and share them. Generally, first names and surnames were combined to provide lists with full forms. However, whenever linguistic constraints were imposed to perform these combinations (e.g., for Baltic languages and Irish) separate lists have been compiled for given names and family names.

[21] https://www.cortedicassazione.it/corte-di-cassazione/

[22] http://www.areiospagos.gr/

5. Toolkit Evaluation

The goal of the evaluation performed during MAPA was to evaluate the quality of the entity detection for de-identification.

5.1. Corpus

The MAPA data production activity collected and annotated data, which was split into training, development and test data. These data were used with Version 2 of the MAPA system to produce the evaluation results described here. The MAPA Consortium members first prepared annotated documents in their native languages. Training and testing was then performed on data splits of the "native language corpus" (e.g., Figure 3 shows the results for French medical data). In addition, this corpus was machine-translated to all the other languages addressed by the project (Figures 4 & 5 for medical translated and legal translated data, respectively). The goal was to examine whether the additional data produced this way would be suitable for training and testing the MAPA de-identification system.

5.2. Measures

Various considerations need to be taken into account with respect to the aim of MAPA, which is to provide a de-identification functionality for text documents:

- **Behaviour on whole text** (accuracy) vs **signal detection** (true positives). Accuracy computes the rate of agreement on every input word. Signal detection focuses on the correct detection of target entities (true positives). While accuracy is a convenient metric for use-agnostic, global system behavior, signal detection is more closely related to the intended use of the system.
- **Granularity: word-level** (correct entity type) vs **entity-level** (the detection of boundaries). Word-level evaluation focuses on the correct prediction of whether or not a word is part of an entity, and of which type. Its unit of measurement is the word. Entity-level evaluation additionally aims at determining the correct boundaries of each entity. Its unit of measurement is the entity (that can encompass several words). Entity-level detection, with both types and boundaries, is relevant when post-detection processing depends on the recognition of well-formed, full entities, while word-level evaluation is for other cases.

- **Information Retrieval** (precision, recall, F1-score) vs **Test** (sensitivity, specificity). The main information retrieval measures (precision, recall, and F1-score) used for NER focus on the signal detection task. They measure the rate of correct detection (true positives) against system detection (precision) or against gold standard annotations (recall), and can be summarized with F1-score (the harmonic mean of precision and recall). Test measures (sensitivity and specificity) are typically used to interpret diagnostic tests in medicine. Here, sensitivity (equal to recall) is the probability that an entity in the gold standard is correctly detected by the system. Specificity is the probability that a non-entity according to the gold standard is correctly ignored (not detected) by the system. If sensitivity and specificity can be measured in a continuous way, they can be summarized by the area under the receiver operating characteristic (ROC) curve (AUC). Recall (or sensitivity) relates to the rate of de-identification and is thus important in the present context. Specificity relates to the preservation of information carried by the text beyond directly identifying entities, and is therefore a useful complementary metric.

5.3. Uniform Weights vs Different Weights

Uniform weights (plain named entity recognition) vs **different weights** (related to identifying power) are used for contrasting entity types, for balancing recall vs precision or sensitivity vs specificity. Some entity types (e.g., person name) have higher identifying power than others (e.g., age), it may be relevant to give them a higher weight. Consequently, a high recall (detecting as many identifying entities as possible) is more important here than a high precision (having the highest possible proportion of actually identifying entities among those predicted as identifying) because the consequences of a miss (false negative) have much more impact than removing a general word. Similarly, a high sensitivity (= recall: detecting as many identifying entities as possible) is more important than a high specificity (marking as non-identifying as many non-identifying words as possible) since identifying entities are always less frequent than general words. The importance of recall makes F2-score a more relevant alternative than the balanced F1-score.

5.4. Level of Importance of the Identification of Fine-Grained Entity Types

The MAPA annotation schema is a hierarchy with three levels of entity types. The lower levels define finer-grained types (e.g., *street* or *building* below *address*). Making the right distinction between lower-level entity types (e.g., *building* vs *street*) is less important than detecting the higher-level entity types (e.g., *address* vs *person*). In a more lenient evaluation mode, lower-level types may be converted into levels higher in the entity type hierarchy.

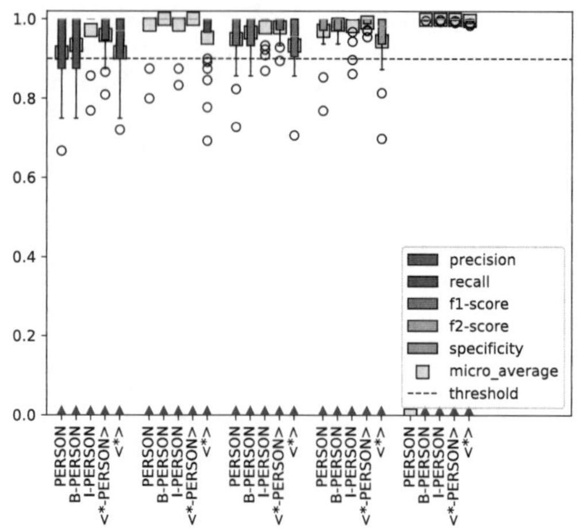

Figure 3: Distribution of precision, recall, F1-score, F2-score, and specificity of PERSON detection evaluation on native documents: French medical, at the entity level (PERSON) and at the word level (boundary-related word labels <B-PERSON> and <I-PERSON>, generic recognition of either of them <*-PERSON>, word-level generic recognition of any type of level-1 entity <*>), for each test document. Specificity is not computed for entity-level labels.

5.5. Distribution of Scores and Aggregation

The MAPA system was tested on a large set of documents of varied nature in different domains and languages. For a given metric, this results in a distribution of scores over individual documents. This distribution can be displayed or summarized in various ways. An average score can be computed globally based on individual results (micro-average) or after computing per-class results (macro-average). Weights can be applied as mentioned above. Because the various selected entity types have different levels of importance for de-identification, computing a plain macro-average is not necessarily optimal. Information on the distribution of values can be obtained through their standard deviation, quartiles, and more generally a histogram of values.

Based upon these considerations, Figures 3–5 show distributions of metrics across documents. The project targeted a threshold of 0.895 in general: a score above this threshold is signaled by a green, up-pointing arrow on the x axis. The figures show that most metrics were above threshold for most documents. The task was more difficult on translated documents and scores were accordingly lower, but recall and F2-score were still above or very close to threshold for most languages in both medical and legal documents.

5.6. Difficulty of Examples

While such scores provide a general idea of the behaviour of these systems, they ignore a key piece of in-

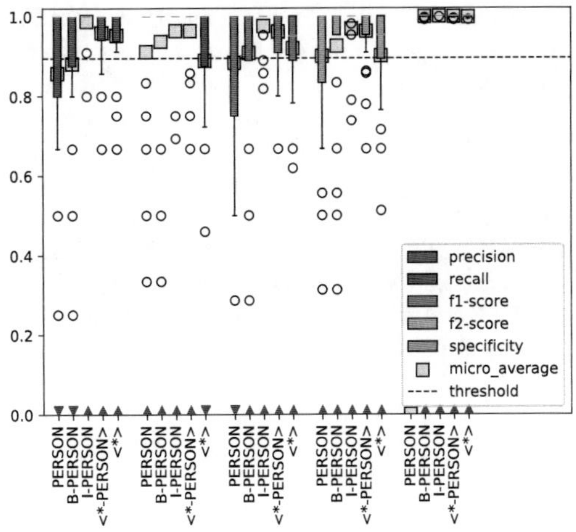

Figure 4: Distribution of precision, recall, F1-score, F2-score and specificity of PERSON detection in documents translated into Bulgarian, with same information as in Fig 3.

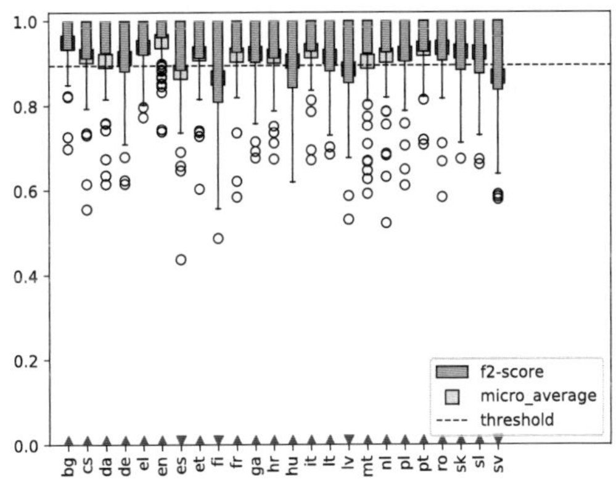

Figure 5: Distribution of F2-score of <∗-PERSON> detection across documents for each language (translated documents).

formation that can be useful for assessing progress and discerning remaining challenges: the relative difficulty of test instances. To address this shortcoming, MAPA designed the notion of differential evaluation which effectively defines a pragmatic partition of instances into gradually more difficult bins by leveraging the predictions made by a set of systems. Comparing systems along these difficulty bins enables us to produce a finer-grained analysis of their relative merits. The methodology is described in (Gianola et al., 2021) with two illustrative examples: a multi-label text classification task (Névéol et al.,) and a comparison of neural models trained for biomedical entity detection (Wei et al., 2016).

6. Conclusions

In this paper we have presented the most relevant outcomes of the MAPA project involving datasets and technology. The project has produced corpora and tools that are available for the community:

- The tools software package produced is shared through Gitlab[23] under an Apache 2.0 licence [24].
- All annotated datasets, raw corpora and name lists produced within MAPA can be downloaded per language package from the ELRA Catalogue[25] and the ELRC-SHARE repository[26], and they will be shortly linked through the ELG catalogue[27].
- The annotation guidelines can be downloaded from the ELRA manual's library[28].

Regarding toolkit evaluation, this paper has focused on the evaluation of entity detection quality on a) a native language French medical data and b) datasets obtained through machine translated data (i.e., using synthetic data). Despite the shortcomings of noise inherited from the synthetic data creation process, both recall and F2-score on held-out data were above a 0.895 threshold for most documents in both legal and medical corpora.

7. Acknowledgements

This work was partially funded by the MAPA project. The MAPA project was an INEA-funded Action for the European Commission under the Connecting Europe Facility (CEF) – Telecommunications Sector with Grant Agreement No INEA/CEF/ICT/A2019/1927065.

The authors wish to acknowledge all MAPA consortium members for their work and contributions.

We would also like to thank (a) the *Cour de Cassation* and their anonymisation team for their fruitful discussions, and (b) the INCEpTION project group for their help with the annotation platform.

Finally, a very big thank you to our colleagues from DCU (Jane Dunne, Teresa Lynn, and Jane O'Connor) and from ILC-CNR (Monica Monachini, Claudia Soria and Tommaso Lo Sterzo) for their very valuable help with the Irish data and the Italian names, respectively.

[23] https://gitlab.com/MAPA-EU-Project/mapa_project

[24] http://www.apache.org/licenses/LICENSE-2.0

[25] http://www.elra.info/en/

[26] https://elrc-share.eu/repository/search/?q=MAPA

[27] https://live.european-language-grid.eu/

[28] http://www.elra.info/media/filer_public/2022/05/10/mapa_annotation-guidelines-v6.pdf

8. Bibliographical References

Ajausks, Ē., Arranz, V., Bié, L., Cerdà-i Cucó, A., Choukri, K., Cuadros, M., Degroote, H., Estela, A., Etchegoyhen, T., García-Martínez, M., García-Pablos, A., Herranz, M., Kohan, A., Melero, M., Rosner, M., Rozis, R., Paroubek, P., Vasiļevskis, A., and Zweigenbaum, P. (2020). The Multilingual Anonymisation Toolkit for Public Administrations (MAPA) Project. In *Proceedings of the 22nd Annual Conference of the European Association for Machine Translation*, pages 471–472, Lisboa, Portugal, November. European Association for Machine Translation.

Cañete, J., Chaperon, G., Fuentes, R., and Pérez, J. (2020). Spanish Pre-Trained BERT Model and Evaluation Data. In *Proceedings of the Practical ML for Developing Countries Workshop at the Eighth International Conference on Learning Representations (ICLR 2020)*, pages 1–9.

de Gibert, O., García-Pablos, A., Cuadros, M., and Melero, M. (2022). Spanish datasets for sensitive entity detection in the legal domain. In Nicoletta Calzolari, et al., editors, *Proceedings of the Thirteenth International Conference on Language Resources and Evaluation (LREC'22)*, Marseille, France, june. European Language Resource Association (ELRA).

Devlin, J., Chang, M.-W., Lee, K., and Toutanova, K. (2019). BERT: Pre-training of Deep Bidirectional Transformers for Language Understanding. In *Proceedings of the 2019 Conference of the North American Chapter of the Association for Computational Linguistics: Human Language Technologies, Volume 1 (Long and Short Papers)*, pages 4171–4186.

Gianola, L., Ēriks Ajausks, Arranz, V., Bendahman, C., Bié, L., Borg, C., Cerdà, A., Choukri, K., Cuadros, M., Gibert, O. D., Degroote, H., Edelman, E., Etchegoyhen, T., Ángela Franco Torres, Hernandez, M. G., Pablos, A. G., Gatt, A., Grouin, C., Herranz, M., Kohan, A. A., Lavergne, T., Melero, M., Paroubek, P., Rigault, M., Rosner, M., Rozis, R., Plas, L. V. D., Vīksna, R., and Zweigenbaum, P., (2020). *Legal Knowledge and Information Systems*, volume 334 of *Frontiers in Artificial Intelligence and Applications*, chapter Automatic Removal of Identifying Information in Official EU Languages for Public Administrations: The MAPA Project, pages 223–226. IOS Press. DOI 10.3233/FAIA200869.

Gianola, L., El Boukkouri, H., Grouin, C., Lavergne, T., Paroubek, P., and Zweigenbaum, P. (2021). Differential Evaluation: a Qualitative Analysis of Natural Language Processing System Behavior Based Upon Data Resistance to Processing. In *Proceedings of the 2nd Workshop on Evaluation and Comparison of NLP Systems*, pages 1–10, Punta Cana, Dominican Republic, November. Association for Computational Linguistics.

Huang, J., Li, C., Subudhi, K., Jose, D., Balakrishnan, S., Chen, W., Peng, B., Gao, J., and Han, J. (2021). Few-Shot Named Entity Recognition: An Empirical Baseline Study. In *Proceedings of the 2021 Conference on Empirical Methods in Natural Language Processing*, pages 10408–10423, Online and Punta Cana, Dominican Republic, November. Association for Computational Linguistics.

Klie, J.-C., Bugert, M., Boullosa, B., Eckart de Castilho, R., and Gurevych, I. (2018). The INCEpTION Platform: Machine-Assisted and Knowledge-Oriented Interactive Annotation. In *Proceedings of the 27th International Conference on Computational Linguistics: System Demonstrations*, pages 5–9, Santa Fe, New Mexico, August. Association for Computational Linguistics.

Yadav, V. and Bethard, S. (2018). A Survey on Recent Advances in Named Entity Recognition from Deep Learning Models. In *Proceedings of the 27th International Conference on Computational Linguistics*, pages 2145–2158, Santa Fe, New Mexico, USA, August. Association for Computational Linguistics.

9. Language Resource References

Grabar, N., Claveau, V., and Dalloux, C. (2018). CAS: French Corpus with Clinical Cases. In *Proc of LOUHI*, Brussels, Belgium.

Grabar, N., Grouin, C., Hamon, T., and Claveau, V. (2019). Recherche et Extraction d'Information dans des Cas Cliniques. Présentation de la Campagne d'Évaluation DEFT 2019. In *Actes de DEFT*, Toulouse, France.

Névéol, A., Robert, A., Grippo, F., Morgand, C., Orsi, C., Pelikán, L., Ramadier, L., Rey, G., , and Zweigenbaum, P.). CLEF eHealth 2018 Multilingual Information Extraction Task Overview: ICD10 Coding of Death Certificates in French, Hungarian and Italian.

Wei, C.-H., Peng, Y., Leaman, R., Davis, A. P., Mattingly, C. J., Li, J., Wiegers, T. C., and Lu, Z. (2016). Assessing the State of the Art in Biomedical Relation Extraction: Overview of the BioCreative V Chemical-Disease Relation (CDR) Task. *Database: The Journal of Biological Databases and Curation*, PMCID:PMC4799720. doi:10.1093/database/baw032.

The Legal and Ethical issues Workshop @LREC2022, pages 73–78
Marseille, 20 June 2022

PRIPA: A Tool for Privacy-Preserving Analytics of Linguistic Data

Jeremie Clos[1], Emma McClaughlin[1], Pepita Barnard[1], Elena Nichele[1], Dawn Knight[2], Derek McAuley[1], Svenja Adolphs[1]
[1] University of Nottingham
{jeremie.clos, emma.mcclaughlin, pepita.barnard, elena.nichele, derek.mccauley, svenja.adolphs}@nottingham.ac.uk
[2] Cardiff University
knightd5@cardiff.ac.uk

Abstract

The days of large amorphous corpora collected with armies of Web crawlers and stored indefinitely are, or should be, coming to an end. There is a wealth of hidden linguistic information that is increasingly difficult to access, hidden in personal data that would be unethical and technically challenging to collect using traditional methods such as Web crawling and mass surveillance of online discussion spaces. Advances in privacy regulations such as GDPR and changes in the public perception of privacy bring into question the problematic ethical dimension of extracting information from unaware if not unwilling participants. Modern corpora need to adapt, be focused on testing specific hypotheses, and be respectful of the privacy of the people who generated its data. Our work focuses on using a distributed participatory approach and continuous informed consent to solve these issues, by allowing participants to voluntarily contribute their own censored personal data at a granular level. We evaluate our approach in a three-pronged manner, testing the accuracy of measurement of statistical measures of language with respect to standard corpus linguistics tools, evaluating the usability of our application with a participant involvement panel, and using the tool for a case study on health communication.

Keywords: privacy-preserving linguistics, corpus linguistics, software tools

1. Introduction

There is a wealth of hidden linguistic information which is increasingly difficult to access, hidden in personal and private data that would be unethical and technically challenging to collect using traditional methods such as Web crawling and mass surveillance of online discussion spaces. Additionally, advances in privacy regulations and changes in the zeitgeist bring into question the problematic ethical dimension of extracting such information from unaware if not unwilling participants.

Since the generation of knowledge from large amounts of empirical data is at the heart of corpus linguistics, its practitioners have long sought ways to protect the privacy of those who have generated it. However, so far the use of privacy-preserving methods has focused on post hoc processing such as automated anonymisation and de-identification. Those automated methods are severely lacking when faced with modern methods of re-identification and de-anonymisation. Non-automated methods on the other hand are not as scalable.

As a first step towards addressing this issue, we developed PRIPA[1], a software tool using a distributed participatory approach and continuous informed consent by allowing participants to stay in control of their data, and only voluntarily contribute their own censored personal data on their own terms (McClaughlin et al., 2022).

We evaluate our prototype by producing a comparison of word frequencies and collocate association scores between two standard state-of-the-art systems and PRIPA, showing that PRIPA is on par with those tools for some of their common features. We produce a small scale quantitative and qualitative evaluation of the tool by users of different levels of expertise, highlighting some key challenges in the production of privacy-preserving linguistic analysis tools.

This paper is structured as follows: In section 2, we discuss the overall methodology of PRIPA: general design for continuous consent, and software architecture. In section 3 we describe our evaluation methodology. We will finally conclude with key challenges and recommendations for further development in section 4.

2. Privacy-Preserving Corpus Linguistics

Privacy-preserving technologies allow for the processing of personal data in a way that minimises risks towards the privacy of the people who generated it (Noble et al., 2019). There are several approaches to privacy-preserving analytics, which rely on different tools to protect this privacy: trusted execution environments, homomorphic encryption, secure multi-party computation, differential privacy, and personal data stores. We opt for the personal data store approach to privacy-preserving analytics because it is the most compatible with the notion of continuous consent and granular sharing of data that is key to PRIPA, however those approaches are not mutually exclusive and further development of the tool will investigate the use of additional privacy layers such as differential privacy for statistics which cannot be computed locally.

[1] `https://c19comms.wp.horizon.ac.uk/pripa`

Other approaches to privacy-preserving analytics use the personal data store approach. Mozilla's Rally project (Mozilla, 2022) for example focuses on passive monitoring of data volunteers for Web-based data. One key difference with PRIPA is that Rally does not differentiate websites of interest, while PRIPA predetermines a set of websites of interest from which statistics are collected. Additionally, Rally monitors a wider set of interactions such as videos watched, time spent on each page, and all domain names of websites visited during the experiment while PRIPA focuses on specific linguistic items.

In the remaining parts of this section, we will describe the overall design principles of PRIPA and contrast them to the requirements of the General Data Protection Regulation (GDPR). We will then describe two key aspects of PRIPA for privacy-preserving corpus linguistics: the software architecture allowing data to be collected according to our key principles, and the user interface design allowing for the informed consent of users to be monitored at each key step of the data collection process.

2.1. Design principles of PRIPA

Being privacy-preserving by design involves the adherence to a set of principles, described in Table 1. Instead of collecting the data on the online discussion platform, we recruit participants who install a plugin into their Web browser. The PRIPA plugin then allows participants to enrol themselves into different experiments. Those experiments specify multiple things: the websites that will be watched, the words that will be observed, and the statistics that will be collected.

The principles used to develop PRIPA aim to be compatible with modern regulations in Internet privacy such as the European Union's General Data Protection Regulation and its United Kingdom counterpart. While it is possible to use PRIPA in a malicious way, the transparency in data collection helps make this more difficult.

P1	Participants are aware of the purpose of the experiment.
P2	Participants are aware of the parameters (web sites, words, time scale) of the data collection.
P3	The features of interest (words, statistical measurements, excerpts) are described in an intelligible way for the participants.
P4	Participants are aware of their right to anonymity.
P5	Participants can consult their data before it is shared with the researchers.
P6	Participants can decide to exclude selected results from the data that is shared with the researchers.
P7	Participants can decide to withdraw completely from a study at any time.
P8	If participants omit to remove personally identifiable information, the researchers should remove it before long-term storage of the data.

Table 1: Key design principles of PRIPA

Principle 1: Lawfulness, Fairness and Transparency According to the first principle of GDPR, a service provider must specify a legal basis in order to collect data. PRIPA only collect data which are specific to an analysis which is agreed to by a participant. Additionally, PRIPA enforces the asking of consent from the user at multiple stages of the analysis, as well as allows a finer-grained control of which datapoints reach the central server. Items 1, 2, 3, 4, 6 and 7 from Table 1 correspond to this principle.

Principle 2: Purpose limitation The linguistic analysis is defined before the collection of the data; purpose limitation is built into PRIPA's core.

Principle 3: Data minimisation According to the third principle of GDPR, a service provider must only collect data that is adequate and limited to the claimed purpose of the system. The data to be collected being defined as part of the experiment, data minimisation is another core principle of PRIPA.

Principle 4: Accuracy By allowing participants to consult their data and choose which datapoint to communicate to the researchers, and by allowing participants to remove their data post collection, PRIPA allows the information to remain accurate. Items 4, 5, 6, 7, 8 from Table 1 correspond to this principle.

Principle 5: Storage limitation The fifth principle of GDPR states that the service provider must not store data for longer than needed for the claimed purpose. This is not enforced in software, but the fact that PRIPA is integrated with the Microsoft Office 365 back-end for storage of results makes it easy to set data storage policies.

Principle 6: Integrity and confidentiality By being integrated in the Microsoft Office 365 back-end for data storage, it is easy to enforce a higher level of security and protect whatever personal data was collected.

Principle 7: Accountability (UK GDPR) The United Kingdom's version of GDPR contains a seventh principle: accountability. The principle of accountability requires the service provider to take responsibility of the way personal data is used, and have appropriate measures and records to be able to demonstrate compliance. Much like principle 6, being tied to the Office 365 ecosystem means that existing systems for limiting the use of data and logging access to those datasets can be used out of the box.

2.2. Data collection process

PRIPA collects 3 types of linguistic information:

Word frequencies Word frequencies are the raw number of occurrences for words in a specific word list, defined as part of the experiment. The word list is specific to the experiment and as such a participant that does not want to share a specific word frequency needs to withdraw from the experiment in order to preserve the integrity of the data without violating their privacy.

Collocates Collocates are pairs of words of interest (defined in a word list as part of the experiment) along with their strength of association, given a pre-specified window of words. The list of word pairs is specific to the experiment, and, like word frequencies, a participant that does not want to share a specific word pair needs to withdraw from the experiment.

Concordance lines Concordance lines are lines of text showing the context for a particular word, along with the source of that line. The size of the context is specified in the experiment, and the participant can review the list of concordance lines and exclude the ones they do not want to share.

2.3. Architecture and design

PRIPA is built in a client-server architecture, where the server hosts experiments which are defined in a specific format using JSON syntax[2]. Figure 1 describes the format. The query allows for six big types of parameters: (1) the title of the study, (2) meta-instructions which apply for the entire experiment and contain details about the way text is meant to be processed (e.g., punctuation, casing, etc.), (3) an allow list which specifies which websites need to be observed

2.3.1. Client-side data collection

The client of the application sits in a plug-in for Chromium-based Web browsers (e.g., Google Chrome, Microsoft Edge). We make use of the JavaScript regular expression engine in order to process word lists which are downloaded from the experiment server. Once the user selects an experiment they would like to take part in and accept the disclaimers regarding the way their data will be processed and how they can access/modify/remove it, the PRIPA extension downloads an experiment specification file and watches for the opening or closing of specific websites (depending on the specification of the experiment). When such action (open/close) is triggered, PRIPA attempts to extract the core of the webpage by ignoring banner ads and other informational noise, and runs the analysis based on the word lists provided in the experiment file. The data is stored in the Web browser itself, never leaving the participant's device until they have decided to share their data with the researcher.

[2]a lightweight data-interchange format documented at `https://www.json.org`

Monitoring on tab open/close Being able to collect data on either the opening or the closing of a tab/window is an important distinction for linguistic analysis. Since some websites dynamically load data based on user input (e.g., Twitter feed, Facebook messages), collecting data at opening would not be effective. Collecting data at close allows for more flexibility in the data collection process by asking participants, for example, to scroll through a month of Twitter feed before closing the tab to start the analysis.

2.3.2. Server-side aggregation

The statistical measures collected by PRIPA can be aggregated after the fact. Word frequency can be aggregated with a simple sum, and collocate strength is measured using pointwise mutual information (Bouma, 2009) which can be aggregated using simple frequency measures and information about document length. Considering that the Pointwise Mutual Information of two words w_1 and w_2 in a document d can be computed as $PMI(w_1, w_2, d) = log(\frac{P_d(w_1,w_2)}{P_d(w_1)\cdot P_d(w_2)})$ and that $P_d(w) = \frac{\text{freq}(w)}{|d|}$ where $|d|$ is the length of document d, we only need to communicate individual and joint word frequencies as well as length of the web pages in order to aggregate that measure over all participants.

2.3.3. Consent monitoring

In order for PRIPA to adhere to the principles laid out in the beginning of the project, consent of the participants needs to be monitored at regular intervals when user data is manipulated. This is done at the following stages:

During the enrolment stage The first stage of consent is whether the participant wants to enrol in the experiment.

During the activation stage The second stage of consent is whether the participant accepts the collection of data from their device. Participants are asked to explicitly enable the data collection, which will start the monitoring of a specific and explicit set of websites. By explicitly enabling this monitoring, participants are informed that they can disable it at any moment.

During the review stage When reviewing concordance lines, participants can choose to exclude specific data points they do not want to share by simply disabling a checkbox, as shown in Figure 2. A number representing the percentage of data censored by the participant is communicated in the results, so that the researcher can make an informed decision about whether to consider this data point.

At the submission stage As shown in Figure 3, when submitting results to the researchers participants are asked to consent to the process of sending their data, and can instead opt to stop the experiment and delete their data.

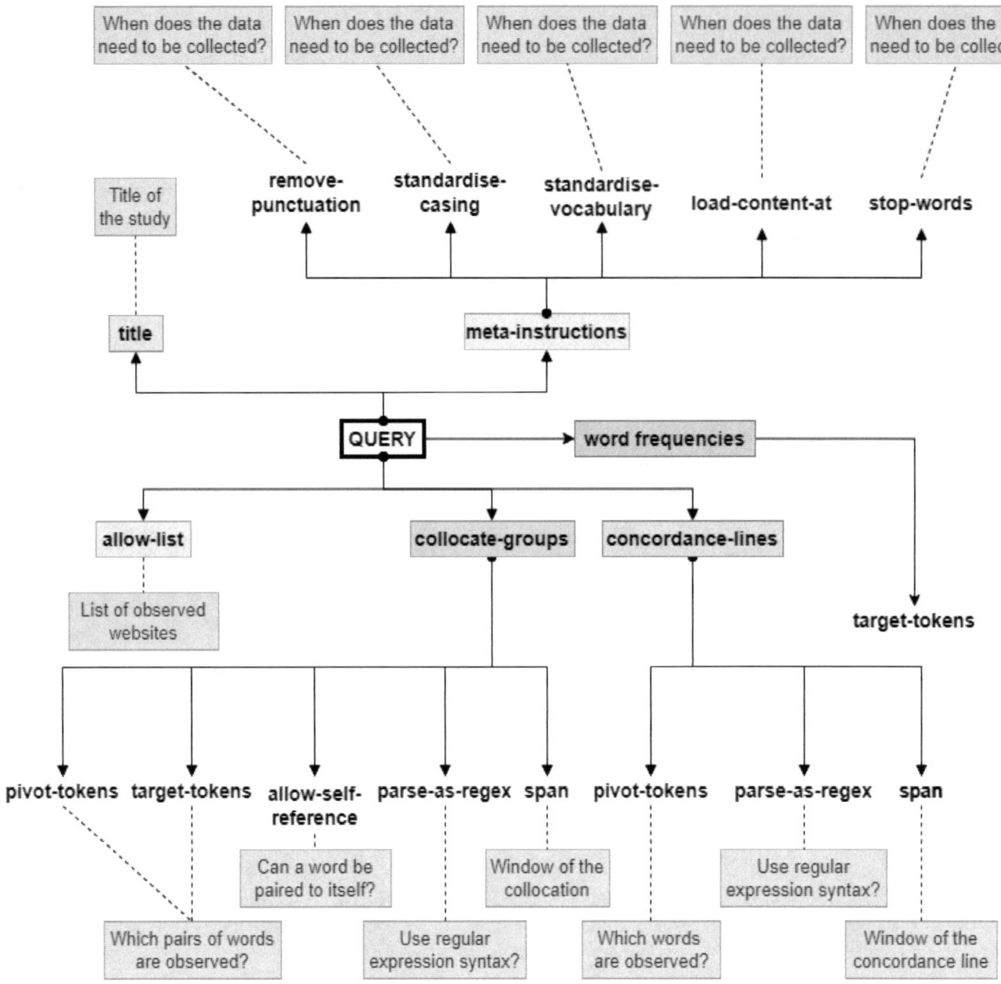

Figure 1: A graphical representation of the experiment file format

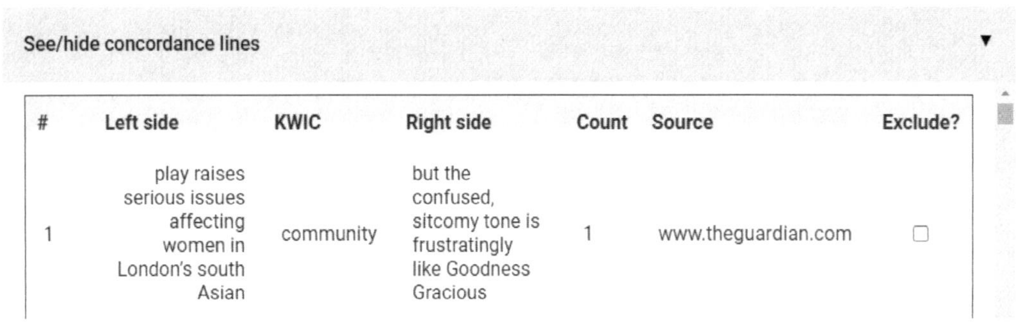

Figure 2: Interface allowing participants to remove individual datapoints

3. Evaluation and results

We evaluated our system in a three-pronged approach:

Accuracy of word counting As pointed out by Anthony (2013), corpus linguistics applications often differ in their measurements due to having different standards in the way they process text. For example, some software would break "We'll" into two word tokens, while some would keep it as a singular word token. Small variations, repeated over large corpora, can lead to vastly different linguistic measurements and affect interpretation. As such, we calibrated our measurement so that it is close to standard tools such as

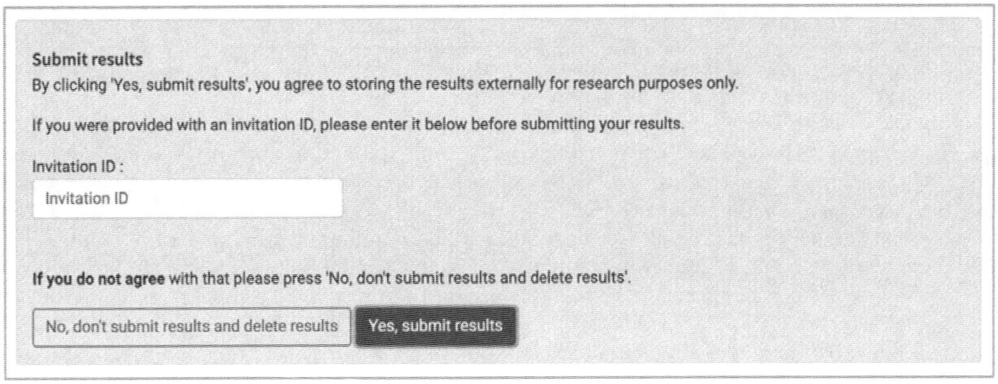

Figure 3: Interface allowing participants to confirm submission of their results, or delete them from the browser

	PRIPA	AntConc	LancsBox
may	33	34	33
might	16	16	15
must	15	15	15
should	29	29	29
would	39	39	39
could	30	30	30
can	93	98	91
will	126	126	125
shall	0	0	0
ought to	0	0	0
total	**381**	**353**	**377**

Table 2: Comparative analysis of PRIPA, AntConc and LancsBox on term frequency of modal verbs on a selected corpus (coloured cells indicate identical counts).

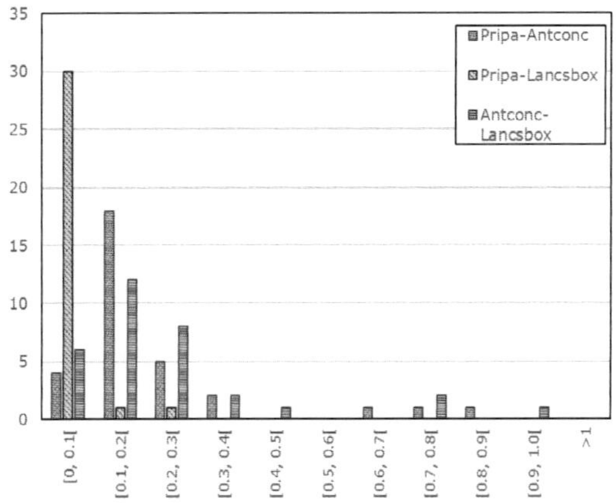

Figure 4: Histogram of differences between PRIPA, AntConc and LancsBox in calculating strength of association between collocates on a sample corpus. Difference between LancsBox and AntConc also provided for baseline.

AntConc (Anthony, 2005) and LancsBox (Brezina et al., 2018). We designed a set of test web pages with minimal noise and hosted them on a university website, analysing them both offline with AntConc and LancsBox and online through PRIPA.

In Table 2 we show a comparison of frequencies of single words when running a study on modal verbs on a pre-selected corpus. We can observe that counts mostly match. A visual inspection determined that readings which were not matching were due to tokenisation differences when handling punctuation and apostrophes.

In Figure 4 we show a comparative histogram of the differences between measurements of collocation strength between PRIPA, AntConc, and LancsBox on an experiment measuring collocation strength between modal verbs and pronouns. We can see from this graph that out of our samples, most measurements fell within $[0, 0.2[$ of LancsBox and $[0, 0.3[$ of AntConc. A visual inspection showed that the readings that did not match were due to tokenisation differences, like with standard term frequencies.

Usability of the software Since participants are rarely researchers themselves, it is important that the software produced is adapted for laypeople and general non-experts. To test this, we ran a usability questionnaire with a small participant involvement panel of 6 people. The quantitative results of the study are summarised in Table 3.

We can see from the data that most participants felt confident in using PRIPA, but had a difficult time understanding the goal of the application. This raises the issue of the importance of a clear user interface and shows that PRIPA can be improved with respect to its first key design principle: participants are aware of the purpose of the experiment. Additionally, we note from the quantitative data reported in Table 3 as well as from qualitative data collected during the same survey that participants were concerned about the privacy of their data. This is partly explained due to the permission model of Chrome-based extensions, which require ask-

	Question	Median
Q1	I think that I would like to use this extension frequently.	3
Q2	I found it difficult to understand what the extension does.	4
Q3	I found it easy to set up and run the project in the extension.	4.5
Q4	I think that I would need the support of a technical person to be able to use this extension	1.5
Q5	I found the analyses and results were clearly explained in the extension	2.5
Q6	I felt very confident using this extension	4
Q7	I would imagine that most people would learn to use this extension very quickly	3.5
Q8	I am concerned about the privacy and security of my personal data (i.e., who may be able to access my personal information and how it is protected) when using the extension	2.5

Table 3: Usability questionnaire given to 6 participants - Median value of the Likert data (1 = strongly disagree, 5 = strongly agree).

ing the participants access to their entire browsing experience and them trusting that we will filter only the websites and the data that is stated in the experiment details. Recent updates in the Chrome permission models allow for fine-grained website permissions at runtime and therefore that problem will soon be patched out of PRIPA.

In-depth study of health communication In order to evaluate our tool in the field, we ran a study of health communication from the British government during the COVID-19 pandemic. We defined a list of websites of interest based on an empirical study of the most visited news websites in the UK, on which to carry out a pilot study to examine modality markers surrounding key terms from health messages (e.g., "mask", "vaccine", "lockdown", and more). Results from our study shows that PRIPA allows us to access language data from the perspective of the people consuming it. However, it also highlighted a weakness of PRIPA in that when dealing with communication-oriented web applications such as Twitter direct messages or Facebook Messenger, it cannot differentiate between language being produced by the participant and language being consumed. Such information would be useful from a linguistic perspective and will therefore be added in future versions of PRIPA.

4. Conclusion

In this paper we present PRIPA, an early prototype of a new family of corpus linguistics tools that allow for collecting personal data in a privacy-preserving way. PRIPA is an early prototype and therefore a work in progress, but its development raised a number of questions and helped us uncover a set of research directions and good practices for a more trustworthy privacy-preserving type of linguistic analysis.

5. Acknowledgements

This research is funded by the Arts and Humanities Research Council (AHRC), grant reference AH/V015125/1 supported by the Horizon Digital Economy Research Institute. The authors would like to thank Tino Tom for his work on the initial prototype browser plugin, on which PRIPA is based.

6. References

Anthony, L. (2005). Antconc: design and development of a freeware corpus analysis toolkit for the technical writing classroom. In *IPCC 2005. Proceedings. International Professional Communication Conference, 2005.*, pages 729–737. IEEE.

Anthony, L. (2013). A critical look at software tools in corpus linguistics. *Linguistic Research*, 30(2):141–161.

Bouma, G. (2009). Normalized (pointwise) mutual information in collocation extraction. *Proceedings of GSCL*, 30:31–40.

Brezina, V., Timperley, M., and McEnery, A. (2018). # lancsbox v. 4. x.

McClaughlin, E., Nichele, E., Adolphs, S., Barnard, P., Clos, J., Knight, D., McAuley, D., Aydt, M., Tom, T., and Lang, A. (2022). Privacy preserving corpus linguistics: Investigating the trajectories of public health messaging online. Technical report.

Mozilla. (2022). Mozilla Rally. `https://rally.mozilla.org`. permanent URL hosted at `https://perma.cc/U9TU-N2XV`.

Noble, A., Cohen, G., Crowcroft, J., Gascón, A., Oswald, M., and Sasse, A. (2019). Protecting Privacy in Pracice: the current use, development and limits of Privacy Enhancing Technologies in data analysis. Technical report, The Royal Society.

The Legal and Ethical issues Workshop @LREC2022, pages 79–83
Marseille, 20 June 2022

Legal and Ethical Challenges in Recording Air Traffic Control Speech

Mickaël Rigault*[1], Claudia Cevenini*[2], Khalid Choukri[1], Martin Kocour[3], Karel Veselý[3], Jan Černocký[3], Igor Szoke[4], Petr Motlíček[5], Juan Zuluaga-Gomez[5], Alexander Blatt[6], Dietrich Klakow[6], Allan Tart[7], Pavel Kolčárek[8],

European Language Resources Association[1], Romagna Tech[2], Brno University of Technology[3], Replaywell[4], Idiap Research Institute[5], Saarland University[6], OpenSky Network[7], Honeywell[8].

9 rue des Cordelières, 75013 Paris, France[1] ; Romagna Tech, Corso Giuseppe Garibaldi 49, Forli 47121, Italy[2] ; Brno University of Technology, 61200 Brno, Czech Republic[3] ; Replaywell, 61200 Brno, Czech Republic[4]; Idiap, 1920 Martigny, Switzerland[5]; Saarland University, 66123 Saarbrücken, Germany[6]; OpenSky Network, 3400 Burgdorf Switzerland[7]; Honeywell, 62700 Brno, Czech Republic[8]

mickael@elda.org, claudia.cevenini@studiocevenini.it*(corresponding authors), choukri@elda.org, ikocour@fit.vutbr.cz, iveselyk@fit.vutbr.cz, szoke@replaywell.com, motlicek@idiap.ch, juan-pablo.zuluaga@idiap.ch, tt@lsv.uni-saarland.de, dklakow@lsv.uni-saarland.de, tart@opensky-network.org, l.kolcarek@honeywell.com, cernocky@fit.vut.cz.

Abstract

In this paper the authors discuss the various legal and ethical issues faced during the ATCO2 (Automatic Transcription and Collection of Air Traffic Control) project. This project has received funding from the Clean Sky 2 Joint Undertaking (JU) under grant agreement No 864702 and support from the European Union's Horizon 2020 programme.

This project is aimed at developing tools to automatically collect and transcribe air traffic conversations, especially conversations between pilots and air controls towers.

The authors will develop issues related to intellectual property, public data, privacy, and general ethics issues related to the collection of air-traffic control speech.

Keywords: Speech, Air Traffic Control, Intellectual Property, Public Data, GDPR, Ethics

1. Definition of Air-Traffic Control Conversations

The aim of the ATCO2 project is to develop a unique platform allowing to collect, organize and pre-process air-traffic control. According to Wikipedia[1], Air Traffic Control (ATC) is a service provided by ground-based air traffic controllers. Its purpose is to prevent collisions and organize the flow of air traffic. It is usually provided by Air Navigation Service Providers (ANSP) or Air Traffic Services Providers (ATSP) in defined sections of the airspace.

In general terms, the airspace is highly regulated by international conventions such as the Convention on International Civil Aviation[2] (known as the Chicago Convention) whose goal is to promote collaboration in the management of the airspace. This convention led to the inception of the International Civil Aviation Organisation, which is directed by 193 governments within the organization of the United Nations.

However, after reading the terms of this Convention and its various annexes we did not manage to find out a single regulation either allowing or disallowing the recording of Air Traffic Control Conversations.

Without specific international regulation we therefore had to turn to national legislations and more general legal concepts to try to define a legal status fitting for Air Traffic Control Conversations.

2. Air Traffic Control Conversation as IP protected material

The first hypothesis we looked at was to consider Air Traffic Control Conversations as material that may be protected by intellectual property rights.

The reason for doing so was that we could think that either ANSP or air companies may have some rights over the conversations in which their employees partake during ATC.

Therefore, the first thing we considered was the protectability of these conversations under basic concepts of Intellectual Property Protection.

2.1 Originality of Air Traffic Control conversation

When considering whether Air Traffic Control Conversations recordings can be defined as original material capable of being protected under intellectual property principles, we need to figure out whether they meet the threshold of originality which is essential in major legal systems to grant creations legal protection

2.2 Originality under US Law

Under Section 102(a) of the US Copyright Act, copyright protection is granted to a list of original works of authorship including in sound recordings.

The United States Supreme Court decided in its landmark case, *Feist Publications, Inc v. Rural Telephone Service*

[1] https://en.wikipedia.org/wiki/Air_traffic_control

[2] https://www.icao.int/publications/Documents/7300_cons.pdf

Co., Inc.[3], that copying of telephone listing without a license did not constitute a copyright infringement.

The Court held that copyright protection necessitates "*independent creation plus a modicum of creativity*" and that facts in themselves are not original and thus are not copyrightable. The Court also decided that compilation of facts however may be original since the author may choose the facts to include, and the arrangement of these facts to allow readers to use those facts.

2.2.1 Originality under EU Law

In the European Union, the Courts have been at the forefront of the definition of the originality criteria.

In two cases the European Court of Justice provided for further details to the definition of originality necessary to pass the threshold of copyright protection.

In *Infopaq International A/S v. Danske Dagblades Forening*[4], a media monitoring company provided summaries of articles published in Danish Newspaper to its customers thanks to a "data capture process" without authorisation. In its judgment, the court held that copyright apply only in relation to a subject matter which is original in the sense that it is the "author's own intellectual creation" (Rec. 37). The author's creativity can express itself through the choice, sequence, and combination of words.

In *Football Association Premier League et al v QC Leisure et al. and Karen Murphy v Media Protection Services Ltd.*[5], certain public places located in the United Kingdom used foreign decoder devices and cards to allow them to receive broadcasts of the English Football Premier League from other EU countries. The Football Association Premier League viewed these activities as harmful for their activities as it undermined the territorial exclusivity of broadcasting rights they grant to a certain territory.

In this context, the Court ruled that football matches were not classifiable as copyright protected works under the Copyright Directive[6], since the rules to the game leave no room for creative freedom (Rec. 98).

2.2.2 Characteristics of ATC Speech

During the ATCO2 project, we observed that ATC speech bore certain characteristics that led us to think that these conversations do not meet the threshold of originality required to be considered as such as protected by Intellectual Property.

The first thing is that air-traffic conversations are broadcast in the airspace, which is part of the public domain. Indeed, it is fairly known that there are community of enthusiasts listening or recording to ATC speech.

Moreover, the conversations held in that context must respect a strict phraseology to ensure proper communication between the parties, for an example refer to the guide published by Eurocontrol, the association of European ANSPs[7].

Finally, the conversation must be made in a purely utilitarian fashion and do not require the controllers or the pilots to perform any sort of choice on the words they use since they must communicate exact information to each other.

Therefore, we can assume that ATC Speech as such cannot be considered Intellectual property material that can be appropriated by either the companies, the ANSPs or the pilots.

2.3 ATC Databases

Even if we can exclude ATC speech as protectable in essence, we thought that the collection of ATC speech in databases may be protected.

Both in US and European Law, collections of works are protected respectively by Section 103 of the Copyright Act and by the Directive on the legal protection of databases[8].

In both legislation databases are defined as collections of independent works or information. In this regard it is the effort made by the producer to compile the database to arrange the data and do not extend to the data itself.

Therefore, we thought that ANSPs may have in their possession databases of recordings of ATC speech. However, after contacting some private ANSPs it appeared that they were not willing to license the rights to use those databases for our purposes.

As example, as detailed in Section 3.2. we tried to contact the National Air Traffic Service which operates in the United Kingdom. However, during our e-mail exchanges with them to try to obtain their records of air-traffic conversations, they declared that they only made available these records upon receipt of a Court order. This would hint that they would have such databases but we could not obtain any detail regarding the extent of these databases.

That is why we tried to figure out a way to obtain the data without asking licenses to ANSPs, leading to our next hypothesis.

3. ATC as public data

Our final hypothesis was to consider ATC speech as public data. This hypothesis rests in the fact that in most cases Air Traffic is considered as a public service which is performed by service providers providing this service under different legal forms.

---

[3] *Feist Publications, Inc v. Rural Telephone Service Co., Inc., 499 U.S. 340*

[4] *Infopaq International A/S v. Danske Dagblades Forening C-5/08*

[5] *Football Association Premier League et al v QC Leisure et al. and Karen Murphy v Media Protection Services Ltd. C-403/08*

[6] Directive (EU) 2001/29/EC on the harmonisation of certain aspects of copyright and related rights in the information society

[7] https://www.easa.europa.eu/sites/default/files/dfu/EGAST_Radiotelephony-guide-for-VFR-pilots.pdf

[8] Directive 96/9/EC on the legal protection of databases

3.1 Public Sector Information Directive

The European Union provides for a harmonized framework for the access and reuse of Public Sector Information (PSI)[9]. This Directive provides for rules facilitating the collection and re-use of documents produced by public sector actors.

This Directive provides that documents produced by public authorities, public enterprises, and other public bodies can be reused by third parties for commercial or non-commercial purposes upon request.

- France

We had a look at France as one of the major countries where the collection is to take place.

Relying on the provisions of the national rules related to the reuse of public sector information we made a request to the "Direction Générale de l'Aviation Civile" (General Directorate for Civil Aviation), which is the public administration in charge of managing French airspace.

In our request we detailed the data that we wanted to obtain as well as the piece of legislation we relied upon to get the data (here Article L.311-1). In the absence of reply we made an appeal to the French "Commission d'Accès aux Documents Administratifs" (Access to Administrative Documents Commission) (CADA). In its opinion number 20205215, the Commission declared that recording controls are public documents and therefore can be communicated to applicants.

However, in its reply to the Commission the DGAC stated that there was no automatic method to differentiate between civilian and military conversations. Moreover, it was added that the conversations would allow to identify the speakers.

Therefore, it was decided that communicating those recordings would pose a threat to national security and privacy, which are valid concerns to withhold communications of public documents under section L.311-5 and L.311-6 of the "Code des Relations entre le Public et l'Administration" (Relations between the Public and the Administrations Code)

3.2 Freedom of Information Legislations

In the United States, the framework rests upon the right to be informed and has been implemented through the Freedom of Information Act[10] (FOIA)

This legislation compels federal agencies to provide copies of all records produced by the agency upon request. However, the applicant makes its request in accordance with the requirements of the agency.

In the following we will go through some of the use case that we encountered during the project for specific countries.

- United States

To obtain records from the United States, we submitted a request under the FOIA to the Federal Aviation Authority (FAA).

We submitted a request for Air traffic records as is made look possible on the website[11]. However, in our following exchanges with the FAA we found out that we had to provide for specific zones to pull the request (either via latitude and longitude or air traffic control centres.

In the follow up of our exchanges we also found out that surveillance data (radar track data) was kept for a long period of time. Nevertheless, it was indicated to us that conversations were kept only for a period of 45 days before being erased unless necessary for security reasons.

- United Kingdom and New Zealand

When we looked at the British legislation, we faced a major legal block. Indeed, the Wireless Telegraphy Act[12] provides in Section 48 that the use of devices to intercept and disclose information relative to the content of a message sent by wireless telegraphy (i.e. radio communications) constitutes a criminal offence.

We also tried to contact the National Air Traffic Service who is United Kingdom's Air Navigation Service Providers, however it refused to make its records available in application of the provisions of the United Kingdom Freedom of Information Act, or the Re-Use of Public Sector Information Regulation which implement the PSI Directive in UK Law.

In New Zealand we also faced a similar block. The section 133A of the Radiocommunications Act prohibits to reproduce and publish the existence of the conversations held in the context of air traffic.

4. Protection of personal data

ATC voice recordings are strongly standardised and concern flight-related issues; thus, they may rarely contain the mentioning of personal data.

This, however, cannot be *a priori* excluded in absolute terms, and even in the absence of personal information, data protection related issues would need to be investigated.

4.1 Applicability of data protection laws

Personal data processing according to Reg. (EU) 2016/679 (GDPR) is a very broad concept. It refers to any action performed to pieces of information, which may – directly or indirectly – identify a person.

Even if there is the slightest chance of processing personal data, then all applicable legal requirements for ethical and legal compliance should be met.

---

[9] Directive 1019/1024/EU on open data and the reuse of public sector information

[10] 5. U.S. Code, §552 available at https://www.justice.gov/sites/default/files/oip/legacy/2014/07/23/foia-final.pdf

[11] https://www.faa.gov/foia/foia_coordinators/ato_service_centers/?section=ato_request

[12] https://www.legislation.gov.uk/ukpga/2006/36/contents

There exist some exceptions that may exempt some data processing in the field of recording air traffic conversations such as the ones detailed below:

- Household exception

ATC voice recordings are often taken by individual enthusiasts, who listen to conversations between airplanes and control towers and can share them on dedicated online platforms.

The GDPR does not apply whenever personal data are processed by a natural person during a purely personal or household activity, without a connection with a commercial or professional activity.

This could include correspondence and the holding of addresses, or social networking and online activity undertaken within the context of such activities.

However, one thing is recording and listening privately to ATC records, a different thing is sharing the recordings with an indefinite number of persons.

In any case, regardless of the applicability of the GDPR, it should be remembered that any activity, even if carried out for purely personal and household purposes, should never cause any damage to third parties.

- Protection of threats to public security

We can also exclude the processing of personal data that is carried out by the ANPSs. We feel they can be excluded on the grounds of an exception. This exception provides that the GDPR is not applicable to processing activities linked to the prevention of threats to public security.

It is not difficult to see how the security of airspace can be closely linked to public security and that recordings of air traffic conversations are necessary to ensure the safety of passengers.

However, this may not apply to the data collected by some of the partners involved in this project therefore as a safety measure we can apply the principles of data protection.

- Use of non-personal data

Researchers could freely use anonymous, non-identifying data. Thus, adopting anonymisation techniques would be an interesting option to be explored.

We may think of solutions that would directly anonymise speech of the air traffic controllers and pilots without degrading the safety of airspace while also maintaining the confidentiality of the speakers involved.

While we did not manage to find implementations of such methods for air traffic control. We feel that any processing of air traffic control conversations imposes the compliance with the legal obligations imposed by GDPR.

4.2 General principles of data protection

When dealing with personal data, the GDPR provides for a whole set of obligations upon the controller of the data who performs the processing of the data.

There are two overarching principles that guide how the data are supposed to be handled by controllers. The first one is a principle of accountability which let rests the responsibility of the processing activities on the controller.

The second principle is one of "privacy by design and by default". According to this principle, controllers are obliged to think about the privacy of the users from the design of the processing and make sure that it is protected from the beginning of the project and at every step.

This in turn is turned into a set of principles that are applicable to any type of processing activities (lawfulness of processing, transparency, data minimisation, purpose limitation, storage limitation, integrity and confidentiality)

The use of pseudonymisation techniques, could be very useful in this sense as they can be regarded as a security measure. Pseudonymised data are in fact still personal data, even if only indirectly identifying.

4.3 Voiceprints and handling of biometric data

Even if recordings contained no personal data at all, they would however have to be managed with caution: voiceprints are biometric data, like a fingerprint.

Not only are they potentially identifying, but they would fall within the "special categories" of data when used to uniquely identify a person.

In this regard they are to be processed only if certain conditions are met. During the project we identified three provisions from Article 9 GDPR that could help provide a legal basis for processing.

- Explicit consent from the data subject
- Processing related to data manifestly made public by the data subject
- Processing necessary for reasons of substantial public interest

From a data protection perspective, biometric technologies, in general, are closely linked to specific physical, physiological, behavioural or even psychological characteristics of a person, and some of them might also reveal sensitive data.

As to the voice, biometrics may concern the analysis of the tone, pitch, cadence and frequency of a person's voice, which can make it possible to determine if a certain person is who he/she declares to be, or the identity of an unknown person, if matched with data from other databases.

Biometric data may also allow for automated tracking, tracing or profiling of persons and, as such, their potential impact on the privacy and the right to data protection of individuals is high, as also observed by the EU data protection authorities.

Moreover, biometric data are irrevocable: a breach concerning biometric data threatens the further safe use of biometrics as identifier and the right to data protection of the concerned persons for which there is no possibility to mitigate the effects of the breach.

5. Conclusions and further work

Future work may include a thorough analysis of the European framework with a specific analysis of the local legislation regarding the availability of Air Traffic Control speech under open data regulations.

As well as an in-depth investigation into the exceptions granted to processing of sensitive data for reasons of public interest as well as their transcription into national legislations.

6. Acknowledgements

The ATCO2 project has received funding from the Clean Sky 2 Joint Undertaking (JU) under grant agreement No 864702. The JU receives support from the European Union's Horizon 2020 research and innovation programme and the Clean Sky 2 JU members other than the Union.

The Legal and Ethical issues Workshop @LREC2022, pages 84–91
Marseille, 20 June 2022

It is not Dance, is Data: Gearing Ethical Circulation of Intangible Cultural Heritage practices in the Digital Space

Jorge P. Yánez [1,2], **Amel Fraisse** [2]
[1] Ghent University, S:PAM - IPEM [2] Univ. Lille, ULR 4073 - GERiiCO
[1]Campus Technicum, Building 4, 2nd floor, B-9000 Ghent, Belgium. [2]F-59000 Lille, France
[1]jorge.povedayanez@ugent.be, [2]amel.fraisse@univ-lille.fr

Abstract

The documentation, protection and dissemination of Intangible Cultural Heritage (ICH) in the digital age pose significant theoretical, technological and legal challenges. Through a multidisciplinary lens, this paper presents new approaches for collecting, documenting, encrypting and protecting ICH-related data for more ethical circulation. Human-movement recognition technologies such as motion capture, allows for the recording, extraction and reproduction of human movement with unprecedented precision. The once indistinguishable or hard-to-trace reproduction of dance steps between their creators and unauthorized third parties becomes patent through the transmission of embodied knowledge, but in the form of data. This new battlefield prompted by digital technologies only adds to the disputes within the creative industries, in terms of authorship, ownership and commodification of body language. For the sake of this paper, we are aiming to disentangle the various layers present in the process of digitisation of the dancing body, to identify its by-products as well as the possible arising ownership rights that might entail. "Who owns what?", the basic premise of intellectual property law, is transposed, in this case, onto the various types of data generated when intangible cultural heritage, in the form of dance, is digitised through motion capture and encrypted with blockchain technologies.

Keywords: intangible cultural heritage, digitization, dance data

1. Introduction

The mutually correspondent dyad of dance and language and its cross-pollinating nature has illuminated the study of both phenomena in academic discourses. Eastern-European ethno-choreologists have focused on disclosing the implicit existent grammar in each dance idiom (Giurchescu and Torp, 1991). And as early as the sixties, Martin and Pesovár (1961) already employed the methodologies of linguistics to perform structural analysis of Hungarian folk dances. In the US., the usage of linguistic-based approaches to illuminate the intricacies of dance can be traced to Kaeppler (1972), who went as far as drawing analogies from phonemes and morphemes to build equivalent analytical units for dance like kinemes and morphokines. In (Hanna, 2001), the author frames dance as a form of language, because of its communicative affordances and its capacity to transmit emotions as well as ideas that range from very concrete to very abstract. Regarding the so-called hard-sciences, different experiments and metrics revitalizing the premise of the 'motor theory of perception' keep linking the mental simulation of bodily movements as the basis for any kind of cognitive operation, ranging from very conceptual tasks to the perception of language (Liberman and Mattingly, 1985). As Godoy (2009) remarks, with the advent of brain imaging techniques, there now seems to be solid evidence in support of the idea of motor involvement in language perception (Luciano Fadiga and Rizzolatti, 2002). It is within this interdisciplinary matrix that dance and movement practices make their entrance into the digital space(s) on the XXI century, but this incursion only spawns never-before-seen tensions regarding creativity, reproduction and embodiment as well as the intellectual property laws that protect them.

We have come a long way since the lawsuits of "Image rights VS free speech in video game" or the "Lindsay Lohan VS Rockstar games" for the alleged misuse of the identity of celebrities and performers in the form of 3D renderings for video- gaming platforms. After a pandemic that has pushed people to abandon the physical dance-floors and join the metaverse, users and content-creators are these days disputing over the dance steps performed by their virtual avatars. Movements and dance steps that used to convey the embodied skills of performers are now reproduced and sold as pieces of data. This is how online interactive video-game platforms like Fortnite, one of the most successful ones in history, make their revenues. By selling its nearly 350 millions of registered users, short sequences of movements or 'emotes' that allow virtual avatars to dance exactly like their favorite celebrity. The circulation of embodied creativity has made a 180 degree turn. After dismissing the four appeals made in US. Courts by dancers who claimed to have their movements stolen by this software and because of the heated feuds that intellectual property laws seem unsuitable to prevent, we raise in this article alternative ways to protect dance steps, maybe not under the category of 'choreography' but as pieces of data. Since the issue of appropriation of kinetic or choreographic material by unauthorised third parties is both a legal problem and an ethical issue, we deploy and disentangle, over the following sections, the various layers that are unleashed when digitising the human body and the language configured by its movements. We will narrow our focus to two instances, the usage of motion capture recording technologies, as the one employed for digitising sign-language (Jantunen et al., 2012); and secondly the encryption of Non-Fungible Tokens (NFTs) on the Blockchain (Pilkington, 2015; Wood, 2014) associated to dance steps. It is pressing to consider all the digital assets and objects that are created throughout these processes, to then move forward to account for the authorial and ownership-related tensions that stem from them.

2. Intangible Cultural Heritage (ICH)

We find value on the notion of 'intangible cultural heritage' as an analytical label to engage with a set of practices and practitioners in the effort to explore the potential that new human language technologies hold for ethically circulating creative products, as it is precisely collective creativity, the one that is in a heightened state of vulnerability. Herein, we introduce several definitions of the term that help map-out embodied practices, specially in their original form, since, as we will see over the upcoming sections, all kinds of movements get equalized into pieces of data once they enter the digital space.

The UNESCO (2003) convention has defined intangible cultural heritage as "the practices, representations, expressions, knowledge, skills – as well as the instruments, objects, artifacts and cultural spaces associated therewith – that communities, groups and, in some cases, individuals recognise as part of their cultural heritage". According to the same convention, such expressions of ICH can be manifested in the form of:(a) oral traditions and expressions, including language as a vehicle of the intangible cultural heritage; (b) performing arts; (c) social practices, rituals and festive events; (d) knowledge and practices concerning nature and the universe; and (e) traditional craftsmanship.

An analogous definition of ICH can be found in the developments of the World Intellectual Property Organisation (WIPO) under their analytical category of Traditional Cultural Expressions (TCE). Such expressions may comprise pre-existing materials dating from the distant past that were once developed by "authors unknown" through to the most recent and contemporary expressions of traditional cultures, with an infinite number of incremental and evolutionary adaptations, imitations, revitalisations, revivals and recreations in between.

As seen, intangible cultural heritage or traditional cultural expressions both, could be effective categories to frame the embodied creativity of communities who put an accent on transmitting knowledge from one generation to the next, within which, language, oral traditions and performing arts become the more relevant cases to be foregrounded for this study.

2.1. Copyright Issues for Dance as a Digital Object

To address the issue of dances being "stolen" across digital spaces, it is necessary to narrow the scope with the question, "what is it that is being appropriated when a virtual dance is being misused"? And to solve such query, it is necessary to first account for the kind of materials that virtual dance steps or choreographies are made of, when they circulate as digital objects. To illustrate these matters, we are choosing the case of motion capture technologies, which are an efficient and very precise way to digitise the dancing body.

Motion capture has been used for an array of digitisation initiatives that range from sign language (Jantunen et al., 2012) to dance (Romarheim, 2014). Notably, this technology does not register or portray images in the same way that regular video recordings do. On the contrary, faces, bodies and gestures are reduced to coordinates and rudimentary skeletons made out of segments and 3D points against a black background. This very anonymisation of the identities of the four plaintiffs described before in the Fortnite cases, has been enough to extinguish their legal aspirations, since they were all dismissed in court; but paradoxically, it was ineffective at derailing the performers from recognising that their creativity was being taken and sold within the video game in the first place. The four plaintiffs in these cases, could not succeed at obtaining protection for their dances because they were 'too short' for qualifying for copyright protection, which is a constrain in the US not necessarily present in other jurisdictions like France. On the other hand, because their dance steps identified in the software were anonymised by the interchangeable avatars and their customisable 'skins' available on the video game, the dance-related data ended up being obscured and indistinguishable in the eyes of decision-makers, which were unable to see the resemblance claimed between the dancers/plaintiffs and the digital avatars dancing their steps. This is not the first time that courts have difficulties grasping or 'seeing' kinetic material as an object of legal value in itself. During the first half of the XX century, Court Houses in the US, were unable to identify the value of dance, as body language material worthy of copyright protection until a technological development such as Labanotation scores, allowed to render it visible in the form of a written notation to reveal its underlying structure(Kraut, 2009). Such conditions have further reiterated the predominance that written language and musical scores have had over embodied creativity when it comes to obtaining protection from the law as they were already fixed over tangible mediums. Now that digital technologies, such as motion capture, can finally apprehend, reproduce and transcribe dance and movement, the evanescent nature of embodied languages has become tangible at last in the form of data. As such, 'stealing steps' from a video or even by learning it from their creators is a phenomenon of a different scale and strain, if compared to the reproducibility of motion capture data, that used to be 'dance' before being digitised, being transposed to the virtually infinite avatars/bodies of the users of online gaming platforms. The former being an illegal human-to-human operation, given that a copyrighted choreography is involved, and the later being an unethical human-to-avatar one by proxy of the digitisation process.

2.2. The problem of "who is the owner ?"

Misappropriation of dance in the 'real' world of dancers made out of flesh and bone, involved the apprehension of kinetic material embodied by the appropriator. Despite the fact that the misappropriation of dance in the form of motion capture data is manifested in virtual bodies or avatars, one could still trace the movements to human bodies whose labour and creativity engendered the movement at some point. Cultural practices have been in dispute already in relation to the UNESCO promulgated system for the Safeguarding of Intangible Cultural Heritage. As Lixinski (2011) points out, inscription of an element on the representative list does not imply exclusivity or constitute a marker of intellectual property rights. With the advent of the digital era, not only metadata of intangible cultural heritage items are circulating across the digital space, but also representations of the practices in themselves. Further advancing the multi-layered prism of data that is spawned by digitization processes, blockchain technologies are now adding up another 'encrypted' layer of information when dance is being digitized. With its tamper-proof- qualities and authenticating possibilities, blockchain related applications for the documentation and digitization of cultural/artistic expressions are flourishing at light-speed. Besides the practical and innovative uses that all these technologies are making available for the creative industries, the truth is that there is little to no clarity about the entailing rights and consequences that follow the digitisation and 'encryption' of the dancing body, its likeness, its movements and image. The WIPO (2019) report published by the Intergovernmental Committee on Intellectual Property and Genetic Resources, Traditional Knowledge and Folklore raised awareness about how difficult it is for intellectual property laws to prevent collective cultural expressions, such as the one held by indigenous peoples across the globe, from being misappropriated. The impossibility to match transient practices, such as dance, when they are sustained by entire communities of practitioners and the protection that intellectual property laws offer, is the subject of several research works (Karjala and Kirkwood, 2003; Gervais, 2003; Long, 1998; Frankel, 2014; Burri, 2008). Despite the agreement that typically conceived intellectual property regimes are not suitable nor intended to cover transient/oral practices that are collectively transmitted from one generation to the next, the issue gets further complicated when such expressions enter the digital space. For this reason, we synthesize in the following section, the complexities around the data produced through motion capture recordings and the blockchain, based on the digitisation of embodied practices, in an effort to start deploying and clearing the new tensions that arise in relation to intellectual property.

2.3. Digitisation and Protection of ICH Data

Several initiatives are currently working to digitise, document and protect human movement that is performed with artistic, ritual, aesthetic, social or religious connotations. The interest behind this archive fever ranges from safeguarding purposes to commercial interests, as will be reviewed over the following lines. With each type of method employed for the digitisation of the human body and its movements, there are not only different possibilities that arise, but also different kinds of data that is engendered, with their correspondent challenges in terms of management, protection, storage, interoperability, and so on. As a matter of fact, objects of a different order arise in the digitisation/tangibilisation of the human body language and its movements: data-sets, assets, files, and encrypted tokens that still need to be reckoned with current intellectual property regimes. As evidence of the profound impact that the seminal texts of Taylor (2003) or Lepecki (2010) have had in the field of the performing arts for reclaiming the epistemic value of movement and performance, there is now a plethora of initiatives devoted to record, abstract, render and reproduce practices related to embodied creativity in the digital space, as proper pieces of embodied knowledge.

2.3.1. Safeguarding initiatives

An example of current projects dealing with the safeguarding of human movement-related practices is "Practicing Odin Teatret's archive: training transmission, interaction and creativity"[1]. Originated as an academic endeavor, the project aims to use new digital technologies to capture the corporeal and vocal training techniques of the members of the iconic company, the "Odin Theatre" of Denmark. The outcome of such digitisation processes is still a work in progress but several VR environments are already on the making, wherein users can train alongside the motion-captured representations of the members of the famous group, that dance, sing and perform right next to them, within digital and immersive spaces. This initiative proposes to create a sustainable model for the development, transmission and distribution of virtually archived theater acting techniques, in which the user becomes in-

[1] https://research.flw.ugent.be/en/projects/practicing-odin-teatrets-archive-training-transmission-interaction-and-creativity

teractively and creatively engaged in the production of knowledge. Similarly, the "Bodies for Empathy Museum" by the Non-Profit Embodying Reconciliation-Colombia is working on developing motion capture-based alternatives for traditional practitioners and communities to digitise their dancing practices in a period marked by the constrains of social isolation. Through a basic motion capture platform that is available on any device, visitants of the Museum are offered the possibility to engage with practices that used to be transmitted physically on one-to-one dynamics, but that now are being extrapolated to the digital space. Projects like this, that are based on the recording, abstraction and reproduction of human-movement through motion capture technologies, are the reverse of video-games like Fortnite since all the performers and actors are consciously participating of the digitisation process of their embodied practices, even though they might employ the same methods and produce the same kinds of data. The 'Terpsichore' project (Anastasios Doulamis, 2017) offers a platform for transforming intangible folkloric performing arts into tangible choreographic digital objects. In the same way, the 'i-Treasures' project (Iris Kico and Liarokapis, 2018) implemented a digital environment for capturing the Intangible Cultural Heritage and Learning the Rare Know-How of Living Human Treasures .

2.3.2. Protecting initiatives

'Protecting' initiatives, as the Intergovernmental Committee on Traditional Knowledge at WIPO has expressed: The word "protection" is understood to mean protection in an IP sense (sometimes referred to as "legal protection"), i.e., protection of human intellectual creativity and innovation against unauthorized use. IP "protection" in this sense is distinguishable from the "safeguarding", "preservation" and "promotion" of cultural heritage (?). Aligned to this aim, the project 'Beauty in the streets' intends to [2] to protect human movement-related practices by 'tokenizing' dance movements and short steps on the Ethereum blockchain. By turning them into NFTs, the project allows performers to sell or circulate their movements as they consider more suitable. Under the same perspective, "Meta-movers" by Dylan Mayoral is an effort to try to gain attribution and stewardship of dance steps, once they start circulating on the metaverse. This initiative involves designing 2D representations of virtual characters performing dance moves that can later be used to mint unique NFTs on the Ethereum blockchain, ready to be sold to collectors and enthusiast of crypto-art. For these last two cases, digitisation strategies of the dancing body go one step further, because on top of recording and reproducing movements for enjoyment, creativity and also profit, the artists behind them are invested in obtaining a degree of ownership over embodied creativity by attaching imperishable certificates of authenticity on the blockchain. Nonetheless, such ownership aspirations are yet to be reckoned with other no-so-cutting-edge frameworks, i.e. intellectual property regimes and related rights.

[2] https://www.beautyinthestreets.com/

3. Our proposition : Between indexicality and commodification

As Auslander (1992) has debated, the issue of disputes of authorship and ownership in the arts is hardly new but its contemporary digital iterations are still waiting to be solved with each generation of creators, consumers, and their corespondent technological affordances and challenges. While walking in this direction it is important to not bring new technologies and possibilities under the restrictive authority of existing legal definitions, which translates into thinking of ethics in-and-out of the law, specially when it comes to intellectual property laws and their spirit of commodification of cultural production. This critical approach towards the premises contained in intellectual property laws does not translate to an animadversion of the possibility to profit from cultural products, should the communities or practitioners behind them render it desirable. In this way, the ideas we raise in the following lines try to grapple with these tensions while recognizing that there are no 'one-size-fits-all' solutions for the issues raised but there are definitely some conclusions that can be raised after the cases and rationale deployed over the previous sections.

3.1. Defining a new Ethical Framework

Stealing someone else's dance steps, specially if they are not protectable under IP law can be done in the 'real world' too. However, the extended reach, fluidity and reproducibility that dance steps (stolen or not) can have in the form of data, as the hundreds of millions of users of platforms like Fortnite bear witness to, should invoke a distinctive treatment. In the same way that ethnographers used to inadvertently win ownership rights over their recordings of folk songs recovered over their fieldwork periods, using motion capture to record the way that someone moves should also be considered as a process worth of discussion and regulation. But since recording, extracting and reproducing the likeness of someone else's movements is not only a legal issue but an ethical one, we propose that in the same way that the GDPR normative regulates the obtention, usage and reproduction of personal data recovered over interviews, motion capture files should be regulated too, specially when salient features or prominent pieces of choreographic material that belongs to an individual or a community are being used for commercial purposes. The field of visibility and power that academic spaces hold wherein researchers and informants hold asymmetric positions, has been already established and discussed but the unequal conditions to enter the digital space(s) to create assets based on human activities such as dance or movement, as well as the distribution of profits that this entails, still needs to be reckoned from an intersectional stance. In the same vein, we raise the possibility of pursuing ownership rights over dances that have been digitised with motion capture, not under the category of 'Choreographic works' that most IP national laws offer, but rather as sets of data protectable through copyright. The result, scope and viability that this would imply are still to be discussed, specially if we consider that dancers themselves very rarely have the access, interest or literacy in these kind of technologies. In other words, recognise the very moment that the corporeal practice of dance is transformed into motion capture data and protect it as such, to try to solve the innovation requirement, which in countries like the US imply the exclusion of dance steps that are 'too short' to be considered worthy of protection. Parallel to the power dynamics mentioned between researcher-informant, the duo animator-dancer also has to be carefully considered, as there is a great risk of well-versed professionals in computerized methods of human movement recording to end up hoarding every dance that enters the digital space in the form of data. As (Brekke and Haase, 2017) signals, computer scientists and tech developers are the new priest caste, "but there is very little awareness of the position of power and influence and very little willingness to accept the responsibilities that come with such a position of power".

In synchronicity to the various and odd intents of choreographers and dancers at the beginning of the XX century to have their craft finally being recognised as worthy of protection by intellectual property techniques, the digitisation of choreographic material could unleash a plethora of new ways to try to gain ownership and stewardship of the resulting data. For example, claiming that a data-set created based off a dance or a human performance should be granted a patent, is an alternative route that could be explored by practitioners around the globe. To support such strategy, it is interesting to recover the provision of Title 35 of the United States Code regarding Patents, which further describes what can be patentable: "First, the invention must be a new and useful process, machine, item of manufacture, or composition(!). The second requirement of your invention that has to be met to get a patent is that it must be non-obvious and reproducible by one skilled in the art."

3.2. Collecting Dance Data through Motion Capture technologies

To disentangle the multiple threads at play in the digitisation of the dancing body, first let us describe the output or the kind of data generated while working on the kinds of digitisation processes that we have narrowed our attention to. When using motion capture technologies to capture and extract movement, the kinetic material or embodied knowledge of the performer is being transformed and recorded as discreet points in a 3D space with coordinates X, Y and Z. Their changing positions are registered as plain numbers that account for the trajectory they travel on the 3 planes. These data sets, that used to be dance steps in their previous form, are usually exported as *.fbx* or *.tsv* files, and can later be re-imported for an infinite number of 3D avatars to perform them across digital spaces, through software packages such as Qualysis. This very possibility of a virtually infinite number of 3D avatars performing the same data extracted from dance steps, was already identified as a key factor preventing Court Houses from recognising any appropriation in cases of unauthorized use of choreographic material. As seen over the Fortnite cases, judges were unable to 'see' what is it that is being misappropriated when Epic Games reproduced the movements of the four plaintiffs on their popular software. Notably, at the official hearing, judges saw virtual avatars performing the dance steps of the plaintiffs under dispute, but given that the software allows for these in-game characters to look like anything from human-size squirrels to robots, the dissonance between the image of the virtual avatars and those of the plaintiffs who claimed to have their moves stolen, was concealing the underlining usage of identical choreographic material. It goes without saying, that such visual inspection of the disputed materials is insufficient as it overlooks the underlying identical reproduction of data, that once was dance steps, being reproduced across different virtual bodies. Particularly because, at the core of the discussions dealing with cases like this, should be the illegitimate reproduction of embodied knowledge, in the form of data, and not the unlawful usage of the likeness of the dancers or performers behind it. This very condition of evaluating data collected based on the movements of human performers, but later 'performed' by seemingly dissimilar virtual avatars, obscures not only the labour and creativity of those who embodied the kinetic material in the first place, but is bracketing and invisibilizing the input and design made by visual-effects creatives as well as computer animators whose work is embedded in these new materials, that mistakenly keep being treated as a regular 'dance' or a 'performance'. This very problem has been already discussed in the context of film studies, when accomplished actor Andy Serki's salient performance as the 'Gollum' in the Lord of the Rings was dismissed by the Oscars, after considering the character as a result of mere animation, instead of the seamless hybridisation of data produced by the human actor, along with the computer-generated images built on top of it by animators. The Gollum problem is one of a series of interrelated scenarios in which digital information derived from a performer is used to create performances, and often performer, with varying degrees of independence from the source.

3.3. Safeguarding Dance Data with Blockchain Technologies

Nonetheless, and even though special attention needs to be granted to the way in which intellectual property systems recognise embodied practices, not all paths of protection of creativity need to rely on governmental authorities or centralized bodies. Herein, we highlight the experimentation that artists are working with within blockchain architectures and their applications. Regarding the blockchain, as a decentralised architecture for encrypted assets, (Greenfield, 2017) describes it rather enthusiastically as a technology that could give people powerful new tools for collective action, unsupervised by the state. Although, it is worth mentioning that the inclusion of a certain creative product on a blockchain platform, by proxy of an Non-fungible Token (NFT), does not equate to gaining copyrights over it, as the World Intellectual Property Organization highlights, it is nevertheless a robust alternative for creators who want to gain a tamper-proof and time-stamped certification of the moment when they 'upload' something onto the blockchain. We foreground these examples as encrypted certificates of authenticity and origin of creative products could work as para-legal strategies to settle disputes of authorship or educate audiences about the 'authentic' creators behind a practice, in the same way that communities of dance practitioners in the 60s used to sustain para-legal or extra-legal stewardship of originality and creativity of dance steps via mutual vigilance (Kraut, 2010). As relevant as such extra-legal strategies could be, they are not exempt of controversy. First, mutual-vigilance and good faith within communities of practitioners can go a long way, until it doesn't. Recognising someone else's authorship or ownership over a creative product, because they hold an NFT which pre-dates use or exploitation by other parties, could be an amicable way to settle misuse or appropriation disputes. However, such encrypted certificates of authenticity and ownership would not stand their ground against an actual copyright registration of the same element of intellectual creativity. In that sense, the law needs to further clarify the value that these new digital assets represent or their harmonisation with regular intellectual property systems. Second, even if the law prompts harmonisation between intellectual property regimes and the possibilities of these new technologies, recognizing the legal value of NFTs to prove authorship and ownership of creative products would not happen without problems, as that would prompt creators to rush into a 'tokenizing race'. In other words, equating holding copyrights or any other intellectual property rights over an element with having an NFT registered on a blockchain connected to it, would embark the creative markets, creators and artists on a race to be the first ones to 'tokenize' cultural expressions. As dystopian as this might sound, projects such as the ones described in the previous section, are already embracing this approach on the quest to 'tokenize' signature dance steps. On the other hand, the summing interest of the creative industries in 'tokenizing' cultural expressions on the blockchain, tend to blur in the gaze of audiences and traders, the different sets of data being produced by these encrypting' strategies, as well as the legal rights they might or might not entail. As exemplified with the aforementioned initiatives, dancers are already intending to increase the degree of ownership and stewardship that they have over the dance steps that they create, maybe in response to the public attention that surrounded the Fortnite cases. What they actually mean when they offer the service of 'tokenizing' a dance step or 'minting' an NFT on the blockchain, is obtaining ERC-721 tokens, whose metadata refers back to the creative product in itself, i.e. the dance steps. Usually these dance steps, or any kind of product being 'tokenized' rests on other digital storage services such as clouds or online repositories. In other words, the dance steps in themselves never really enter the blockchain but only the encrypted certificates that refer to them do. And as Iaconesi (2021) has straightforwardly point out, NFTs are not attached to the actual entities they represent, as we can find NFTs circulating even for the Trevi Fountain of Italy. In this sense, the current craze surrounding NFTs for the exchange of art pieces, along with the possibility of trusted digital evidence of their ownership, is at this point, and until new legal amendments, more of a euphemism. This is not to say that NFTs are not effective and successful, as people are already commodifying and selling their creativity with their help. As a complement, in the next section, we try to articulate the potentialities and shortcomes of the crypto-space with other technologies and systems in the quest for more ethically-minded paths of circulation of embodied creativity across the new digital spaces.

4. Conclusion

Intangible cultural heritage practices, indigenous embodied creativity or dance, as a Western practice, they all hold different aesthetic, cultural and legal statuses; however, once that their are extrapolated to the digital spaces, facilitated by motion capture technologies or blockchain architectures, they are all equalized as data. The conversion of any of these practices of embodied creativity to sets of data needs to be aligned with broader strategies of safeguarding and protection, considering the legal limitations and constrains identified in the stewardship of intangible cultural heritage practices, even in their previous form before any digitisation process. Some initiatives for the digitisation of the dancing body aim to obtain a degree of ownership or stewardship of the related practices, precisely because of the unsuitability of intellectual property regimes to protect embodied knowledge in its manifold manifestations. We have described several lines of work that could articulate different kinds of technologies in-and-out of the law for enhancing the agency that artist have regarding the ways in which their embodied practices circulate. Even though embodied practices can end up being equalized as pieces of data once they are digitized, it is pressing to think of what happens before such incursion on the digital space, what is necessary to do so, or if even that is the path that marginalised communities of practitioners want for their own intangible cultural heritage practices. On top of discussing the issue of the potentialities and shortcomings of new technologies of human-movement recognition, accessibility issues need to be reckoned as well. Indigenous communities and other communities of traditional practitioners could end up on a double state of vulnerability, both by not being able to be granted protection for their practices by intellectual property laws, neither benefiting from the para-legal strategies of protection and safeguarding that new technologies could afford. Finally, and as an extension of the scope of this paper, it would be relevant to differentiate the legal regimes from one country to another, to identify the consequences that would entail obtaining actual protection for short sequences of movement as the ones involved in the Fortnite cases, in terms of the extent of such protection. Complementary to this, further attention needs to be paid to the ramifications of protecting dance as data, in terms on the kind of limitations that such approach would entail for other practitioners within the metaverse, and even more intriguingly, for those physical dancers that want to replicate the steps underlining such sets of data, in the 'real world'.

5. Acknowledgements

This project is co-financed by the Research Foundation Flanders (FWO) under the Fundamental Research scheme, file number 91950.

6. Bibliographical References

Anastasios Doulamis, Athanasios Voulodimos, N. D. S. S. A. L. (2017). Transforming intangible folkloric performing arts into tangible choreographic digital objects: The terpsichore approach. In ScitePress, editor, *Proceedings of the 12th International Joint Conference on Computer Vision, Imaging and Computer Graphics Theory and Applications*, pages 451–460, Porto, Portugal, March.

Auslander, P. (1992). Intellectual property meets the cyborg: Performance and the cultural politics of technology. *Performing Arts Journal*, 14(1):30–42.

Brekke, J. K. and Haase, E., (2017). *Breaking Chains and Busting Blocks: Commentary on the Satoshi. (Hippocratic) Oath for Blockchain Developers*, pages 91–95. Torque Editions.

Burri, M., (2008). *The long tail of the rainbow serpent: New technologies and the protection and promotion of traditional cultural expressions*, pages 205–37.

Frankel, S., (2014). *Ka Mate Ka Mate' and the Protection of Traditional Knowledge*, pages 23–46.

Gervais, D. (2003). Spiritual but not intellectual? the protection of sacred intangible traditional knowledge. *Cardozo Journal of International and Comparative Law*, 11:468–495.

Giurchescu, A. and Torp, L. (1991). Theory and methods in dance research: A european approach to the holistic study of dance. *Yearbook for Traditional Music*.

Godoy, R. I., (2009). *Gestural Affordances of Musical Sound*, pages 103–25. Routledge.

Greenfield, A. (2017). *Radical Technologies: The Design of Everyday Life*. Verso, London.

Hanna, J. L. (2001). The language of dance. *Journal of Physical Education Recreation Dance*.

Iaconesi, S. (2021). Nft what could possibly go wrong? the financialization of life. *Medium*.

Iris Kico, Nikos Grammalidis, Y. C. and Liarokapis, F. (2018). Digitisation and visualisation of folk dances in cultural heritage: A review. *Inventions*, 3(4):72–95.

Jantunen, T., Burger, B., Weerdt, D. D., Seilola, I., and Wainio, T. (2012). Experiences collecting motion capture data on continuous signing. In *Proceedings of the 5th Workshop on the Representation and Processing of Sign Languages: Interactions between Corpus and Lexicon colocated with LREC'12*, Istanbul, Turkey, may.

Kaeppler, A. (1972). Method and theory in analyzing dance structure with an analysis of tongan dance. *Ethnomusicology*.

Karjala, D. and Kirkwood, R. (2003). Looking beyond intellectual property in resolving protection of intangible cultural heritage of indigenous peoples. *Cardozo Journal of International and Comparative Law*, 11:633–671.

Kraut, A., (2009). *Race-ing choreographic copyright*, pages 76–96. Palgrave Macmillan.

Kraut, A. (2010). Stealing steps and signature moves: Embodied theories of dance as intellectual property. *Theatre Journal*.

Lepecki, A. (2010). The body as archive: Will to re-enact and the afterlives of dances. *Dance Research Journal*, 42.

Liberman, A. M. and Mattingly, I. G. (1985). The motor theory of speech perception revised. *Cognition*.

Lixinski, L. (2011). Selecting heritage: The interplay of art, politics and identity. *European Journal of International Law*, 22(1):81–100.

Long, D. (1998). The impact of foreign investment on indigenous culture: An intellectual property perspective,. *North Carolina Journal of International Law and Commercial Regulation*, 23(2):229–40.

Luciano Fadiga, Laila Craighero, G. B. and Rizzolatti, G. (2002). Speech listening specifically modulates the excitability of tongue muscles: a tms study. *The European Journal of Neuroscience*, 15(2):399–402.

Martin, G. and Pesovár, E. (1961). A structural analysis of the hungarian folk dance" (a methodological sketch). *Acta Ethnographica*.

Pilkington, M. (2015). Blockchain technology: Principles and applications. In F. Xavier Olleros et al., editors, *Research Handbook on Digital Transformations*, chapter 11, page 225–253.

Romarheim, M. (2014). Studying rhythmical structures in norwegian folk music and dance using motion capture technology: a case study of norwegian telespringar. *Musikk og tradisjon*, 28.

Taylor, D. (2003). *The Archive and the Repertoire*. Duke University Press.

UNESCO. (2003). Convention for safeguarding the intangible cultural hertiage. Paris. UNESCO.

WIPO. (2019). The protection of traditional cultural expressions: Updated draft gap analysis. Technical Report WIPO/GRTKF/IC/39/7, WIPO, Géneve.

Wood, G. (2014). Ethereum: A secure decentralised generalised transaction ledger. *Ethereum Project Yellow Paper, 151*.

Author Index

Association for Computational Linguistics
209 N. Eighth Street
Stroudsburg, Pennsylvania 18360

ISBN 978-1-7138-6126-3

CURRAN ASSOCIATES INC.
proceedings.com